Campaigns of a Non-Combatant, and His Romaunt Abroad During the War
by George Alfred Townsend

Civil War in U. S. A.

PRESENTED

BY

JOHN S. PIERSON,

NEW YORK.

CAMPAIGNS

OF

A NON-COMBATANT,

AND HIS

ROMAUNT ABROAD DURING THE WAR.

BY

GEO. ALFRED TOWNSEND.

———————•———————

NEW YORK:
BLELOCK & COMPANY,
19 BEEKMAN STREET,
1866.

SCRYMGEOUR, WHITCOMB & CO.,

Stereotypers,

15 WATER STREET, BOSTON.

TO

" Miles O'Reilly,"

WHO saw the war as vividly as he sang it; and whose aims for the peace that has ensued, are even nobler than the noble influence he exerted during the struggle, these chapters of travel are inscribed by his friend and colleague.

PREFACE.

In the early part of 1863, while I was resident in London, — the first of the War Correspondents to go abroad, — I wrote, at the request of Mr. George Smith, publisher of the Cornhill Magazine, a series of chapters upon the Rebellion, thus introduced : —

"Few wars have been so well chronicled, as that now desolating America. Its official narratives have been copious; the great newspapers of the land have been represented in all its campaigns; private enterprise has classified and illustrated its several events, and delegates of foreign countries have been allowed to mingle freely with its soldiery, and to observe and describe its battles. The pen and the camera have accompanied its bayonets, and there has not probably been any skirmish, however insignificant, but a score of zealous scribes have remarked and recorded it.

"I have employed some leisure hours afforded me in Europe, to detail those parts of the struggle which I witnessed in a civil capacity. The Sketches which follow are entirely personal, and dwell less upon routine incidents, plans, and statistics, than upon those lighter phases of war which fall beneath the dignity of severe history and are seldom related. I have endeavored to reproduce not only the adventures, but the impressions of a novitiate, and I have described not merely the army and its operations, but the country invaded, and the people who inhabit it.

"The most that I have hoped to do, is so to simplify a campaign

(7)

that the reader may realize it as if he had beheld it, travelling at will, as I did, and with no greater interest than to see how fields were fought and won."

To those chapters, I have added in this collection, some estimates of American life in Europe, and some European estimates of American life; with my ultimate experiences in the War after my return to my own country. I cannot hope that they will be received with the same favor, either here or abroad, as that which greeted their original publication. But no man ought to let the first four years of his majority slip away unrecorded. I would rather publish a tolerable book now than a possibly good one hereafter.

CAMPAIGNS OF A NON-COMBATANT,

AND HIS

Romaunt abroad during the War.

CHAPTER I.

MY IMPRESSMENT.

" Here is a piece of James Franklin's printing press, Mr. Townsend," said Mr. Pratt to me, at Newport the other day, — " Ben. Franklin wrote for the paper, and set type upon it. The press was imported from England in 1730, or thereabouts."

He produced a piece of wood, a foot in length, and then laid it away in its drawer very sacredly.

" I should like to write to that press, Mr. Pratt," I said, — " there would be no necessity in such a case of getting off six columns for to-night's mail."

" Well ! " said Mr. Pratt, philosophically, " I have a theory that a man grows up to machinery. As your day so shall your strength be. I believe you have telegraphed up to a House instrument, haven't you ? "

" Mr. Pratt," cried I, with some indignation, " your memory is too good. This is Newport, and I have come down to see the surf. Pray, do not remind me of hot hours in a newspaper office, the click of a Morse dispatch, and work far into the midnight ! "

So I left Mr. Pratt, of the Newport *Mercury*, with an

ostentation of affront, and bade James Brady, the boatman, hoist sail and carry me over to Dumpling Rocks.

On the grassy parapet of the crumbling tower which once served the purposes of a fort, the transparent water hungering at its base, the rocks covered with fringe spotting the channel, the ocean on my right hand lost in its own vastness, and Newport out of mind save when the town bells rang, or the dip of oars beat in the still swell of Narragansett, —— I lay down, chafing and out of temper, to curse the only pleasurable labor I had ever undertaken.

To me all places were workshops: the seaside, the springs, the summer mountains, the cataracts, the theatres, the panoramas of islet-fondled rivers speeding by strange cities. I was condemned to look upon them all with mercenary eyes, to turn their gladness into torpid prose, and speak their praises in turgid columns. Never nepenthe, never *abandonne*, always wide-awake, and watching for saliences, I had gone abroad like a falcon, and roamed at home like a hungry jackal. Six fingers on my hand, one long and pointed, and ever dropping gall; the ineradicable stain upon my thumb; the widest of my circuits, with all my adventure, a paltry sheet of foolscap; and the world in which I dwelt, no place for thought, or dreaminess, or love-making, — only the fierce, fast, flippant existence of NEWS!

And with this inward execration, I lay on Dumpling Rocks, looking to sea, and recalled the first fond hours of my newspaper life.

To be a subject of old Hoe, the most voracious of men, I gave up the choice of three sage professions, and the sweet alternative of idling husbandry.

The day I graduated saw me an *attaché* of the Philadelphia *Chameleon*. I was to receive three dollars a week and be the heir to lordly prospects. In the long course of persevering years I might sit in the cushions of the night-editor, or speak of the striplings around me as "*my* reporters."

"There is nothing which you cannot attain," said Mr.

Axiom, my employer, — "think of the influence you exercise! — more than a clergyman; Horace Greeley was an editor; so was George D. Prentice; the first has just been defeated for Congress; the last lectured last night and got fifty dollars for it."

Hereat I was greatly encouraged, and proposed to write a leader for next day's paper upon the evils of the Fire Department.

"Dear me," said Mr. Axiom, "you would ruin our circulation at a wink; what would become of our ball column? in case of a fire in the building we couldn't get a hose to play on it. Oh! no, Alfred, writing leaders is hard and dangerous; I want you first to learn the use of a beautiful pair of scissors."

I looked blank and chopfallen.

"No man can write a good hand or a good style," he said, "without experience with scissors. They give your palm flexibility and that is soon imparted to the mind. But perfection is attained by an alternate use of the scissors and the pen; if a little paste be prescribed at the same time, cohesion and steadfastness is imparted to the man."

His reasoning was incontrovertible; but I damned his conclusions.

So, I spent one month in slashing several hundred exchanges a day, and paragraphing all the items. These reappeared in a column called "THE LATEST INFORMATION," and when I found them copied into another journal, a flush of satisfaction rose to my face.

The editor of the *Chameleon* was an old journalist, whose face was a sealed book of Confucius, and who talked to me, patronizingly, now and then, like the Delphic Oracle. His name was Watch, and he wore a prodigious pearl in his shirt-bosom. He crept up to the editorial room at nine o'clock every night, and dashed off an hour's worth of glittering generalities, at the end of which time two or three gentlemen, blooming at the nose, and with cheeks resembling a map drawn in red ink, sounded the pipe below stairs, and Mr. Watch said —

"Mr. Townsend, I look to you to be on hand to-night; I am called away by the Water-Gas Company."

Then, with enthusiasm up to blood-heat, aroused by this mark of confidence, I used to set to, and scissor and write till three o'clock, while Mr. Watch talked water-gas over brandy and water, and drew his thirty dollars punctually on Saturdays.

So it happened that my news paragraphs, sometimes pointedly turned into a reflection, crept into the editorial columns, when water-gas was lively. Venturing more and more, the clipper finally indited a leader; and Mr. Watch, whose nose water-gas was reddening, applauded me, and told me in his sublime way, that, as a special favor, I might write all the leaders the next night. Mr. Watch was seen no more in the sanctum for a week, and my three dollars carried on the concern.

When he returned, he generously gave me a dollar, and said that he had spoken of me to the Water-Gas Company as a capital secretary. Then he wrote me a pass for the Arch Street Theatre, and told me, benevolently, to go off and rest that night.

For a month or more the responsibility of the *Chameleon* devolved almost entirely upon me. Child that I was, knowing no world but my own vanity, and pleased with those who fed its sensitive love of approbation rather than with the just and reticent, I harbored no distrust till one day when Axiom visited the office, and I was drawing my three dollars from the treasurer, I heard Mr. Watch exclaim, within the publisher's room —

"Did you read my article on the Homestead Bill?"

"Yes," answered Axiom; "it was quite clever; your leaders are more alive and epigrammatic than they were."

I could stand it no more. I bolted into the office, and cried —

" The article on the Homestead Bill is mine, so is every other article in to-day's paper.   Mr. Watch does not tell the truth ; he is ungenerous ! "

" What's this, Watch ? " said Axiom.

" Alfred," exclaimed Mr. Watch, majestically, "adopts my suggestions very readily, and is quite industrious.   I recommend that we raise his salary to five dollars a week. That is a large sum for a lad."

That night the manuscript was overhauled in the composing room.   Watch's dereliction was manifest ; but not a word was said commendatory of my labor ; it was feared I might take " airs," or covet a further increase of wages.   I only missed Watch's hugh pearl, and heard that he had been discharged, and was myself taken from the drudgery of the scissors, and made a reporter.

All this was very recent, yet to me so far remote, that as I recall it all, I wonder if I am not old, and feel nervously of my hairs.   For in the five intervening years I have ridden at Hoe speed down the groove of my steel-pen.

The pen is my traction engine ; it has gone through worlds of fancy and reflection, dragging me behind it ; and long experience has given it so great facility, that I have only to fire up, whistle, and fix my couplings, and away goes my locomotive with no end of cars in train.

Few journalists, beginning at the bottom, do not weary of the ladder ere they climb high.   Few of such, or of others more enthusiastic, recall the early associations of " the office " with pleasure.   Yet there is no world more grotesque, none, at least in America, more capable of fictitious illustration.   Around a newspaper all the dramatis personæ of the world congregate ; within it there are staid idiosyncratic folk who admit of all kindly caricature.

I summon from that humming and hurly-burly past, the ancient proof-reader.   He wears a green shade over his eyes and the gas burner is drawn very low to darken the bald and wrinkled contour of his forehead.   He is severe in

2

judgment and spells rigidly by the Johnsonian standard.
He punctuates by an obdurate and conscientious method,
and will have no italics upon any pretext.   He will lend
you money, will eat with you, drink with you, and encour-
age you ; but he will not punctuate with you, spell with
you, nor accept any of your suggestions as to typography
or paragraphing whatsoever.   He wears slippers and smokes
a primitive clay pipe ; he has everything in its place, and
you cannot offend him more than by looking over any proof
except when he is holding it.   A chip of himself is the copy-
holder at his side, — a meagre, freckled, matter of fact
youth, who reads your tenderest sentences in a rapid monotone, and is never known to venture any opinion or suggestion whatever.   This boy, I am bound to say, will follow
the copy if it be all consonants, and will accompany it if it
flies out of the window.

The office clerk was my bane and admiration.   He was
presumed by the verdant patrons of the paper to be its
owner and principal editor, its type-setter, pressman, and
carrier.   His hair was elaborately curled, and his ears were
perfect racks of long and dandyfied pens ; a broad, shovel-
shaped gold pen lay forever opposite his high stool ; he had
an arrogant and patronizing address, and was the perpetual
cabbager of editorial perquisites.   Books, ball-tickets, sea-
son-tickets, pictures, disappeared in his indiscriminate fist,
and he promised notices which he could not write to no end
of applicants.   He was to be seen at the theatre every night,
and he was the dashing escort of the proprietor's wife, who
preferred his jaunty coat and highly-polished boots to the
less elaborate wardrobe of us writers.   That this noble and
fashionable creature could descend to writing wrappers, and
to waiting his turn with a bank-book in the long train of a
sordid teller, passed all speculation and astonishment.   He
made a sorry fag of the office boy, and advised us every day
to beware of cutting the files, as if that were the one vice
of authors.   To him we stole, with humiliated faces, and

begged a trifling advance of salary.   He sternly requested us not to encroach behind the counter — his own indisputable domain — but sometimes asked us to watch the office while he drank with a theatrical agent at the nearest bar. He was an inveterate gossip, and endowed with a damnable love of slipshod argument ; the only oral censor upon our compositions, he hailed us with all the complaints made at his solicitation by irascible subscribers, and stood in awe of the cashier only, who frequently, to our delight and surprise, combed him over, and drove him to us for sympathy.

The foreman was still our power behind the throne ; he left out our copy on mechanical grounds, and put it in for our modesty and sophistry.   In his broad, hot room, all flaring with gas, he stood at a flat stone like a surgeon, and took forms to pieces and dissected huge columns of pregnant metal, and paid off the hands with fabulous amounts of uncurrent bank bills.   His wife and he went thrice a year on excursions to the sea-side, and he was forever borrowing a dollar from somebody to treat the lender and himself.

The ship-news man could be seen towards the small-hours, writing his highly imaginative department, which showed how the Sally Ann, Master Todd, arrived leaky in Bombay harbor ; and there were stacks of newsboys asleep on the boilers, fighting in their dreams for the possession of a fragment of a many-cornered blanket.

These, like myself, went into the halcyon land of Nod to the music of a crashing press, and swarmed about it at the dawn like so many gad flies about an ox, to carry into the awakening city the rhetoric and the rubbish I had written.

And still they go, and still the great press toils along, and still am I its slave and keeper, who sit here by the proud, free sea, and feel like Sinbad, that to a terrible old man I have sold my youth, my convictions, my love, my life !

CHAPTER II.

THE WAR CORRESPONDENT'S FIRST DAY.

Looking back over the four years of the war, and noting how indurated I have at last become, both in body and in emotion, I recall with a sigh that first morning of my correspondentship when I set out so light-hearted and yet so anxious. It was in 1861. I was accompanied to the War department by an *attaché* of the United States Senâte. The new Secretary, Mr. Edwin M. Stanton, referred me to a Mr. Sanford, "Military Supervisor of Army Intelligence," and after a brief delay I was requested to sign a parole and duplicate, specifying my loyalty to the Federal Government, and my promise to publish nothing detrimental to its interests. I was then given a circular, which stated explicitly the kind of news termed contraband, and also a printed pass, filled in with my name, age, residence, and newspaper connection. The latter enjoined upon all guards to pass me in and out of camps; and authorized persons in Government employ to furnish me with information.

Our Washington Superintendent sent me a beast, and in compliment to what the animal might have been, called the same a horse. I wish to protest, in this record, against any such misnomer. The creature possessed no single equine element. Experience has satisfied me that horses stand on four legs; the horse in question stood upon three. Horses may either pace, trot, run, rack, or gallop; but mine made all the five movements at once. I think I may call his gait an eccentric stumble.   That he had endurance I admit ; for he survived perpetual beating ; and his beauty might have been apparent to an anatomist, but would be scouted by the world at large.   I asked, ruefully, if I was expected to go into battle so mounted ; but was peremptorily forbidden, as a valuable property might be endangered thereby.   I was assigned to the Pennsylvania Reserve Corps in the antici- pated advance, and my friend, the *attaché*, accompanied me to its rendezvous at Hunter's Mills.   We started at two o'clock, and occupied an hour in passing the city limits.   I calculated that, advancing at the same ratio, we should ar- rive in camp at noon next day.   We presented ludicrous figures to the grim sabremen that sat erect at street corners, and ladies at the windows of the dwellings smothered with suppressed laughter as we floundered along.   My friend had the better horse ; but I was the better rider ; and if at any time I grew wrathful at my sorry plight, I had but to look at his and be happy again.   He appeared to be riding on the neck of his beast, and when he attempted to deceive me with a smile, his face became horribly contorted.   Di- rectly his breeches worked above his boots, and his bare calves were objects of hopeless solicitude.   Caricatures, rather than men, we toiled bruisedly through Georgetown, and falling in the wake of supply teams on the Leesburg turnpike, rode between the Potomac on one side and the dry bed of the canal on the other, till we came at last to Chain Bridge.

There was a grand view from the point of Little Falls above, where a line of foamy cataracts ridged the river, and the rocks towered gloomily on either hand : and of the city below, with its buildings of pure marble, and the yellow earthworks that crested Arlington Heights.   The clouds over the Potomac were gorgeous in hue, but forests of mel- ancholy pine clothed the sides of the hills, and the roar of the river made such beautiful monotone that I almost thought it could be translated to words.   Our passes were now de-

2*

manded by a fat, bareheaded officer, and while he panted through their contents, two privates crossed their bayonets before us.

"News?" he said, in the shortest remark of which he was capable. When assured that we had nothing to reveal, he seemed immeasurably relieved, and added—"Great labor, reading!" At this his face grew so dreadfully purple that I begged him to sit down, and tax himself with no further exertion. He wiped his forehead, in reply, gasping like a triton, and muttering the expressive direction, "right!" disappeared into a guard-box. The two privates winked as they removed their muskets, and we both laughed immoderately when out of hearing. Our backs were now turned to the Maryland shore, and jutting grimly from the hill before us, the black guns of Fort Ethan Allen pointed down the bridge. A double line of sharp abattis protected it from assault, and sentries walked lazily up and down the parapet. The colors hung against the mast in the dead calm, and the smoke curled straight upward from some log-huts within the fort. The wildness of the surrounding land-scape was most remarkable. Within sight of the Capital of the Republic, the fox yet kept the covert, and the farms were few and far apart. It seemed to me that little had been done to clear the country of its primeval timber, and the war had accomplished more to give evidence of man and industry, than two centuries of occupation. A military road had been cut through the solid rocks here; and the original turnpike, which had been little more than a cart track, was now graded and macadamized. I passed multitudes of teams, struggling up the slopes, and the carcasses of mules littered every rod of the way. The profanity of the teamsters was painfully apparent. I came unobserved upon one who was berating his beasts with a refinement of cruelty. He cursed each of them separately, swinging his long-lashed whip the while, and then damned the six in mass. He would have made a dutiful overseer. The soldiers had shown quite as little consideration for the residences along the way. I came to one dwelling where some pertinacious Vandal had even pried out the window-frames, and imperilled his neck to tear out the roof-beams ; a dead vulture was pinned over the door by pieces of broken bayonets.

"Langley's," — a few plank-houses, clustering around a tavern and a church, — is one of those settlements whose sounding names beguile the reader into an idea of their importance. A lonesome haunt in time of peace, it had lately been the winter quarters of fifteen thousand soldiers, and a multitude of log huts had grown up around it. I tied my horse to the window-shutter of a dwelling, and picked my way over a slimy sidewalk to the ricketty tavern-porch. Four or five privates lay here fast asleep, and the bar-room was occupied by a bevy of young officers, who were emptying the contents of sundry pocket-flasks. Behind the bar sat a person with strongly-marked Hebrew features, and a watchmaker was plying his avocation in a corner. Two great dogs crouched under a bench, and some highly-colored portraits were nailed to the wall. The floor was bare, and some clothing and miscellaneous articles hung from beams in the ceiling.

"Is this your house?" I said to the Hebrew.

"I keepsh it now."

"By right or by conquest?"

"By ze right of conquest," he said, laughing; and at once proposed to sell me a bootjack and an India-rubber overcoat. I compromised upon a haversack, which he filled with sandwiches and sardines, and which I am bound to say fell apart in the course of the afternoon. The watchmaker was an enterprising young fellow, who had resigned his place in a large Broadway establishment, to speculate in cheap jewelry and do itinerant repairing. He says that he followed the "Army Paymasters, and sold numbers of watches, at good premiums, when the troops had money."

Soldiers, he informed me, were reckless spendthrifts; and the prey of sutlers and sharpers. When there was nothing at hand to purchase, they gambled away their wages, and most of them left the service penniless and in debt. He· thought it perfectly legitimate to secure some silver while "going," but complained that the value of his stock rendered him liable to theft and murder. "There are men in every regiment," said he, "who would blow out my brains in any lonely place to plunder me of these watches."

At this point, a young officer, in a fit of bacchanal laughter, staggered rather roughly against me.

"Begurpardon," he said, with an unsteady bow, "never ran against person in life before."

I smiled assuringly, but he appeared to think the offence unpardonable.

"Do asshu a, on honor of gentlemand officer, not in custom of behaving offensively. Azo! leave it to my friends. Entirely due to injuries received at battle Drainesville."

As the other gentlemen laughed loudly here, I took it for granted that my apologist had some personal hallucination relative to that engagement.

"What giggling for, Bob?" he said; "honor concerned in this matter, Will! Do asshu a, fell under Colonel's horse, and Company A walked over small of my back." The other officers were only less inebriated and most of them spoke boastfully of their personal prowess at Drainesville. This was the only engagement in which the Pennsylvania Reserves had yet participated, and few officers that I met did not ascribe the victory entirely to their own individual gallantry. I inquired of these gentlemen the route to the new encampments of the Reserves. They lay five miles south of the turnpike, close to the Loudon and Hampshire railroad, and along both sides of an unfrequented lane. They formed in this position the right wing of the Army of the Potomac, and had been ordered to hold themselves in hourly readiness for an advance. By this time, my friend

S. came up, and leaving him to restore his mortified body, I crossed the road to the churchyard and peered through the open door into the edifice. The seats of painted pine had been covered with planks, and a sick man lay above every pew. At the ringing of my spurs in the threshold, some of the sufferers looked up through the red eyes of fever, and the faces of others were spectrally white. A few groaned as they turned with difficulty, and some shrank in pain from the glare of the light. Medicines were kept in the altar-place, and a doctor's clerk was writing requisitions in the pulpit. The sickening smell of the hospital forbade me to enter, and walking across the trampled yard, I crept through a rent in the paling, and examined the huts in which the Reserves had passed the winter. They were built of logs, plastered with mud, and the roofs of some were thatched with straw. Each cabin was pierced for two or more windows; the beds were simply shelves or berths; a rough fireplace of stones and clay communicated with the wooden chimney; and the floors were in most cases damp and bare. Streets, fancifully designated, divided the settlement irregularly; but the tenements were now all deserted save one, where I found a whole family of " contrabands " or fugitive slaves. These wretched beings, seven in number, had escaped from a plantation in Albemarle county, and travelling stealthily by night, over two hundred miles of precipitous country, reached the Federal lines on the thirteenth day. The husband said that his name was "Jeems," and that his wife was called "Kitty;" that his youngest boy had passed the mature age of eight months, and that the "big girl, Rosy," was "twelve years Christmas comin'." While the troops remained at Langley's, the man was employed at seventy-five cents a week to attend to an officer's horse. Kitty and Rose cooked and washed for soldiers, and the boys ran errands to Washington and return, —twenty-five miles! The eldest boy, Jefferson, had been given the use of a crippled team-horse, and traded in newspapers, but having confused ideas of the relative value of coins, his profits were only moderate. The nag died before the troops removed, and a sutler, under pretence of securing their passage to the North, disappeared with the little they had saved. They were quite destitute now, but looked to the future with no foreboding, and huddled together in the straw, made a picture of domestic felicity that impressed me greatly with the docility, contentment, and unfailing good humor of their dusky tribe. The eyes of the children were large and lustrous, and they revealed the clear pearls beneath their lips as they clung bashfully to their mother's lap. The old lady was smoking a clay pipe ; the man running over some castaway jackets and boots. I remarked particularly the broad shoulders and athletic arms of the woman, whose many childbirths had left no traces upon her comeliness. She asked me, wistfully : "Masser, how fur to de nawf?"

"A long way," said I, "perhaps two hundred miles."

"Lawd!" she said, buoyantly — "is dat all? Why, Jeems, couldn't we foot it, honey?"

"You a most guv out before, ole 'oman," he replied ; "got a good ruff over de head now. Guess de white massar won't let um starve."

I tossed some coppers to the children and gave each a sandwich.

"You get up dar, John Thomas!" called the man vigorously ; "you tank de gentleman, Jefferson, boy! I wonda wha your manners is. Tank you, massar! know'd you was a gentleman, sar! Massar, is your family from ole Virginny?"

It was five o'clock when I rejoined S., and the greater part of our journey had yet to be made. I went at his creeping pace until courtesy yielded to impatience, when spurring my Pegasus vigorously, he fell into a bouncing amble and left the *attaché* far behind. My pass was again demanded above Langley's by a man who ate apples as he examined it, and who was disposed to hold a long parley.

I entered a region of scrub timber further on, and met with nothing human for four miles, at the end of which distance I reached Difficult Creek, flowing through a rocky ravine, and crossed by a military bridge of logs. Through the thick woods to the right, I heard the roar of the Potomac, and a finger-board indicated that I was opposite Great Falls. Three or four dead horses lay at the roadside beyond the stream, and I recalled the place as the scene of a recent cavalry encounter. A cartridge-box and a torn felt hat lay close to the carcasses: I knew that some soul had gone hence to its account.

The road now kept to the left obliquely, and much of my ride was made musical by the stream. Darkness closed solemnly about me, with seven miles of the journey yet to accomplish, and as, at eight o'clock, I turned from the turnpike into a lonesome by-road, full of ruts, pools, and quicksands, a feeling of delicious uneasiness for the first time possessed me. Some owls hooted in the depth of the woods, and wild pigs, darting across the road, went crashing into the bushes. The phosphorescent bark of a blasted tree glimmered on a neighboring knoll, and as I halted at a rivulet to water my beast, I saw a solitary star floating down the ripples. Directly I came upon a clearing where the moonlight shone through the rents of a crumbling dwelling, and from the far distance broke the faint howl of farm dogs. A sense of insecurity that I would not for worlds have resigned, now tingled, now chilled my blood. At last, climbing a stony hill, the skies lay beneath me reddening with the flame of camps and flaring and falling alternately, like the beautiful Northern lights. I heard the ring of hoofs as I looked entranced, and in a twinkling, a body of horsemen dashed past me and disappeared. A little beyond, the road grew so thick that I could see nothing of my way; but trusting doubtfully to my horse, a deep challenge came directly from the thicket, and I saw the flash of a sabre, as I stammered a reply. Led to a cabin close at hand, my pass was examined by candle-light, and I learned that the nearest camp of the Reserves was only a mile farther on, and the regiment of which I was in quest about two miles distant. After another half hour, I reached Ord's brigade, whose tents were pitched in a fine grove of oaks ; the men talking, singing, and shouting, around open air fires ; and a battery of brass Napoleons unlimbered in front, pointing significantly to the West and South. For a mile and a half I rode by the light of continuous camps, reaching at last the quarters of the —— th, commanded by a former newspaper associate of mine, with whom I had gone itemizing, scores of times. His regiment had arrived only the same afternoon, and their tents were not yet pitched. Their muskets were stacked along the roadside, and the men lay here and there wrapped in their blankets, and dozing around the fagots. The Colonel was asleep in a wagon, but roused up at the summons of his Adjutant, and greeting me warmly, directed the cook to prepare a supper of coffee and fried pork. Too hungry to feel the chafing of my sores and bruises, I fell to the oleaginous repast with my teeth and fingers, and eating ravenously, asked at last to be shown to my apartments. These consisted of a covered wagon, already occupied by four teamsters, and a blanket which had evidently been in close proximity to the hide of a horse. A man named "Coggle," being nudged by the Colonel, and requested to take other quarters, asked dolorously if it was time to turn out, and roared " woa," as if he had some consciousness of being kicked. When I asked for a pillow, the Colonel laughed, and I had an intuition that the man " Coggle " was looking at me in the darkness with intense disgust. The Colonel said that he had once put a man on double duty for placing his head on a snowball, and warned me satirically that such luxuries were preposterous in the field. He recommended me not to catch cold if I could help it, but said that people in camp commonly caught several colds at once, and added grimly that if I wished to be shaved in the morning, there was a man close by, who had ground a sabre down to the nice edge of a razor, and who could be made to accommodate me. There were cracks in the bottom of the wagon, through which the cold came like knives, and I was allotted a space four feet in length, by three feet in width.

Being six feet in height, my relation to these Procrustean quarters was most embarassing; but I doubled up, chatteringly, and lay my head on my arm. In a short time I experienced a sensation akin to that of being guillotined, and sitting bolt upright, found the teamsters in the soundest of Lethean conditions. As the man next to me snored very loudly, I adopted the brilliant idea of making a pillow of his thigh; which answered my best expectations. I was aroused after a while, by what I thought to be the violent hands of this person, but which, to my great chagrin, proved to be S., intent upon dividing my place with me. Resistance was useless. I submitted to martyrdom with due resignation, but half resolved to go home in the morning, and shun, for the future, the horrible romance of camps.

3

CHAPTER III.

A GENERAL UNDER THE MICROSCOPE.

When I awoke at Colonel Taggert's tent the morning afterward, I had verified the common experience of camps by "catching several colds at once," and felt a general sensation of being cut off at the knees. Poor S., who joined me at the fire, states that he believed himself to be tied in knots, and that he should return afoot to Washington. Our horses looked no worse, for that would have been manifestly impossible. We were made the butts of much jesting at breakfast; and S. said, in a spirit of atrocity, that camp wit was quite as bad as camp "wittles." I bade him adieu at five o'clock A. M., when he had secured passage to the city in a sutler's wagon. Remounting my own fiery courser, I bade the Colonel a temporary farewell, and proceeded in the direction of Meade's and Reynold's brigades. The drum and fife were now beating *reveillé,* and volunteers in various stages of undress were limping to roll-call. Some wore one shoe, and others appeared shivering in their linen. They stood ludicrously in rank, and a succession of short, dry coughs ran up and down the line, as if to indicate those who should escape the bullet for the lingering agonies of the hospital. The ground was damp, and fog was rising from the hollows and fens. Some signal corps officers were practising with flags in a ploughed field, and negro stewards were stirring about the cook fires. A few supply wagons that I passed the previous day were just creaking into camp,

(26)

having travelled most of the night. I saw that the country was rude, but the farms were close, and the dwellings in many cases inhabited. The vicinity had previously been unoccupied by either army, and rapine had as yet appropriated only the fields for camps and the fences for fuel. I was directed to the headquarters of Major-General M'Call, — a cluster of wall tents in the far corner of a grain-field, concealed from public view by a projecting point of woods. A Sibley tent stood close at hand, where a soldier in blue overcoat was reading signals through a telescope. I mistook the tent for the General's, and riding up to the soldier was requested to stand out of the way. I moved to his rear, but he said curtly that I was obstructing the light. I then dismounted, and led my horse to a clump of trees a rod distant.

"Don't hitch there," said the soldier; "you block up the view."

A little ruffled at this manifest discourtesy, I asked the man to denote some point within a radius of a mile where I would *not* interfere with his operations. He said in reply, that it was not his business to denote hitching-stalls for anybody. I thought, in that case, that I should stay where I was, and he politely informed me that I might stay and be — jammed. I found afterward that this individual was troubled with a kind of insanity peculiar to all headquarters, arising out of an exaggerated idea of his own importance. I had the pleasure, a few minutes afterward, of hearing him ordered to feed my horse. A thickset, gray-haired man sat near by, undergoing the process of shaving by a very nervous negro. The thickset man was also exercising the privileges of his rank; but the more he berated his attendant's awkwardness, the more nervous the other became. I addressed myself mutually to master and man, in an inquiry as to the precise quarters of the General in command. The latter pointed to a wall tent contiguous, and was cursed by the thickset man for not minding his business. The thickset man remarked substantially, that he didn't know anything about it, and was at that moment cut by the negro, to my infinite delight.   Before the wall tent in question stood a tall, broad-shouldered gentleman in shirt-sleeves and slippers, warming his back and hands at a fire.   He was watching, through an aperture in the tent, the movements of a private who was cleaning his boots.   I noticed that he wore a seal ring, and that he opened and shut his eyes very rapidly.   He was, otherwise, a very respectable and digni- fied gentleman.

"Is this General M'Call?" said I, a little discomposed. The gentleman looked abstractedly into my eyes, opening and shutting his own several times, as if doubtful of his personality, and at last decided that he *was* General M'Call.

"What is it?" he said gravely, but without the slightest curiosity.

"I have a letter for you, sir, I believe."

He put the letter behind his back, and went on warming his hands.   Having winked several times again, apparently forgetting all about the matter, I ventured to add that the letter was merely introductory.   He looked at it, mechan- ically.

"Who opened it?" he said.

"Letters of introduction are not commonly sealed, Gen- eral."

"Who are you?" he asked, indifferently.

I told him that the contents of the letter would explain my errand; but he had, meantime, relapsed into abstract- edness, and winked, and warmed his hands, for at least, five minutes.   At the end of that time, he read the letter very deliberately, and said that he was glad to see me in camp. He intimated, that if I was not already located, I could be provided with bed and meals at headquarters.   He stated, in relation to my correspondence, that all letters sent from the Reserve Corps, must, without any reservations, be submit- ted to him in person.   I was obliged to promise compliance, but had gloomy forebodings that the General would occupy a fortnight in the examination of each letter. He invited me to breakfast, proposed to make me acquainted with his staff, and was, in all respects, a very grave, prudent, and affable soldier. I may say, incidentally, that I adopted the device of penning a couple of gossipy epistles, the length and folly of which, so irritated General M'Call, that he released me from the penalty of submitting my compositions for the future.

I took up my permanent abode with quartermaster Kingwalt, a very prince of old soldiers, who had devoted much of a sturdy life to promoting the militia interests of the populous county of Chester. When the war-fever swept down his beautiful valley, and the drum called the young men from villages and farms, this ancient yeoman and miller — for he was both — took a musket at the sprightly age of sixty-five, and joined a Volunteer company. Neither ridicule nor entreaty could bend his purpose; but the Secretary of War, hearing of the case, conferred a brigade quartermastership upon him. He threw off the infirmities of age, stepped as proudly as any youngster, and became, emphatically, the best quartermaster in the Division. He never delayed an advance with tardy teams, nor kept the General tentless, nor penned irregular requisitions, nor wasted the property of Government. The ague seized him, occasionally, and shook his grey hairs fearfully; but he always recovered to ride his black stallion on long forages, and his great strength and bulk were the envy of all the young officers.

He grasped my hand so heartily that I positively howled, and commanded a tall sergeant, rejoicing in the name of Clover, to take away my horse and split him up for kindling wood.

"We must give him the blue roan, that Fogg rides," said the quartermaster, to the great dejection of Fogg, a short stout youth, who was posting accounts. I was glad

3*

to see, however, that Fogg was not disposed to be angry, and when informed that a certain iron-gray nag was at his disposal, he was in a perfect glow of good humor. The other *attachés* were a German, whose name, as I caught it, seemed to be Skyhiski; and a pleasant lad called Owen, whose disposition was so mild, that I wondered how he had adopted the bloody profession of arms. A black boy belonged to the establishment, remarkable, chiefly, for getting close to the heels of the black stallion, and being frequently kicked; he was employed to feed and brush the said stallion, and the antipathy between them was intense.

The above curious military combination, slept under a great tarpaulin canopy, originally used for covering commissary stores from the rain. Our meals were taken in the open air, and prepared by Skyhiski; but there was a second tent, provided with desk and secretary, where Mr. Fogg performed his clerk duties, daily. When I had relieved my Pegasus of his saddle, and penned some paragraphs for a future letter, I strolled down the road with the old gentleman, who insisted upon showing me Hunter's mill, a storm-beaten structure, that looked like a great barn. The mill-race had been drained by some soldiers for the purpose of securing the fish contained in it, and the mill-wheel was quite dry and motionless. Difficult Creek ran impetuously across the road below, as if anxious to be put to some use again; and the miller's house adjoining, was now used as a hospital, for Lieutenant-Colonel Kane, and some inferior officers. It was a favorite design of the Quartermaster's to scrape the mill-stone, repair the race, and put the great breast-wheel to work. One could see that the soldier had not entirely obliterated the miller, and as he related, with a glowing face, the plans that he had proposed to recuperate the tottering structure, and make it serviceable to the army, I felt a regret that such peaceful ambitions should have ever been overruled by the call to arms.

While we stood at the mill window, watching the long stretches of white tents and speculating upon the results of war, we saw several men running across the road toward a hill-top cottage, where General Meade made his quarters. A small group was collected at the cottage, reconnoitring something through their telescopes. As I hastened in that direction, I heard confused voices, thus: "No, it isn't!" "It is!" "Can you make out his shoulder-bar?" "What is the color of his coat?" "Gray!" "No, it's butternut!" "Has he a musket!" "Yes, he is levelling it!" At this the group scattered in every direction. "Pshaw!" said one, "we are out of range; besides, it is a telescope that he has. By ——, it is a Rebel, reconnoitring our camp!" There was a manifest sensation here, and one man wondered how he had passed the picket. Another suggested that he might be accompanied by a troop, and a third convulsed the circle by declaring that there were six other Rebels visible in a woods to the left. Mr. Fogg had meantime come up and proffered me a field-glass, through which I certainly made out a person in gray, standing in the middle of the road just at the ridge of a hill. When I dropped my glass I saw him distinctly with the naked eye. He was probably a mile distant, and his gray vesture was little relieved by the blue haze of the forest.

"He is going," exclaimed a private, excitedly; "where's the man that was to try a lead on him?" Several started impulsively for their pieces, and some officers called for their horses. "There go his knees!" "His body is behind the hill!" "Now his head——"

"Crack! crack! crack!" spluttered musketry from the edge of the mill, and like as many rockets darted a score of horsemen through the creek and up the steep. Directly a faint hurrah pealed from the camp nearest the mill. It passed to the next camp and the next; for all were now earnestly watching; and finally a medley of cheers shook the air and the ear. Thousands of brave men were shouting the requiem of one paltry life. The rash fool had bought with his temerity a bullet in the brain. When I

saw him — dusty and still bleeding — he was beset by a
full regiment of idlers, to whom death had neither awe nor
respect. They talked of the delicate shot, as connoisseurs
in the art of murder, — and two men dug him a grave on
the green before the mill, wherein he was tossed like a dog
or a vulture, to be lulled, let us hope, by the music of the
grinding, when grain shall ripen once more.

I had an opportunity, after dinner, to inspect the camp of
the " Bucktails," a regiment of Pennsylvania backwoods-
men, whose efficiency as skirmishers has been adverted to
by all chroniclers of the civil war. They wore the common
blue blouse and breeches, but were distinguished by squirrel tails fastened to their caps. They were reputed to be
the best marksmen in the service, and were generally
allowed, in action, to take their own positions and fire at
will. Crawling through thick woods, or trailing ser-
pent-like through the tangled grass, these mountaineers
were for a time the terror of the Confederates ; but when
their mode of fighting had been understood, their adversaries improved upon it to such a degree that at the date of
this writing there is scarcely a Corporal's guard of the original Bucktail regiment remaining. Slaughtered on the field,
perishing in prison, disabled or paroled, they have lost both
their prestige and their strength. I remarked among these
worthies a partiality for fisticuffs, and a dislike for the
manual of arms. They drilled badly, and were reported to
be adepts at thieving and unlicensed foraging.

The second night in camp was pleasantly passed. Some
sociable officers — favorites with Captain Kingwalt — congregated under the tarpaulin, after supper-hour, and when a
long-necked bottle had been emptied and replenished, there
were many quaint stories related and curious individualities
revealed. I dropped asleep while the hilarity was at its
height, and Fogg covered me with a thick blanket as I lay.
The enemy might have come upon us in the darkness ; but
if death were half so sound as my slumber afield, I should
have bid it welcome.

CHAPTER IV.

A FORAGING ADVENTURE.

THERE was a newsboy named "Charley," who slept at Captain Kingwalt's every second night, and who returned my beast to his owner in Washington. The aphorism that a Yankee can do anything, was exemplified by this lad; for he worked my snail into a gallop. He was born in Chelsea, Massachusetts, and appeared to have taken to speculation at the age when most children are learning A B C. He was now in his fourteenth year, owned two horses, and employed another boy to sell papers for him likewise. His profits upon daily sales of four hundred journals were about thirty-two dollars. He had five hundred dollars in bank, and was debating with Captain Kingwalt the propriety of founding an army express and general agency. Such a self-reliant, swaggering, far-sighted, and impertinent boy I never knew. He was a favorite with the Captain's black-boy, and upon thorough terms of equality with the Commanding General. His papers cost him in Washington a cent and a half each, and he sold them in camp for ten cents each. I have not the slightest doubt that I shall hear of him again as the proprietor of an overland mail, or the patron and capitalist of Greenland emigration.

I passed the second and third days quietly in camp, writing a couple of letters, studying somewhat of fortification, and making flying visits to various officers. There was but one other Reporter with this division of the army. He represented a New York journal, and I could not but contrast his fine steed and equipments with the scanty accommodations that my provincial establishment had provided for me. His saddle was a cushioned McClellan, with spangled breast-strap and plump saddle-bags, and his bridle was adorned with a bright curb bit and twilled reins. He wore a field-glass belted about his body, and was plentifully provided with money to purchase items of news, if they were at any time difficult to obtain. I resolved inwardly to seize the first opportunity of changing establishments, so that I might be placed upon as good a footing. My relations with camp, otherwise, were of the happiest character; for the troops were State-people of mine, and, as reporters had not yet abused the privileges accorded them, my profession was held in some repute. I made the round of various "messes," and soon adopted the current dissipations of the field, — late hours, long stories, incessant smoking, and raw spirits. There were some restless minds about me, whose funds of anecdote and jest were apparently inexhaustible. I do not know that so many eccentric, adventurous, and fluent people are to be found among any other nationality of soldiers, not excepting the Irish.

The blue roan of which friend Fogg had been deprived, exhibited occasional evidences of a desire to break my neck. I was obliged to dispense with the spur in riding him, but he nevertheless dashed off at times, and put me into an agony of fear. On those occasions I managed to retain my seat, and gained thereby the reputation of being a very fine equestrian. As there were few civilians in camp, and as I wore a gray suit, and appeared to be in request at head-quarters, a rumor was developed and gained currency that I was attached to the Division in the capacity of a scout. When my horse became unmanageable, therefore, his speed was generally accelerated by the cheers of soldiers, and I became an object of curiosity in every quarter, to my infinite mortification and dread.

The Captain was to set off on the fourth day, to purchase or seize some hay and grain that were stacked at neighboring farms. We prepared to go at eight o'clock, but were detained somewhat by reason of Skyhiski being inebriated the night before, and thereby delaying the breakfast, and afterward the fact that the black stallion had laid open the black-boy's leg. However, at a quarter past nine, the Captain, Sergeant Clover, Fogg, Owen, and myself, with six four-horse wagons, filed down the railroad track until we came to a bridge that some laborers were repairing, where we turned to the left through some soggy fields, and forded Difficult Creek. As there was no road to follow, we kept straight through a wood of young maples and chestnut-trees. Occasionally a trunk or projecting branch stopped the wagons, when the teamsters opened the way with their axes. After two hours of slow advance, we came to the end of the wood, and climbed a succession of hilly fields. From the summit of the last of these, a splendid sweep of farm country was revealed, dotted with quaint Virginia dwellings, stackyards, and negro-cabins, and divided by miles of tortuous worm-fence. The eyes of the Quartermaster brightened at the prospect, though I am afraid that he thought only of the abundant forage; but my own grew hazy as I spoke of the peaceful people and the neglected fields. The plough had furrowed none of these acres, and some crows, that screamed gutturally from a neighboring ash-tree, seemed lean and pinched for lack of their plunder of corn.

Many of the dwellings were guarded by soldiers; but of the resident citizens only the women and the old men remained. I did not need to ask where the young men were exiled. The residue that prayed with their faces toward Richmond, told me the story with their eyes. There was, nevertheless, no melodramatic exhibition of feeling among the bereaved. I did not see any defiant postures, nor hear any melting apostrophies. Marius was not mouthing by the ruins of Carthage, nor even Rachel weeping for her Hebrew children.   But there were on every hand manifestations of adherence to the Southern cause, except among a few males who feared unutterable things, and were disposed to cringe and prevaricate.   The women were not generally handsome ; their face was indolent, their dress slovenly, and their manner embarrassed.   They lopped off the beginnings and the ends of their sentences, generally commencing with a verb, as thus : " Told soldiers not to carr' off the rye ; declared they would ; said they bound do jest what they pleased.   Let 'em go ! "

The Captain stopped at a spruce residence, approached by a long lane, and on knocking at the porch with his ponderous fist, a woman came timidly to the kitchen window.

" Who's thar ? " she said, after a moment.

" Come out young woman," said the Captain, soothingly ; " we don't intend to murder or rob you, ma'am ! "

There dropped from the doorsill into the yard, not one, but three young women, followed by a very deaf old man, who appeared to think that the Captain's visit bore some reference to the hencoop.

" I wish to buy for the use of the United States Government," said the Captain, " some stacks of hay and corn fodder, that lie in one of your fields."

" The last hen was toted off this morning before breakfast," said the old man ; " they took the turkeys yesterday, and I was obliged to kill the ducks or I shouldn't have had anything to eat."

Here Fogg so misdemeaned himself, as to laugh through his nose, and the man Clover appeared to be suddenly interested in something that lay in a mulberry-tree opposite.

" I am provided with money to pay liberally for your produce, and you cannot do better than to let me take the stacks : leaving you, of course, enough for your own horses and cattle."

Here the old man pricked up his ears, and said that he

hadn't heard of any recent battle ; for his part, he had never been a politician ; but thought that both parties were a little wrong ; and wished that peace would return : for he was a very old man, and was sorry that folks couldn't let quiet folks' property alone. How far his garrulity might have betrayed him, could be conjectured only by one of the girls taking his hand and leading him submissively into the house.

The eldest daughter said that the Captain might take the stacks at his own valuation, but trusted to his honor as a soldier, and as he seemed, a gentleman, to deal justly by them. There could be no crop harvested for a twelve-month, and beggary looked them in the face. I have never beheld anything more chivalrously gallant, than the sturdy old quartermaster's attitude. He blended in tone and face the politeness of a diplomat and the gentleness of a father. They asked him to return to the house, with his *officers*, when he had loaded the wagons ; for dinner was being prepared, and they hoped that Virginians could be hospitable, even to their enemies. As to the hay and fodder, none need be left ; for the Confederates had seized their horses some months before, and driven off their cows when they retired from the neighborhood.

I so admired the queer gables and great brick ovens of the house, that I resolved to tie my horse, and rest under the crooked porch. The eldest young lady had taken me to be a prisoner, and was greatly astonished that the Quartermaster permitted me to go at large. She asked me to have a chair in the parlor, but when I made my appearance there, the two younger sisters fled precipitately. The old man was shaking his head sadly by the fireplace. Some logs burned on the andirons with a red flame. The furniture consisted of a mahogany sideboard, table, and chairs, — ponderous in pattern ; and a series of family portraits, in a sprawling style of art, smirked and postured on the wall. The floor was bare, but shone by reason of repeated scrub-

4

bing, and the black mantel-piece was a fine specimen of colonial carving in the staunchest of walnut-wood.

Directly the two younger girls — though the youngest must have been twenty years of age — came back with averted eyes and the silliest of giggles. They sat a little distance apart, and occasionally nodded or signalled like school children.

"Wish you *would* stop, Bell !" said one of these misses, — whose flaxen hair was plastered across her eyebrows, and who was very tall and slender.

"See if I don't tell on you," said the other, — a dark miss with roguish eyes and fat, plump figure, and curls that shook ever so merrily about her shoulders.

"Declar' I never said so, if he asks me ; declar' I will."

"Tell on you, — you see ! Won't he be jealous ? How he will car' on !"

I made out that these young ladies were intent upon publishing their obligations to certain sweethearts of theirs, who, as it afterward seemed, were in the army at Manassas Junction. I said to the curly-haired miss, that she was endangering the life of her enamored ; for it would become an object with all the anxious troops in the vicinity to shorten his days. The old man roused up here, and remarked that his health certainly was declining ; but he hoped to survive a while longer for the sake of his children ; that he was no politician, and always said that the negroes were very ungrateful people. He caught his daughter's eye finally, and cowered stupidly, nodding at the fire.

I remarked to the eldest young woman, — called Prissy (Priscilla) by her sister, — that the country hereabout was pleasantly wooded. She said, in substance, that every part of Virginia was beautiful, and that she did not wish to survive the disgrace of the old commonwealth.

"Become right down hateful since Yankees invaded it !" exclaimed Miss Bell. *Some* Yankee's handsome sister," said Miss Bessie, the proprietor of the curls, "think some Yankees puffick gentlemen !"

" Oh, you traitor ! " said the other, — " wish *Henry* heard you say that ! "

Miss Bell intimated that she should take the first opportunity of telling him the same, and I eulogized her good judgment. Priscilla now begged to be excused for a moment, as, since the flight of the negro property, the care of the table had devolved mainly upon her. A single aged servant, too feeble or too faithful to decamp, still attended to the menial functions, and two mulatto children remained to relieve them of light labor. She was a dignified, matronly young lady, and, as one of the sisters informed me, plighted to a Major in the Confederate service. The others chattered flippantly for an hour, and said that the old place was dreadfully lonesome of late. Miss Bell was *sure* she should die if another winter, similar to the last, occurred. She loved company, and had always found it *so* lively in Loudon before ; whereas she had positively been but twice to a neighbor's for a twelvemonth, and had quite forgotten the road to the mill. She said, finally, that, rather than undergo another such isolation, she would become a *Vivandiere* in the Yankee army. The slender sister was altogether wedded to the idea of her lover's. " *Wouldn't* she tell Henry ? and *shouldn't* she write to Jeems ? and oh, Bessie, you would not *dare* to repeat that before *him.*" In short, I was at first amused, and afterwards annoyed, by this young lady, whereas the roguish-eyed miss improved greatly upon acquaintance.

After a while, Captain Kingwalt came in, trailing his spurs over the floor, and leaving sunshine in his wake. There was something galvanic in his gentleness, and infectious in his merriment. He told them at dinner of his own daughters on the Brandywine, and invented stories of Fogg's courtships, till that young gentleman first blushed, and afterward dropped his plate. Our meal was a frugal one, consisting mainly of the ducks referred to, some vegetables, corn-bread, and coffee made of wasted rye. There were neither sugar, spices, nor tea, on the premises, and the salt before us was the last in the dwelling. The Captain promised to send them both coffee and salt, and Fogg volunteered to bring the same to the house, whereat the Captain teased him till he left the table.

At this time, a little boy, who was ostensibly a waiter, cried : "Miss Prissy, soldiers is climbin' in de hog-pen."

"I knew we should lose the last living thing on the property," said this young lady, much distressed.

The Captain went to the door, and found three strolling Bucktails looking covetously at the swine. They were a little discomposed at his appearance, and edged off suspiciously.

"Halt !" said the old man in his great voice, "where are you men going ?"

"Just makin' reconnoissance," said one of the freebooters ; "s'pose a feller has a right to walk around, hain't he ?"

"Not unless he has a pass," said the Quartermaster ; "have you written permission to leave camp ?"

"Left'nant s'posed we might. Don't know as it's your business. Never see *you* in the regiment."

"It is my business, as an officer of the United States, to see that no soldier strays from camp unauthorizedly, or depredates upon private property. I will take your names, and report you, first for straggling, secondly for insolence !"

"Put to it, Bill !" said the speaker of the foragers ; "run, Bob ! go it hearties !" And they took to their heels, cleared a pair of fences, and were lost behind some outbuildings. The Captain could be harsh as well as generous, and was about mounting his horse impulsively, to overtake and punish the fugitives, when Priscilla begged him to refrain, as an enforcement of discipline on his part might bring insult upon her helpless household. I availed myself of a pause in the Captain's wrath, to ask Miss Priscilla if she would allow me to lodge in the dwelling. Five nights' experience in camp had somewhat reduced my enthusiasm, and I already wearied of the damp beds, the hard fare, and the coarse conversation of the bivouac. The young lady assented willingly, as she stated that the presence of a young man would both amuse and protect the family. For several nights she had not slept, and had imagined footsteps on the porch and the drawing of window-bolts. There was a bed, formerly occupied by her brother, that I might take, but must depend upon rather laggard attendance. I had the satisfaction, therefore, of seeing the Captain and retinue mount their horses, and wave me a temporary good by. Poor Fogg looked back so often and so seriously that I expected to see him fall from the saddle. The young ladies were much impressed with the Captain's manliness, and Miss Bell wondered *how* such a *puffick* gentleman could *reconcile* himself to the Yankee cause. She had felt a desire to speak to him upon that point as she was *sure* he was of fine stock, and entirely averse to the invasion of such territory as that of *dear* old Virginia. There was something in his manner that *so* reminded her of some one who should be *nameless* for the present; but the "nameless" was, *of course*, young, *handsome*, and *so* brave. I ruthlessly dissipated her theory of the Captain's origin, by stating that he was of humble German descent, so far as I knew, and had probably never beheld Virginia till preceded by the bayonets of his neighbors.

After tea Miss Bessie produced a pitcher of rare cider, that came from a certain mysterious quarter of the cellar. A chessboard was forthcoming at a later hour, when we amused ourselves with a couple of games, facetiously dubbing our chessmen Federals and Confederates. Miss Bell, meanwhile, betook herself to a diary, wherein she minutely related the incidents and sentiments of successive days. The quantity of words underscored in the same autobiography would have speedily exhausted the case of italics, if the printer had obtained it. I was so beguiled by these pa-

4*

triarchal people, that I several times asked myself if the circumstances were real. Was I in a hostile country, surrounded by thousands of armed men? Were the incidents of this evening portions of an historic era, and the ground about me to be commemorated by bloodshed? Was this, in fact, revolution, and were these simple country girls and their lovers revolutionists? The logs burned cheerily upon the hearth, and the ancestral portraits glowered contemplatively from the walls. Miss Prissy looked dreamily into the fire, and the old man snored wheezily in a corner. A gray cat purred in Miss Bell's lap, and Miss Bessie was writing some nonsense in my note-book.

A sharp knock fell upon the door, and something that sounded like the butt of a musket shook the porch without. The girls turned pale, and I think that Miss Bessie seized my arm and clung to it. I think also, that Miss Bell attempted to take the other arm, to which I demurred.

"Those brutal soldiers again!" said Priscilla, faintly

"I think one of the andirons has fallen down, darter!" said the old man, rousing up.

"Tremble for my life," said Miss Bell; "*sure* shall die if it's *a man*."

I opened the door after a little pause, when a couple of rough privates in uniform confronted me.

"We're two guards that General Meade sent to protect the house and property," said the tallest of these men; "might a feller come in and warm his feet!"

I understood at once that the Quartermaster had obtained these persons; and the other man coming forward, said —

"I fetched some coffee over, and a bag o' salt, with Corporal Fogg's compliments."

They deposited their muskets in a corner, and balanced their boots on the fender. Nothing was said for a time.

"Did you lose yer poultry?" said the tall man, at length.

"All," said Miss Priscilla.

"Fellers loves poultry!" said the man, smacking his lips.

"Did you lose yer sheep?" said the same man, after a little silence.

"The Bucktails cut their throats the first day that they encamped at the mill," said Miss Priscilla.

"Them Bucktails great fellers," said the tall man; "them Bucktails awful on sheep: they loves 'em so!"

He relapsed again for a few minutes, when he continued:

"You don't like fellers to bag yer poultry and sheep, do you?"

Miss Priscilla replied that it was both dishonest and cruel. Miss Bell intimated that none but Yankees would do it.

"P'raps not," said the tall soldier, drily; "did you ever grub on fat pork, Miss? No? Did you ever gnaw yer hard tack after a spell o' sickness, and a ten-hour march? No? P'raps you might like a streak o' mutton arterwards! P'raps you might take a notion for a couple o' chickens or so! No? How's that, Ike? What do you think, pardner? (to me) I ain't over and above cruel, mum. I don't think the Bucktails is over and above dishonest to home, mum. But, gosh hang it, I think I *would* bag a chicken any day! I say that above board. Hey, Ike?"

When the tall man and his inferior satellite had warmed their boots till they smoked, they rose, recovered their muskets, and bowed themselves into the yard. Soon afterward I bade the young ladies good night, and repaired to my room. The tall man and his associate were pacing up and down the grass-plot, and they looked very cold and comfortless, I thought. I should have liked to obtain for them a draught of cider, but prudently abstained; for every man in the army would thereby become cognizant of its existence. So I placed my head once more upon a soft pillow, and pitied the chilled soldiers who slept upon the turf. I thought of Miss Bessie with her roguish eyes, and wondered what themes were now engrossing her. I asked myself if this was the romance of war, and if it would bear relating to one's children when he grew as old and as deaf as the wheezy gentleman down-stairs. In fine, I was a little sentimental, somewhat reflective, and very drowsy. So, after a while, processions of freebooting soldiers, foraging Quartermasters, deaf gentlemen, Fogg's regiment, and multitudes of ghosts from Manassas, drifted by in my dreams. And, in the end, Miss Bessie's long curls brushed into my eyes, and I found the morning, ruddy as her cheeks, blushing at the window.

CHAPTER V.

WHAT A MARCH IS IN FACT.

I FOUND at breakfast, that Miss Bessie had been placed beside me, and I so far forgot myself as to forget all other persons at the table. Miss Priscilla asked to be helped to the corn-bread, and I deposited a quantity of the same upon Miss Bessie's plate. Miss Bell asked if I did not love *dear* old Virginia, and I replied to Miss Bessie that it had lately become very attractive, and that, in fact, I was decidedly rebellious in my sympathy with the distressed Virginians. I *did* except, however, the man darkly mooted as "Henry," and hoped that he would be disfigured — not killed — at the earliest engagement. The deaf old gentleman bristled up here and asked *who* had been killed at the recent engagement. There was a man named Jeems Lee, — a distant connection of the Lightfoots, — not the Hampshire Lightfoots, but the Fauquier Lightfoots, — who had distinctly appeared to the old gentleman for several nights, robed in black, and carrying a coffin under his arm. Since I had mentioned his name, he recalled the circumstance, and hoped that Jeems Lightfoot had not disgraced his ancestry. Nevertheless, the deaf gentleman was not to be understood as expressing any opinion upon the merits of the war. For *his* part he thought both sides a little wrong, and the crops were really in a dreadful state. The negroes were very ungrateful people and property should be held sacred by all belligerents.

At this point he caught Miss Priscilla's eye, and was transfixed with conscious guilt.

I had, meantime, been infringing upon Miss Bessie's feet, — very pretty feet they were ! — which expressive but not very refined method of correspondence caused her to blush to the eyes. Miss Bell, noticing the same, was determined to tell 'Henry' at once, and I hoped in my heart that she would set out for Manassas to further that purpose.

The door opened here, and the rubicund visage of Mr. Fogg appeared like the head of the Medusa. He said that 'Captain' had ordered the blue roan to be saddled and brought over to me, but I knew that this was a cunning device on his part, to revisit the dwelling. Miss Bell, somehow caught the idea that Fogg was enamored of her, and the poor fellow was subjected to a volley of tender innuendos and languishing glances, that by turn mortified and enraged him.

I bade the good people adieu at eight o'clock, promising to return for dinner at five ; and Miss Bessie accompanied me to the lane, where I took leave of her with a secret whisper and a warm grasp of the hand. One of her rings had somehow adhered to my finger, which Fogg remarked with a bilious expression of countenance. I had no sooner got astride of the blue roan than he darted off like the wind, and subjected me to great terror, alternating to chagrin, when I turned back and beheld all the young ladies waving their handkerchiefs. They evidently thought me an unrivalled equestrian.

I rode to a picket post two miles from the mill, passing over the spot where the Confederate soldier had fallen. The picket consisted of two companies or one hundred and sixty men. Half of them were sitting around a fire concealed in the woods, and the rest were scattered along the edges of a piece of close timber. I climbed a lookout-tree by means of cross-strips nailed to the trunk, and beheld from the summit a long succession of hazy hills, valleys, and forests, with the Blue Ridge Mountains bounding the distance, like some mighty monster, enclosing the world in its coils. This was the country of the enemy, and a Lieutenant obligingly pointed out to me the curling smoke of their pickets, a few miles away. The cleft of Manassas was plainly visible, and I traced the line of the Gap Railway to its junction with the Orange and Alexandria road, below Bull Run. For aught that I knew, some concealed observer might now be watching me from the pine-tops on the nearest knoll. Some rifleman might be running his practised eye down the deadly groove, to topple me from my perch, and send me crashing through the boughs. The uncertainty, the hazard, the novelty of my position had at this time an indescribable charm : but subsequent exposures dissipated the romance and taught me the folly of such adventures.

The afternoon went dryly by : for a drizzling rain fell at noon ; but at four o'clock I saddled the blue roan and went to ride with Fogg. We retraced the road to Colonel T ——s, and crossing a boggy brook, turned up the hills and passed toward the Potomac. Fogg had been a schoolmaster, and many of his narrations indicated keen perception and clever comprehension. He so amused me on this particular occasion that I quite forgot my engagement for dinner, and unwittingly strolled beyond the farthest brigade.

Suddenly, we heard a bugle-call from the picket-post before us, and, at the same moment, the drums beat from the camp behind. Our horses pricked up their ears and Fogg stared inquiringly. As we turned back we heard approaching hoofs and the blue roan exhibited intentions of running away. I pulled his rein in vain. He would neither be soothed nor commanded. A whole company of cavalry closed up with him at length, and the sabres clattered in their scabbards as they galloped toward camp at the top of their speed. With a spring that almost shook me from the saddle and drove the stirrups flying from my feet, the blue roan dashed the dust into the eyes of Fogg, and led the race.

Not the wild yager on his gait to perdition, rode so fearfully. Trees, bogs, huts, bushes, went by like lightning. The hot breath of the nag rose to my nostrils and at every leap I seemed vaulting among the spheres.

I speak thus flippantly now, of what was then the agony of death. I grasped the pommel of my saddle, mechanically winding the lines about my wrist, and clung with the tenacity of sin clutching the world. Some soldiers looked wonderingly from the wayside, but did not heed my shriek of "stop him, for God's sake !" A ditch crossed the lane, — deep and wide, — and I felt that my moment had come : with a spring that seemed to break thew and sinew, the blue roan cleared it, pitching upon his knees, but recovered directly and darted onward again. I knew that I should fall headlong now, to be trampled by the fierce horsemen behind, but retained my grasp though my heart was choking me. The camps were in confusion as I swept past them. A sharp clearness of sense and thought enabled me to note distinctly the minutest occurrences. I marked long lines of men cloaked, and carrying knapsacks, drummer-boys beating music that I had whistled in many a ramble, — field-officers shouting orders from their saddles, and cannon limbered up as if ready to move, — tents taken down and teams waiting to be loaded; all the evidences of an advance, that I alas should never witness, lying bruised and mangled by the roadside. A cheer saluted me as I passed some of Meade's regiments. "It is the scout that fetched the orders for an advance !" said several, and one man remarked that "that feller was the most reckless rider he had ever beheld." The crisis came at length : a wagon had stopped the way ; my horse in turning it, stepped upon a stake, and slipping rolled heavily upon his side, tossing me like an acrobat, over his head, but without further injury than a terrible nervous shock and a rent in my pantaloons.

I employed a small boy to lead the blue roan to Captain Kingwalt's quarters, and as I limped wearily after, some regiments came toward me through the fields. General McCall responded to my salute ; he rode in the advance. The Quartermaster's party was loading the tents and utensils. The rain fell smartly as dusk deepened into night, and the brush tents now deserted by the soldiers, were set on fire. Being composed of dry combustible material, they burned rapidly and with an intense flame. The fields in every direction were revealed, swarming with men, horses, batteries, and wagons. Some of the regiments began the march in silence ; others sang familiar ballads as they moved in column. A few, riotously disposed, shrieked, whistled, and cheered. The standards were folded ; the drums did not mark time ; the orders were few and short. The cannoneers sat moodily upon the caissons, and the cavalry-men walked their horses sedately. Although fifteen thousand men comprised the whole corps, each of its three brigades would have seemed as numerous to a novice. The teams of each brigade closed up the rear, and a quartermaster's guard was detailed from each regiment to march beside its own wagons. When the troops were fairly under way, and the brush burning along from continuous miles of road, the effect was grand beyond all that I had witnessed. The country people gathered in fright at the cottage doors, and the farm-dogs bayed dismally at the unwonted scene. I refused to ride the blue roan again, but transferred my saddle to a team horse that appeared to be given to a sort of equine somnambulism, and once or twice attempted to lie down by the roadside. At nine o'clock I set out with Fogg, who slipped a flask of spirits into my haversack. Following the tardy movement of the teams, we turned our faces toward Washington. I was soon wet to the skin, and my saddle cushion was soaking with water. The streams crossing the road were swollen with rain, and the great team wheels clogged on the slimy banks. We were sometimes delayed a half hour by a single wagon, the storm beating pitilessly in our faces the while. During the stoppages, the Quartermaster's guards burned all the fence rails in the vicinity, and some of the more indurated sat round the fagots and gamed with cards.

Cold, taciturn, miserable, I thought of the quiet farm. house, the ruddy hearth-place, and the smoking supper. I wondered if the roguish eyes were not a little sad, and the trim feet a little restless, the chessmen somewhat stupid, and the good old house a trifle lonesome. Alas! the intimacy so pleasantly commenced, was never to be renewed. With the thousand and one airy palaces that youth builds and time annihilates, my first romance of war towered to the stars in a day, and crumbled to earth in a night.

At two o'clock in the morning we halted at Metropolitan Mills, on the Alexandria and Leesburg turnpike. A bridge had been destroyed below, and the creek was so swollen that neither artillery nor cavalry could ford it. The meadows were submerged and the rain still descended in torrents. The chilled troops made bonfires of some new panel fence, and stormed all the henroosts in the vicinity. Some pigs, that betrayed their whereabouts by inoportune whines and grunts, were speedily confiscated, slaughtered, and spitted. We erected our tarpaulin in a ploughed field, and Fogg laid some sharp rails upon the ground to make us a dry bed. Skyhiski fried a quantity of fresh beef, and boiled some coffee; but while we ate heartily, theorizing as to the destination of the corps, the poor Captain was terribly shaken by his ague.

I woke in the morning with inflamed throat, rheumatic limbs, and every indication of chills and fever. Fogg whispered to me at breakfast that two men of Reynold's brigade had died during the night, from fatigue and exposure. He advised me to push forward to Washington and await the arrival of the division, as, unused to the hardships of a march, I might, after another day's experience, become dangerously ill. I set out at five o'clock, resolving to ford the creek, resume the turnpike, and reach Long Bridge at noon. Passing over some dozen fields in which my horse at every step sank to the fetlocks, I travelled along the brink of the stream till I finally reached a place that seemed to be shallow. Bracing myself firmly in the saddle, I urged my unwilling horse into the waters, and emerged half drowned on the other side. It happened, however, that I had crossed only a branch of the creek and gained an island. The main channel was yet to be attempted, and I saw that it was deep, broad, and violent. I followed the margin despairingly for a half-mile, when I came to a log footbridge, where I dismounted and swam my horse through the turbulent waters. I had now so far diverged from the turnpike that I was at a loss to recover it, but straying forlornly through the woods, struck a wagon track at last, and pursued it hopefully, until, to my confusion, it resolved itself to two tracks, that went in contrary directions. My horse preferred taking to the left, but after riding a full hour, I came to some felled trees, beyond which the traces did not go. Returning, weak and bewildered, I adopted the discarded route, which led me to a worm-fence at the edge of the woods. A house lay some distance off, but a wheat-field intervened, and I might bring the vengeance of the proprietor upon me by invading his domain. There was no choice, however; so I removed the rails, and rode directly across the wheat to some negro quarters, a little removed from the mansion. They were deserted, all save one, where a black boy was singing some negro hymns in an uproarious manner. The words, as I made them out, were these : —

> " Stephen came a runnin',
> His Marster fur to see;
> But Gabriel says he is not yar';
> He gone to Calvary !
>   O, — O, — Stephen, Stephen,
>   Fur to see;
>   Stephen, Stephen, get along up Calvary ! "

I learned from this person two mortifying facts, — that I was farther from Washington than at the beginning of my journey, and that the morrow was Sunday. War, alas! knows no Sabbaths, and the negro said, apologetically —

" I was a seyin' some ole hymns, young Mars'r. Sence dis yer war we don't have no more meetin's, and a body mos' forgits his pra'rs. Dere hain't been no church in all Fairfax, sah, fur nigh six months."

Washington was nineteen miles distant, and another creek was to be forded before gaining the turnpike. The negro sauntered down the lane, and opened the gate for me. " You jes keep from de creek, take de mill road, and enqua' as ye get furder up," said he ; " it's mighty easy, sah, an' you can't miss de way."

I missed the way at once, however, by confounding the mill road with the mill lane, and a shaggy dog that lay in a wagon shed pursued me about ¼ mile. The road was full of mire ; no dwellings adjoined it, and nothing human was to be seen in any direction. I came to a crumbling negro cabin after two plodding hours, and, seeing a figure flit by the window, called aloud for information. Nobody replied, and when, dismounting, I looked into the den, it was, to my confusion, vacant.

The soil, hereabout, was of a sterile red clay, spotted with scrub cedars. Country more bleak and desolate I have never known, and when, at noon, the rain ceased, a keen wind blew dismally across the barriers. I reached a turnpike at length, and, turning, as I thought, toward Alexandria, goaded my horse into a canter. An hour's ride brought me to a wretched hamlet, whose designation I inquired of a cadaverous old woman —

" Drainesville," said she.

" Then I am not upon the Alexandria turnpike ? "

" No. You're sot for Leesburg. This is the George- town and Chain Bridge road."

With a heavy heart, I retraced my steps, crossed Chain

Bridge at five o'clock, and halted at Kirkwood's at seven. After dinner, falling in with the manager of the Washington Sunday morning *Chronicle,* I penned, at his request, a few lines relative to the movements of the Reserves; and, learning in the morning that they had arrived at Alexandria, set out on horseback for that city.

Many hamlets and towns have been destroyed during the war. But, of all that in some form survive, Alexandria has most suffered. It has been in the uninterrupted possession of the Federals for twenty-two months, and has become essentially a military city. Its streets, its docks, its warehouses, its dwellings, and its suburbs, have been absorbed to the thousand uses of war.

I was challenged thrice on the Long Bridge, and five times on the road, before reaching the city. I rode under the shadows of five earthworks, and saw lines of white tents sweeping to the horizon. Gayly caparisoned officers passed me, to spend their Sabbath in Washington, and trains laden with troops, ambulances, and batteries, sped along the line of railway, toward the rendezvous at Alexandria. A wagoner, looking forlornly at his splintered wheels; a slovenly guard, watching some bales of hay; a sombre negro, dozing upon his mule; a slatternly Irish woman gossiping with a sergeant at her cottage door; a sutler in his "dear-born," running his keen eye down the limbs of my beast; a spruce civilian riding for curiosity; a gray-haired gentleman, in a threadbare suit, going to camp on foot, to say good by to his boy, — these were some of the personages that I remarked, and each was a study, a sermon, and a story. The Potomac, below me, was dotted with steamers and shipping. The bluffs above were trodden bare, and a line of dismal marsh bordered some stagnant pools that blistered at their bases. At points along the river-shore, troops were embarking on board steamers; transports were taking in tons of baggage and subsistence. There was a schooner, laden to the water-line with locomotive engines and burden car-

5*

riages ; there, a brig, shipping artillery horses by a steam derrick, that lifted them bodily from the shore and deposited them in the hold of the vessel. Steamers, from whose spaⓒus saloons the tourist and the bride have watched the picturesque margin of the Hudson, were now black with clusters of rollicking volunteers, who climbed into the yards, and pitched headlong from the wheel-houses. The "grand movement," for which the people had waited so long, and which McClellan had promised so often, was at length to be made. The Army of the Potomac was to be transferred to Fortress Monroe, at the foot of the Chesapeake, and to advance by the peninsula of the James and the York, upon the city of Richmond.

I rode through Washington Street, the seat of some ancient residences, and found it lined with freshly arrived troops. The grave-slabs in a fine old churchyard were strewn with weary cavalry-men, and they lay in some side yards, soundly sleeping. Some artillery-men chatted at doorsteps, with idle house-girls ; some courtesans flaunted in furs and ostrich feathers, through a group of coarse engineers ; some sergeants of artillery, in red trimmings, and caps gilded with cannon, were reining their horses to leer at some ladies, who were taking the air in their gardens ; and at a wide place in the street, a Provost-Major was manœuvring some companies, to the sound of the drum and fife. There was much drunkenness, among both soldiers and civilians ; and the people of Alexandria were, in many cases, crushed and demoralized by reason of their troubles. One man of this sort led me to a sawmill, now run by Government, and pointed to the implements.

"I bought 'em and earned 'em," he said. "My labor and enterprise set 'em there ; and while my mill and machinery are ruined to fill the pockets o' Federal sharpers, I go drunk, ragged, and poor about the streets o' my native town. My daughter starves in Richmond ; God knows I can't get to her. I wish to h—l I was dead."

Further inquiry developed the facts that my acquaintance had been a thriving builder, who had dotted all Northeastern Virginia with evidences of his handicraft. At the commencement of the war, he took certain contracts from the Confederate government, for the construction of barracks at Richmond and Manassas Junction; returning inopportunely to Alexandria, he was arrested, and kept some time in Capitol-Hill prison; he had not taken the oath of allegiance, consequently, he could obtain no recompense for the loss of his mill property. Domestic misfortunes, happening at the same time, so embittered his days that he resorted to dissipation. Alexandria is filled with like ruined people; they walk as strangers through their ancient streets, and their property is no longer theirs to possess, but has passed into the hands of the dominant nationalists. My informant pointed out the residences of many leading citizens: some were now hospitals, others armories and arsenals; others offices for inspectors, superintendents, and civil officials. The few people that remained upon their properties, obtained partial immunity, by courting the acquaintance of Federal officers, and, in many cases, extending the hospitalities of their homes to the invaders. I do not know that any Federal functionary was accused of tyranny, or wantonness, but these things ensued, as the natural results of civil war; and one's sympathies were everywhere enlisted for the poor, the exiled, and the bereaved.

My dinner at the City Hotel was scant and badly prepared. I gave a negro lad who waited upon me a few cents, but a burly negro carver, who seemed to be his father, boxed the boy's ears and put the coppers into his pocket. The proprietor of the place had voluntarily taken the oath of allegiance, and had made more money since the date of Federal occupation than during his whole life previously. He said to me, curtly, that if by any chance the Confederates should reoccupy Alexandria, he could very well afford to relinquish his property. He employed a smart barkeeper, who led guests by a retired way to the drinking-rooms. Here, with the gas burning at a taper point, cobblers, cocktails, and juleps were mixed stealthily and swallowed in the darkness. The bar was like a mint to the proprietor; he only feared discovery and prohibition. It would not accord with the chaste pages of this narrative to tell how some of the noblest residences in Alexandria had been desecrated to licentious purposes ; nor how, by night, the parlors of cosey homes flamed with riot and orgie. I stayed but a little time, having written an indiscreet paragraph in the Washington Chronicle, for which I was pursued by the War Department, and the management of my paper, lacking heart, I went home in a pet.

CHAPTER VI.

DOWN THE CHESAPEAKE.

DISAPPOINTED in the unlucky termination of my adventures afield, I now looked ambitiously toward New York. As London stands to the provinces, so stands the empire city to America. Its journals circulate by hundreds of thousands; its means are only rivalled by its enterprise; it is the end of every young American's aspiration, and the New Bohemia for the restless, the brilliant, and the industrious. It seemed a great way off when I first beheld it, but I did not therefore despair. Small matters of news that I gathered in my modest city, obtained space in the columns of the great metropolitan journal, the ————. After a time I was delegated to travel in search of special incidents, and finally, when the noted Tennessee Unionist, "Parson" Brownlow, journeyed eastward, I joined his *suite*, and accompanied him to New York. The dream of many months now came to be realized. A correspondent on the ————'s staff had been derelict, and I was appointed to his division. His horse, saddle, field-glasses, blankets, and pistols were to be transferred, and I was to proceed without delay to Fortress Monroe, to keep with the advancing columns of McClellan.

At six in the morning I embarked; at eleven I was whirled through my own city, without a glimpse of my friends; at three o'clock I dismounted at Baltimore, and at five was gliding down the Patapsco, under the shadows of

Fort Federal Hill, and the white walls of Fort McHenry. The latter defence is renowned for its gallant resistance to a British fleet in 1813, and the American national anthem, "The Star-Spangled Banner," was written to commemorate that bombardment.   Fort Carroll, a massive structure of hewn stone, with arched bomb-proof and three tiers of mounted ordnance, its smooth walls washed by the waves, and its unfinished floors still ringing with the trowel and the adze, — lies some miles below, at a narrow passage in the stream.   Below, the shores diverge, and at dusk we were fairly in the Chesapeake, under steam and sail, speeding due southward.

The *Adelaide* was one of a series of boats making daily trips between Baltimore and Old Point.   Fourteen hours were required to accomplish the passage, and we were not to arrive till seven o'clock next morning.   I was so fortunate as to obtain a state-room, but many passengers were obliged to sleep upon sofas or the cabin floor.   These boats monopolized the civil traffic between the North and the army, although they were reputed to be owned and managed by Secessionists.   None were allowed to embark unless provided with Federal passes ; but there were, nevertheless, three or four hundred people on board.   About one fourth of these were officers and soldiers ; one half sutlers, traders, contractors, newsmen, and idle civilians, anxious to witness a battle, or stroll over the fields of Big Bethel, Lee's Mills, Yorktown, Gloucester, Williamsburg, or West Point ; the rest were females on missions of mercy, on visits to sons, brothers, and husbands, and on the way to their homes at Norfolk, Suffolk, or Hampton.   Some of these were citizens of Richmond, who believed that the Federals would occupy the city in a few days, and enable them to resume their professions and homes.   The lower decks were occupied by negroes.   The boat was heavily freighted, and among the parcels that littered the hold and steerage, I noticed scores of box coffins for the removal of corpses from the field to the North. There were quantities of spirits, consigned mainly to Quartermasters, but evidently the property of certain Shylocks, who watched the barrels greedily. An embalmer was also on board, with his ghostly implements. He was a sallow man, shabbily attired, and appeared to look at all the passengers as so many subjects for the development of his art. He was called "Doctor" by his admirers, and conversed in the blandest manner of the triumphs of his system.

"There are certain pretenders," he said, " who are at this moment imposing upon the Government. I regret that it is necessary to repeat it, but the fact exists that the Government is the prey of harpies. And in the art of which I am an humble disciple, — that of injecting, commonly called embalming, — the frauds are most deplorable. There was Major Montague, — a splendid subject, I assure you, — a subject that any *Professor* would have beautifully preserved, — a subject that one esteems it a favor to obtain, — a subject that I in particular would have been proud to receive ! But what were the circumstances ? I do assure you that a person named Wigwart, — who I have since ascertained to be a veterinary butcher; in plain language, a doctor of horses and asses, — imposed upon the relatives of the deceased, obtained the body, and absolutely ruined it ! — absolutely *mangled* it ! I may say, shamefully disfigured it ! He was a man, sir, six feet two, — about your height, I think ! (to a bystander.) About your weight, also ! Indeed quite like you ! And allow me to say that, if you should fall into my hands, I would leave your friends no cause for offence ! (Here the bystander trembled perceptibly, and I thought that the doctor was about to take his life.) Well ! *I* should have operated thus : — "

Then followed a description of the process, narrated with horrible circumstantiality. A fluid holding in solution pounded glass and certain chemicals, was, by the doctor's "system," injected into the bloodvessels, and the subject at the same time bled at the neck. The body thus became hard and stony, and would retain its form for years. He had, by his account, experimented for a lifetime, and said that little "Willie," the son of President Lincoln, had been so preserved that his fond parents must have enjoyed his decease.

It seemed to me that the late lamented practitioners, Messrs. Burke and Hare, were likely to fade into insignificance, beside this new light of science.

I went upon deck for some moments, and marked the beating of the waves; the glitter of sea-lights pulsing on the ripples; the sweep of belated gulls through the creaking rigging; the dark hull of a passing vessel with a grinning topmast lantern; the vigilant pilot, whose eyes glared like a fiend's upon the waste of blackness; the foam that the panting screw threw against the cabin windows; the flap of fishes caught in the threads of moonlight; the depths over which one bent, peering half wistfully, half abstractedly, almost crazily, till he longed to drop into their coolness, and let the volumes of billow roll musically above him.

A woman approached me, as I stood against the great anchor, thus absorbed. She had a pale, thin face, and was scantily clothed, and spoke with a distrustful, timorous voice : —

"You don't know the name of the surgeon-general, do you sir!"

"At Washington, ma'am?"

"No, sir; at Old Point."

I offered to inquire of the Captain : but she stopped me, agitatedly. "It's of no consequence," she said, — "that is, it is of great consequence to me; but perhaps it would be best to wait." I answered, as obligingly as I could, that any service on my part would be cheerfully rendered.

"The fact is, sir," she said, after a pause, "I am going to Williamsburg, to — find — the — the body — of my — boy."

Here her speech was broken, and she put a thin, white

hand tremulously to her eyes. I thought that any person in the Federal service would willingly assist her, and said so.

" He was not a Federal soldier, sir. He was a Confederate ! "

This considerably altered the chances of success, and I was obliged to undeceive her somewhat. " I am sure it was not my fault," she continued, "that he joined the Rebellion. You don't think they'll refuse to let me take his bones to Baltimore, do you, sir ? He was my oldest boy, and his brother, my second son, was killed at Ball's Bluff: *He* was in the Federal service. I hardly think they will refuse me the poor favor of laying them in the same grave."

I spoke of the difficulty of recognition, of the remoteness of the field, and of the expense attending the recovery of any remains, particularly those of the enemy, that, left hastily behind in retreat, were commonly buried in trenches without headboard or record. She said, sadly, that she had very little money, and that she could barely afford the journey to the Fortress and return. But she esteemed her means well invested if her object could be attained.

" They were both brave boys, sir ; but I could never get them to agree politically. William was a Northerner by education, and took up with the New England views, and James was in business at Richmond when the war commenced. So he joined the Southern army. It's a sad thing to know that one's children died enemies, isn't it ? And what troubles me more than all, sir, is that James was at Ball's Bluff where his brother fell. It makes me shudder to think, sometimes, that *his* might have been the ball that killed him."

The tremor of the poor creature here was painful to behold. I spoke soothingly and encouragingly, but with a presentiment that she must be disappointed. While I was speaking the supper-bell rang, and I proposed to get her a seat at the table.

6

"No, thank you," she replied, "I shall take no meals on the vessel; I must travel economically, and have prepared some lunch that will serve me. Good by, sir!"

Poor mothers looking for dead sons! God help them! I have met them often since; but the figure of that pale, frail creature flitting about the open deck, — alone, hungry, very poor, — troubles me still, as I write. I found, afterward, that she had denied herself a state-room, and intended to sleep in a saloon chair. I persuaded her to accept my berth, but a German, who occupied the same apartment, was unwilling to relinquish his bed, and I had the power only to give her my pillow.

Supper was spread in the forecabin, and at the signal to assemble the men rushed to the tables like as many beasts of prey. A captain opposite me bolted a whole mackerel in a twinkling, and spread the half-pound of butter that was to serve the entire vicinity upon a single slice of bread. A sutler beside me reached his fork across my neck, and plucked a young chicken bodily, which he ate, to the great disgust of some others who were eyeing it. The waiter advanced with some steak, but before he reached the table, a couple of Zouaves dragged it from the tray, and laughed brutally at their success. The motion of the vessel caused a general unsteadiness, and it was absolutely dangerous to move one's coffee to his lips. The inveterate hate with which corporations are regarded in America was here evidenced by a general desire to empty the ship's larder.

"Eat all you can," said a soldier, ferociously, — "fare's amazin' high. Must make it out in grub."

"I always gorges," said another, "on a railroad or a steamboat. Cause why? You must eat out your passage, you know!"

Among the passengers were a young officer and his bride. They had been married only a few days, and she had obtained permission to accompany him to Old Point. Very pretty, she seemed, in her travelling hat and flowing robes;

and he wore a handsome new uniform with prodigious shoulder-bars. There was a piano in the saloon, where another young lady of the party performed during the evening, and the bride and groom accompanied her with a song. It was the popular Federal parody of " Gay and Happy : "

> " Then let the South fling aloft what it will, —
> We are for the Union still !
>   For the Union ! For the Union !
> We are for the Union still ! "

The bride and groom sang alternate stanzas, and the concourse of soldiers, civilians, and females swelled the chorus. The reserve being thus broken, the young officer sang the " Star-Spangled Banner," and the refrain must have called up the mermaids. Dancing ensued, and a soldier volunteered a hornpipe. A young man with an astonishing compass of lungs repeated something from Shakespeare, and the night passed by gleefully and reputably. One could hardly realize, in the cheerful eyes and active figures of the dance, the sad uncertainties of the time. Youth trips lightest, somehow, on the brink of the grave.

The hilarities of the evening so influenced the German quartered with me, that he sang snatches of foreign ballads during most of the night, and obliged me, at last, to call the steward and insist upon his good behavior.

In the gray of the morning I ventured on deck, and, following the silvery line of beach, made out the shipping at anchor in Hampton Roads. The *Minnesota* flag-ship lay across the horizon, and after a time I remarked the low walls and black derricks of the Rip Raps. The white tents at Hampton were then revealed, and finally I distinguished Fortress Monroe, the key of the Chesapeake, bristling with guns, and floating the Federal flag. As we rounded to off the quay, I studied with intense interest the scene of so many historic events. Sewall's Point lay to the south, a

stretch of woody beach, around whose western tip the
dreaded *Merrimac* had so often moved slowly to the encounter. The spars of the *Congress* and the *Cumberland*
still floated along the strand, but, like them, the invulnerable monster had become the prey of the waves. The guns
of the Rip Raps and the terrible broadsides of the Federal
gunboats, had swept the Confederates from Sewall's Point,
— their flag and battery were gone, — and farther seaward,
at Willoughby Spit, some figures upon the beach marked
the route of the victorious Federals to the city of Norfolk.

The mouth of the James and the York were visible from
the deck, and long lines of shipping stretched from each
to the Fortress. The quay itself was like the pool in the
Thames, a mass of spars, smoke-stacks, ensigns and swelling
hills. The low deck and quaint cupola of the famous *Monitor* appeared close into shore, and near at hand rose the
thick body of the *Galena*. Long boats and flat boats went
hither and thither across the blue waves : the grim ports of
the men of war were open and the guns frowned darkly
from their coverts ; the seamen were gathering for muster
on the flagship, and drums beat from the barracks on shore ;
the Lincoln gun, a fearful piece of ordnance, rose like the
Sphynx from the Fortress sands, and the sodded parapet,
the winding stone walls, the tops of the brick quarters
within the Fort, were some of the features of a strangely
animated scene, that has yet to be perpetuated upon canvas, and made historic.

At eight o'clock the passengers were allowed to land, and
a provost guard marched them to the Hygeia House, — of
old a watering-place hotel, — where, by groups, they were
ushered into a small room, and the oath of allegiance admin-
istered to them. The young officer who officiated, repeated
the words of the oath, with a broad grin upon his face, and
the passengers were required to assent by word and by
gesture. Among those who took the oath in this way, was
a very old sailor, who had been in the Federal service for

the better part of his life, and whose five sons were now in the army. He called "Amen" very loudly and fervently, and there was some perceptible disposition on the part of other ardent patriots, to celebrate the occasion with three cheers. The quartermaster, stationed at the Fortress gave me a pass to go by steamer up the York to White House, and as there were three hours to elapse before departure, I strolled about the place with our agent. In times of peace, Old Point was simply a stone fortification, and one of the strongest of its kind in the world. Many years and many millions of dollars were required to build it, but it was, in general, feebly garrisoned, and was, altogether, a stupid, tedious locality, except in the bathing months, when the beauty and fashion of Virginia resorted to its hotel. A few cottages had grown up around it, tenanted only in "the season;" and a little way off, on the mainland, stood the pretty village of Hampton.

By a strange oversight, the South failed to seize Fortress Monroe at the beginning of the Rebellion; the Federals soon made it the basis for their armies and a leading naval station. The battle of Big Bethel was one of the first occurrences in the vicinity. Then the dwellings of Hampton were burned and its people exiled. In rapid succession followed the naval battles in the Roads, the siege and surrender of Yorktown, the flight of the Confederates up the Peninsula to Richmond, and finally the battles of Williamsburg, and West Point, and the capture of Norfolk. These things had already transpired; it was now the month of May; and the victorious army, following up its vantages, had pursued the fugitives by land and water to "White House," at the head of navigation on the Pamunkey river. Thither it was my lot to go, and witness the turning-point of their fortunes, and their subsequent calamity and repulse.

I found Old Point a weary place of resort, even in the busy era of civil war. The bar at the Hygeia House was

6*

beset with thirsty and idle people, who swore instinctively, and drank raw spirits passionately. The quantity of shell, ball, ordnance, camp equipage, and war munitions of every description piled around the fort, was marvellously great. It seemed to me that Xerxes, the first Napoleon, or the greediest of conquerors, ancient or modern, would have beheld with amazement the gigantic preparations at command of the Federal Government. Energy and enterprise displayed their implements of death on every hand. One was startled at the prodigal outlay of means, and the reckless summoning of men. I looked at the starred and striped ensign that flaunted above the Fort, and thought of Madame Roland's appeal to the statue by the guillotine.

The settlers were numbered by regiments here. Their places of business were mainly structures or "shanties" of rough plank, and most of them were the owners of sloops, or schooners, for the transportation of freight from New York, Philadelphia, or Baltimore, to their depots at Old Point. Some possessed a dozen wagons, that plied regularly between these stores and camps. The traffic was not confined to men; for women and children kept pace with the army, trading in every possible article of necessity or luxury. For these— disciples of the dime and the dollar— war had no terrors. They took their muck-rakes, like the man in Bunyan, and gathered the almighty coppers, from the pestilential camp and the reeking battle-field.

CHAPTER VII.

ON TO RICHMOND.

YORKTOWN lies twenty-one miles northwestward from Old Point, and thither I turned my face at noon, resolving to delay my journey to "White House," till next day morning. Crossing an estuary of the bay upon a narrow causeway, I passed Hampton, — half burned, half desolate, — and at three o'clock came to "Big Bethel," the scene of the battle of June 11, 1861. A small earthwork marks the site of Magruder's field-pieces, and hard by the slain were buried. The spot was noteworthy to me, since Lieutenant Greble, a fellow alumnus, had perished here, and likewise, Theodore Winthrop, the gifted author of "Cecil Dreeme" and "John Brent." The latter did not live to know his exaltation. That morning never came whereon he "woke, and found himself famous."

The road ran parallel with the deserted defences of the Confederates for some distance. The country was flat and full of swamps, but marked at intervals by relics of camps. The farm-houses were untenanted, the fences laid flat or destroyed, the fields strewn with discarded clothing, arms, and utensils. By and by, we entered the outer line of Federal parallels, and wound among lunettes, crémaillères, redoubts, and rifle-pits. Marks of shell and ball were frequent, in furrows and holes, where the clay had been upheaved. Every foot of ground, for fifteen miles henceforward, had been touched by the shovel and the pick. My

(67)

companion suggested that as much digging, concentred upon one point, would have taken the Federals to China. The sappers and miners had made their stealthy trenches, rod by rod, each morning appearing closer to their adversaries, and finally, completed their work, at less than a hundred yards from the Confederate defences.   Three minutes would have sufficed from the final position, to hurl columns upon the opposing outworks, and sweep them with the bayonet.   Ten days only had elapsed since the evacuation (May 4), and the siege guns still remained in some of the batteries.   McClellan worshipped great ordnance, and some of his columbiads, that were mounted in the water battery, yawned cavernously through their embrasures, and might have furnished sleeping accommodations to the gunners. A few mortars stood in position by the river side, and there were Parrott, Griffin, and Dahlgren pieces in the shore batteries.

However numerous and powerful were the Federal fortifications, they bore no comparison, in either respect, to those relinquished by the revolutionists. Miniature mountain ranges they seemed, deeply ditched, and revetted with sods, fascines, hurdles, gabions or sand bags. Along the York riverside there were water batteries of surpassing beauty, that seemed, at a little distance, successions of gentle terraces. Their pieces were likewise of enormous calibre, and their number almost incredible.   The advanced line of fortifications, sketched from the mouth of Warwick creek, on the South, to a point fifteen miles distant on the York : one hundred and forty guns were planted along this chain of defences ; but there were two other concentric lines, mounting, each, one hundred and twenty, and two hundred and forty guns.   The remote series consisted of six forts of massive size and height, fronted by swamps and flooded meadows, with frequent creeks and ravines interposing ; sharp *fraise* and *abattis* planted against scarp and slope, pointed cruelly eastward.   There were two water batteries, of six and four thirty-two columbiads respectively, and the town itself, which stands upon a red clay bluff, was encircled by a series of immense rifled and smooth-bore pieces, including a powerful pivot-gun, that one of McClellan's shells struck during the first day's bombardment, and split it into fragments. At Gloucester Point, across the York river, the great guns of the *Merrimac* were planted, it is said, and a fleet of fire-rafts and torpedo-ships were moored in the stream. By all accounts, there could have been no less than five hundred guns behind the Confederate entrenchments, the greater portion, of course, field-pieces, and, as the defending army was composed of one hundred thousand men, we must add that number of small arms to the list of ordnance. If we compute the Federals at so high a figure, — and they could scarcely have had less than a hundred thousand men afield, — we must increase the enormous amount of their field, siege, and small ordnance, by the naval guns of the fleet, that stood anchored in the bay. It is probable that a thousand cannon and two hundred thousand muskets were assembled in and around Yorktown during this memorable siege. The mind shudders to see the terrible deductions of these statistics. The monster, who wished that the world had but one neck, that he might sever it, would have gloated at such realization ! How many days or hours would have here sufficed to annihilate all the races of men ? Happily, the world was spared the spectacle of these deadly mouths at once aflame. Beautiful but awful must have been the scene, and the earth must have staggered with the shock. One might almost have imagined that man, in his ambition, had shut his God in heaven, and besieged him there.

While the fortifications defending it amazed me, the village of Yorktown disappointed me. I marvelled that so paltry a settlement should have been twice made historic. Here, in the year 1783, Lord Cornwallis surrendered his starving command to the American colonists and their French allies. But the entrenchments of that earlier day had been almost obliterated by these recent labors.   The field, where the Earl delivered up his sword, was trodden bare, and dotted with ditches and ramparts ; while a small monument, that marked the event, had been hacked to fragments by the Southerners, and carried away piecemeal.   Yet, strange to say, relics of the first bombardment had just been discovered, and, among them, a gold-hilted sword.

I visited, in the evening, the late quarters of General Hill, a small white house with green shutters, and also the famous "Nelson House," a roomy mansion where, of old, Cornwallis slept, and where, a few days past, Jefferson Davis and General Lee had held with Magruder, and his associates, a council of war.   It had been also used for hospital purposes, but some negroes were now the only occupants.

The Confederates left behind them seventy spiked and shattered cannon, some powder, and a few splintered wagons ; but in all material respects, their evacuation was thorough and creditable.   Some deserters took the first tidings of the retreat to the astonished Federals, and they raised the national flag within the fortifications, in the gray of the morning of the 4th of May.   Many negroes also escaped the vigilance of their taskmasters, and remained to welcome the victors.   The fine works of Yorktown are monuments to negro labor, for *they* were the hewers and the diggers.   Every slave-owner in Eastern Virginia was obliged to send one half of his male servants between the ages of sixteen and fifty to the Confederate camps, and they were organized into gangs and set to work.   In some cases they were put to military service and made excellent sharpshooters.   The last gun discharged from the town was said to have been fired by a negro.

I slept on board a barge at the wharf that evening, and my dreams ran upon a thousand themes.   To every American this was hallowed ground.   It had been celebrated by the pencil of Trumbull, the pen of Franklin, and the eloquence of Jefferson. Scarce eighty years had elapsed since those great minds established a fraternal government; but the site of their crowning glory was now the scene of their children's shame. Discord had stolen upon their councils and blood had profaned their shrine.

I visited next day a bomb-proof postern, or subterranean passage, connecting the citadel with the outworks, and loitered about the fortifications till noon, when I took passage on the mail steamer, which left the Fortress at eleven o'clock, and reached White House at dusk the same evening. The whole river as I ascended was filled with merchant and naval craft. They made a continuous line from Old Point to the mouth of York River, and the masts and spars environing Yorktown and Gloucester, reminded one of a scene on the Mersey or the Clyde. At West Point, there was an array of shipping scarcely less formidable, and the windings of the interminably crooked Pamunkey were marked for leagues by sails, smoke-stacks, and masts. The landings and wharves were besieged by flat-boats and sloops, and Zouaves were hoisting forage and commissary stores up the red bluffs at every turn of our vessel.

The Pamunkey was a beautiful stream, densely wooded, and occasional vistas opened up along its borders of wheat-fields and meadows, with Virginia farm-houses and negro quarters on the hilltops. Some of the houses on the river banks appeared to be tenanted by white people, but the majority had a haunted, desolate appearance, the only signs of life being strolling soldiers, who thrust their legs through the second story windows, or contemplated the river from the chimney-tops, and groups of negroes who sunned themselves on the piazza, or rushed to the margin to gaze and grin at the passing steamers. There were occasional residences not unworthy of old manorial and baronial times, and these were attended at a little distance by negro quarters of logs, arranged in rows, and provided with mud chimneys built against their gables. Few of the Northern navigable rivers were so picturesque and varied.

We passed two Confederate gunboats, that had been half completed, and burned on the stocks. Their charred elbows and ribs, stared out, like the remains of some extinct monsters; a little delay might have found each of them armed and manned, and carrying havoc upon the rivers and the seas. West Point was simply a tongue, or spit of land, dividing the Mattapony from the Pamunkey river at their junction; a few houses were built upon the shallow, and some wharves, half demolished, marked the terminus of the York and Richmond railroad. A paltry water-battery was the sole defence. Below Cumberland (a collection of huts and a wharf), a number of schooners had been sunk across the river, and, with the aid of an island in the middle, these constituted a rather rigid blockade. The steamboat passed through, steering carefully, but some sailing vessels that followed required to be towed between the narrow apertures. The tops only of the sunken masts could be discerned above the surface, and much time and labor must have been required to place the boats in line and sink them. Vessels were counted by scores above and below this blockade, and at Cumberland the masts were like a forest; clusters of pontoons were here anchored in the river, and a short distance below we found three of the light-draught Federal gunboats moored in the stream. It was growing dark as we rounded to at "White House;" the camp fires of the grand army lit up the sky, and edged the tree-boughs on the margin with ribands of silver. Some drums beat in the distance; sentries paced the strand; the hum of men, and the lowing of commissary cattle, were borne towards us confusedly; soldiers were bathing in the river; team-horses were drinking at the brink; a throng of motley people were crowding about the landing to receive the papers and mails. I had at last arrived at the seat of war, and my ambition to chronicle battles and bloodshed was about to be gratified.

At first, I was troubled to make my way; the tents had

just been pitched; none knew the location of divisions other than their own, and it was now so dark that I did not care to venture far. After a vain attempt to find some flat-boats where there were lodgings and meals to be had, I struck out for general head-quarters, and, undergoing repeated snubbings from pert members of staff, fell in at length, with a very tall, spare, and angular young officer, who spoke broken English, and who heard my inquiries, courteously; he stepped into General Marcy's tent, but the Chief of Staff did not know the direction of Smith's division; he then repaired to Gen. Van Vleet, the chief Quartermaster, but with ill success. A party of officers were smoking under a " fly," and some of these called to him, thus —

"Captain! Duke! De Chartres! What do you wish?

It was, then, the Orleans Prince who had befriended me, and I had the good fortune to hear that the division, of which I was in search, lay a half mile up the river. I never spoke to the Bourbon afterward, but saw him often; and that he was as chivalrous as he was kind, all testimony proved.

A private escorted me to a Captain Mott's tent, and this officer introduced me to General Hancock. I was at once invited to mess with the General's staff, and in the course of an hour felt perfectly at home. Hancock was one of the handsomest officers in the army; he had served in the Mexican war, and was subsequently a Captain in the Quartermaster's department. But the Rebellion placed stars in many shoulder-bars, and few were more worthily designated than this young Pennsylvanian. His first laurels were gained at Williamsburg; but the story of a celebrated charge that won him the day's applause, and McClellan's encomium of the " Superb Hancock," was altogether fictitious. The musket, not the bayonet, gave him the victory. I may doubt, in this place, that any extensive bayonet charge has been known during the war. Some have gone so far as to deny that the bayonet has ever been used at all.

7

Hancock's regiments were the 5th Wisconsin, 49th Pennsylvanian, 43d New York, and 6th Maine. They represented widely different characteristics, and I esteemed myself fortunate to obtain a position where I could so eligibly study men, habits, and warfare. During the evening I fell in with the Colonel of each of these regiments, and from the conversation that ensued, I gleaned a fair idea of them all.

The Wisconsin regiment was from a new and ambitious State of the Northwest. The men were rough-mannered, great-hearted farmers, wood-choppers, and tradesmen. They had all the impulsiveness of the Yankee, with less selfishness, and quite as much bravery. The Colonel was named Cobb, and he had held some leading offices in Wisconsin. A part of his life had been adventurously spent, and he had participated in the Mexican war. He was an ardent Republican in politics, and had been Speaker of a branch of the State Legislature. He was an attorney in a small county town when the war commenced, and his name had been broached for the Governorship. In person he was small, lithe, and capable of enduring great fatigue. His hair was a little gray, and he had no beard. He did not respect appearances, and his sword, as I saw, was antique and quite different in shape from the regulation weapon. He had penetrating gray eyes, and his manners were generally reserved. One had not to regard him twice to see that he was both cautious and resolute. He was too ambitious to be frank, and too passionate not to be brave. In the formula of learning he was not always correct; but few were of quicker perception or more practical and philosophic. He might not, in an emergency, be nicely scrupulous as to means, but he never wavered in respect to objects. His will was the written law to his regiment, and I believed his executive abilities superior to those of any officer in the brigade, not excepting the General's.

The New York regiment was commanded by a young officer named Vinton. He was not more than thirty-five years of age, and was a graduate of the United States Military Academy. Passionately devoted to engineering, he withdrew from the army, and passed five years in Paris, at the study of his art. Returning homeward by way of the West Indies, he visited Honduras, and projected a filibustering expedition to its shores from the States. While perfecting the design, the Rebellion commenced, and his old patron, General Scott, secured him the colonelcy of a volunteer regiment. He still cherished his scheme of "Colonization," and half of his men were promised to accompany him. Personally, Colonel Vinton was straight, dark, and handsome. He was courteous, affable, and brave, — but wedded to his peculiar views, and, as I thought, a thorough "Young American."

The Maine regiment was fathered by Colonel Burnham, a staunch old yeoman and soldier, who has since been made a General. His probity and good-nature were adjuncts of his valor, and his men were of the better class of New Englanders. The fourth regiment fell into the hands of a lawyer from Lewistown, Pennsylvania. He had been also in the Mexican war, and was remarkable mainly for strictness with regard to the sanitary regulations of his camps. He had wells dug at every stoppage, and his tents were generally fenced and canopied with cedar arbors. General Hancock's staff was composed of a number of young men, most of whom had been called from civil life. His brigade constituted one of three commanded by General Smith. Four batteries were annexed to the division so formed; the entire number of muskets was perhaps eight thousand. The Chief of Artillery was a Captain Ayres, whose battery saved the three months' army at Bull Run. It so happened that he came into the General's during the evening, and recited the particulars of a gunboat excursion, thirty miles up the Pamunkey, wherein he had landed his men, and burned a quantity of grain, some warehouses, and shipping. I pencilled the facts at once, made up my letter, and mailed it early in the morning.

CHAPTER VIII.

RUSTICS IN REBELLION.

At White House, I met some of the mixed Indians and negroes from Indiantown Island, which lies among the osiers in the stream. One of these ferried me over, and the people received me obsequiously, touching their straw hats, and saying, "Sar, at your service!" They were all anxious to hear something of the war, and asked, solicitously, if they were to be protected. Some of them had been to Richmond the previous day, and gave me some unimportant items happening in the city. I found that they had Richmond papers of that date, and purchased them for a few cents. They knew little or nothing of their own history, and had preserved no traditions of their tribe. There was, however, I understood, a very old woman extant, named "Mag," of great repute at medicines, pow-wows, and divination. I expressed a desire to speak with her, and was conducted to a log-house, more ricketty and ruined than any of the others. About fifty half-breeds followed me in respectful curiosity, and they formed a semicircle around the cabin. The old woman sat in the threshold, barefooted, and smoking a stump of clay pipe.

"Yaw's one o' dem Nawden soldiers, Aunt Mag!" said my conductor. "He wants to talk wid ye."

"Sot down, honey," said the old woman, producing a wooden stool; "is you a Yankee, honey? Does you want you fauchun told by de ole 'oman?"

(76)

I perceived that the daughter of the Delawares smelt strongly of fire-water, and the fumes of her calumet were most unwholesome. She was greatly disappointed that I did not require her prophetic services, and said, appealingly—

"Why, sar, all de gen'elmen an' ladies from Richmond has dere fauchuns told. I tells 'em true. All my fauchuns comes out true. Ain't dat so, chillen?"

A low murmur of assent ran round the group, and I was obviously losing caste in the settlement.

"Here is a dime," said I, "that I will give you, to tell me the result of the war. Shall the North be victorious in the next battle? Will Richmond surrender within a week? Shall I take my cigar at the Spotswood on Sunday fortnight?"

"I'se been a lookin' into dat," she said, cunningly; "I'se had dreams on dat ar'. Le'um see how de armies stand!"

She brought from the house a cup of painted earthenware containing sediments of coffee. I saw her crafty white eyes look up to mine as she muttered some jargon, and pretended to read the arrangement of the grains.

"Honey," she said, "gi' me de money, and let de ole 'oman dream on it once mo'! It ain't quite clar' yit, young massar. Tank you, honey! Tank you! Let de old 'oman dream! Let de ole 'oman dream!"

She disappeared into the house, chuckling and chattering, and the sons of the forest, loitering awhile, dispersed in various directions. As I followed my conductor to the riverside, and he parted the close bushes and boughs to give us exit, the glare of the camp-fires broke all at once upon us. The ship-lights quivered on the water; the figures of men moved to and fro before the fagots; the stars peeped timorously from the vault; the woods and steep banks were blackly shadowed in the river. Here was I, among the aborigines; and as my dusky acquaintance sent his canoe

7*

skimming across the ripples, I thought how inexplicable were the decrees of Time and the justice of God. Two races united in these people, and both of them we had wronged. From the one we had taken lands; from the other liberties. Two centuries had now elapsed. But the little remnant of the African and the American were to look from their Island Home upon the clash of our armies and the murder of our braves.

By the 19th of May the skirts of the grand army had been gathered up, and on the 20th the march to Richmond was resumed. The troops moved along two main roads, of which the right led to New Mechanicsville and Meadow Bridges, and the left to the railroad and Bottom Bridges. My division formed the right centre, and although the Chickahominy fords were but eighteen miles distant, we did not reach them for three days. On the first night we encamped at Tunstall's, a railroad-station on Black Creek; on the second at New Cold Harbor, a little country tavern, kept by a cripple; and on the night of the third day at Hogan's farm, on the north hills of the Chickahominy. The railroad was opened to Despatch Station at the same time, but the right and centre were still compelled to "team" their supplies from White House. In the new position, the army extended ten miles along the Chickahominy hills; and while the engineers were driving pile, tressel, pontoon, and corduroy bridges, the cavalry was scouring the country, on both flanks, far and wide.

The advance was full of incident, and I learned to keep as far in front as possible, that I might communicate with scouts, contrabands, and citizens. Many odd personages were revealed to me at the farm-houses on the way, and I studied, with curious interest, the native Virginian character. They appeared to be compounds of the cavalier and the boor. There was no old gentleman who owned a thousand barren acres, spotted with scrub timber; who lived in a weather-beaten barn, with a multiplicity of porch and a quantity of chimney; whose means bore no proportion to his pride, and neither to his indolence, — that did not talk of his ancestry, proffer his hospitality, and defy me to an argument. I was a civilian, — they had no hostility to me, — but the blue-coats of the soldiers seared their eyeballs. In some cases their daughters remained upon the property; but the sons and the negroes always fled, — though in contrary directions. The old men used to peep through the windows at the passing columns; and as their gates were wrenched from the hinges, their rails used to pry wagons out of the mud, their pump-handles shaken till the buckets splintered in the shaft, and their barns invaded by greasy agrarians, they walked to and fro, half-weakly, half-wrathfully, but with a pluck, fortitude, and devotion that wrung my respect. Some aged negro women commonly remained, but these were rather incumbrances than aids, and they used the family meal to cook bread for the troops. An old, toothless, grinning African stood at every lane and gate, selling buttermilk and corn-cakes. Poor mortal, sinful old women! They had worked for nothing through their threescore and ten, but avarice glared from their shrivelled pupils, and their last but greatest delight lay in the coppers and the dimes. One would have thought that they had outlived the greed of gold; but wages deferred make the dying miserly.

The lords of the manors were troubled to know the number of our troops. For several days the columns passed with their interminable teams, batteries, and adjuncts, and the old gentlemen were loth to compute us at less than several millions.

"Why, look yonder," said one, pointing to a brigade; "I declar' to gracious, there ain't no less than ten thousand in *them!*"

"Tousands an' tousands!" said a wondering negro at his elbow. "I wonda if dey'll take Richmond dis yer day?"

Many of them hung white flags at their gate-posts, imply-
ing neutrality ; but nobody displayed the Federal colors.   If
there were any covert sympathizers with the purposes of the
army, they remembered the vengeance of the neighbors and
made no demonstrations.   There was a prodigious number
of stragglers from the Federal lines, as these were the bane
of the country people.   They sauntered along by twos and
threes, rambling into all the fields and green-apple orchards,
intruding their noses into old cabins, prying into smoke-
houses, and cellars, looking at the stock in the stables, and
peeping on tiptoe into the windows of dwellings.   These
stragglers were true exponents of Yankee character, —
always wanting to know, — averse to discipline, eccentric
in their orbits, entertaining profound contempt for everything that was not up to the measure of " to hum."
"Look here, Bill, I say ! " said one, with a great grin on
his face ; " did you ever, neow !   I swan ! they call that a
plough down in these parts."
"Devilishest people I ever see ! " said Bill, " stick their
meetin'-houses square in the woods !   Build their chimneys
first and move the houses up to 'em !   All the houses
breakin' out in perspiration of porch !   All their machinery
with Noah in the ark ! Pump the soil dry !   Go to sleep a
milkin' a keow !   Depend entirely on Providence and the
nigger ! "
There was a mill on the New Bridge road, ten miles from
White House, with a tidy farm-house, stacks, and cabins
adjoining.   The road crossed the mill-race by a log bridge,
and a spreading pond or dam lay to the left, — the water
black as ink, the shore sandy, and the stream disappearing
in a grove of straight pines.   A youngish woman, with
several small children, occupied the dwelling, and there remained, besides, her fat sister-in-law and four or five faithful
negroes.   I begged the favor of a meal and bed in the place
one night, and shall not forget the hospitable table with its
steaming biscuit ; the chubby baby, perched upon his high

stool ; the talkative elderly woman, who took snuff at the fireplace ; the contented black-girl, who played the Hebe ; and above all, the trim, plump, pretty hostess, with her brown eyes and hair, her dignity and her fondness, sitting at the head of the board. When she poured the bright coffee into the capacious bowl, she revealed the neatest of hands and arms, and her dialect was softer and more musical than that of most Southerners. In short, I fell almost in love with her ; though she might have been a younger playmate of my mother's, and though she was the wife of a Quartermaster in a Virginia regiment. For, somehow, a woman seems very handsome when one is afield ; and the contact of rough soldiers, gives him a partiality for females. It must have required some courage to remain upon the farm ; but she hoped thereby to save the property from spoliation: I played a game of whist with the sister-in-law, arguing all the while ; and at nine o'clock the servant produced some hard cider, shellbarks, and apples. We drank a cheery toast : "an early peace and old fellowship !" — to which the wife added a sentiment of "always welcome," and the baby laughed at her knee. How brightly glowed the fire ! I wanted to linger for a week, a month, a year, — as I do now, thinking it all over, — and when I strolled to the porch, — hearing the pigeons cooing at the barn ; the water streaming down the dam ; the melancholy monotony of the pine boughs ; — there only lacked the humming mill-wheel, and the strong grip of the miller's hand, to fill the void corner of one's happy heart.

But this was a time of war, when dreams are rudely broken, and mine could not last. The next day some great wheels beat down the bridge, and the teams clogged the road for miles ; the waiting teamsters saw the miller's sheep, and the geese, chickens, and pigs, rashly exposed themselves in the barnyard ; these were killed and eaten, the mill stripped of flour and meal, and the garden despoiled of its vegetables. A quartermaster's horse foundered, and he demanded the miller's, giving therefor a receipt, but specifying upon the same the owner's relation to the Rebellion; and, to crown all, a group of stragglers, butchered the cows, and heaped the beef in their wagons to feed their regimental friends. When I presented myself, late in the afternoon, the yard and porches were filled with soldiers; the wife sat within, her head thrown upon the window, her bright hair unbound, and her eyes red with weeping. The baby had cried itself to sleep, the sister-in-law took snuff fiercely, at the fire; the black girl cowered in a corner.

"There is not bread in the house for my children," she said; "but I did not think they could make me shed a tear."

If there were Spartan women, as the story-books say, I wonder if their blood died with them! I hardly think so.

If I learned anything from my quiet study of this and subsequent campaigns, it was the heartlessness of war. War brutalizes! The most pitiful become pitiless afield, and those who are not callous, must do cruel duties. If the quartermaster had not seized the horses, he would have been accountable for his conduct; had he failed to state the miller's disloyalty in the receipt, he would have been punished. The men were thieves and brutes, to take the meal and meat; but they were perhaps hungry and weary, and sick of camp food; on the whole, I became a devotee of the George Fox faith, and hated warfare, though I knew nothing to substitute for it, in *crises*.

Besides, the optimist might have seen much to admire. Individual merits were developed around me; I saw shopkeepers and mechanics in the ranks, and they looked to be better men. Here were triumphs of engineering; there perfections of applied ingenuity. I saw how the weakest natures girt themselves for great resolves, and how fortitude outstripped itself. It is a noble thing to put by the fear of death. It was a grand spectacle, this civil soldiery of both sections, supporting their principles, ambitions, or whatever instigated them, with their bodies; and their bones, lie where they will, must be severed, when the plough-share some day heaves them to the ploughman.

One morning a friend asked me to go upon a scout.

"Where are your companies?" said I.

"There are four behind, and we shall be joined by six at Old Cold Harbor."

I saw, in the rear, filing through a belt of woods, the tall figures of the horsemen, approaching at a canter.

"Do you command?" said I again.

"No! the Major has charge of the scout, and his orders are secret."

I wheeled beside him, as the cavalry closed up, waved my hand to Plumley, and the girls, and went forward to the rendezvous, about six miles distant. The remaining companies of the regiment were here drawn up, watering their nags. The Major was a thick, sunburnt man, with grizzled beard, and as he saw us rounding a corner of hilly road, his voice rang out—

"Attention! Prepare to mount!"

Every rider sprang to his nag; every nag walked instinctively to his place; every horseman made fast his girths, strapped his blankets tightly, and lay his hands upon bridle-rein and pommel.

"Attention! Mount!"

The riders sprang to their seats; the bugles blew a lively strain; the horses pricked up their ears; and the long array moved briskly forward, with the Captain, the Major, and myself at the head. We were joined in a moment by two pieces of flying artillery, and five fresh companies of cavalry. In a moment more we were underway again, galloping due northward, and, as I surmised, toward Hanover Court House. If any branch of the military service is feverish, adventurous, and exciting, it is that of the cavalry. One's heart beats as fast as the hoof-falls; there is no music like the

winding of the bugle, and no monotone so full of meaning
as the clink of sabres rising and falling with the dashing
pace. Horse and rider become one, — a new race of Centaurs, — and the charge, the stroke, the crack of carbines,
are so quick, vehement, and dramatic, that we seem to be
watching the joust of tournaments or following fierce Sala-
dins and Crusaders again. We had ridden two hours at a
fair canter, when we came to a small stream that crossed
the road obliquely, and gurgled away through a sandy valley into the deepnesses of the woods. A cart-track, half
obliterated, here diverged, running parallel with the creek,
and the Major held up his sword as a signal to halt; at the
same moment the bugle blew a quick, shrill note.

"There are hoof-marks here!" grunted the Major, —
"five of 'em. The Dutchman has gone into the thicket.
Hulloo!" he added, precipitately — "there go the carbines!"

I heard, clearly, two explosions in rapid succession; then
a general discharge, as of several persons firing at once,
and at last, five continuous reports, fainter, but more regular, and like the several emptyings of a revolver. I had
scarcely time to note these things, and the effect produced
upon the troop, when strange noises came from the woods
to the right : the floundering of steeds, the cries and curses
of men, and the ringing of steel striking steel. Directly
the boughs crackled, the leaves quivered, and a horse and
rider plunged into the road, not five rods from my feet.
The man was bareheaded, and his face and clothing were
torn with briars and branches. He was at first riding fairly
upon our troops, when he beheld the uniform and standards,
and with a sharp oath flung up his sword and hands.

"I surrender!" he said; "I give in! Don't shoot!"

The scores of carbines that were levelled upon him at
once dropped to their rests at the saddles; but some unseen
avenger had not heeded the shriek; a ball whistled from the
woods, and the man fell from his cushion like a stone. In

another instant, the German sergeant bounded through the gap, holding his sabre aloft in his right hand; but the left hung stiff and shattered at his side, and his face was deathly white. He glared an instant at the dead man by the roadside, leered grimly, and called aloud —

" Come on, Major ! Dis vay ! Dere are a squad of dem ahead ! "

The bugle at once sounded a charge, the Major rose in the stirrups, and thundered " Forward ! " I reined aside, intuitively, and the column dashed hotly past me. With a glance at the heap of mortality littering the way, I spurred my nag sharply, and followed hard behind. The riderless horse seemed to catch the fever of the moment, and closed up with me, leaving his master the solitary tenant of the dell. For perhaps three miles we galloped like the wind, and my brave little traveller overtook the hindmost of the troop, and retained the position. Thrice there were discharges ahead ; I caught glimpses of the Major, the Captain, and the wolfish sergeant, far in the advance ; and once saw, through the cloud of dust that beset them, the pursued and their individual pursuers, turning the top of a hill. But for the most part, I saw nothing ; I *felt* all the intense, consuming, burning ardor of the time and the event. I thought that my hand clutched a sabre, and despised myself that it was not there. I stood in the stirrups, and held some invisible enemy by the throat. In a word, the bloodiness of the chase was upon me. I realized the fierce infatuation of matching life with life, and standing arbiter upon my fellow's body and soul. It seemed but a moment, when we halted, red and panting, in the paltry Court House village of Hanover ; the field-pieces hurled a few shells at the escaping Confederates, and the men were ordered to dismount.

It seemed that a Confederate picket had been occupying the village, and the creek memorized by the skirmish was

8

an outpost merely. Two of the man Otto's party had been slain in the woods, where also lay as many Southerners.

Hanover Court House is renowned as the birthplace of Patrick Henry, the colonial orator, called by Byron the "forest Demosthenes." In a little tavern, opposite the old Court House building, he began his humble career as a measurer of gills to convivials, and *in* the Court House, — a small stone edifice, plainly but quaintly constructed, — he gave the first exhibitions of his matchless eloquence. Not far away, on a by-road, the more modern but not less famous orator, Henry Clay, was born. The region adjacent to his father's was called the "Slashes of Hanover," and thence came his appellation of the "Mill Boy of the Slashes." I had often longed to visit these shrines; but never dreamed that the booming of cannon would announce me. The soldiers broke into both the tavern and courthouse, and splintered some chairs in the former to obtain relics of Henry. I secured Richmond newspapers of the same morning, and also some items of intelligence. With these I decided to repair at once to White House, and formed the rash determination of taking the direct or Pamunkey road, which I had never travelled, and which might be beset by Confederates. The distance to White House, by this course, was only twenty miles; whereas it was nearly as far to head-quarters; and I believed that my horse had still the persistence to carry me. It was past four o'clock; but I thought to ride six miles an hour while daylight lasted, and, by good luck, get to the depot at nine. The Major said that it was foolhardiness; the Captain bantered me to go. I turned my back upon both, and bade them good by.

CHAPTER IX.

PUT UNDER ARREST.

While daylight remained, I had little reason to repent my wayward resolve. The Pamunkey lay to my left, and the residences between it and the road were of a better order than others that I had seen. This part of the country had not been overrun, and the wheat and young corn were waving in the river-breeze. I saw few negroes, but the porches were frequently occupied by women and white men, who looked wonderingly toward me. There were some hoof-marks in the clay, and traces of a broad tire that I thought belonged to a gun-carriage. The hills of King William County were but a little way off, and through the wood that darkened them, sunny glimpses of vari-colored fields and dwellings now and then appeared. I came to a shabby settlement called New Castle, at six o'clock, where an evil-looking man walked out from a frame-house, and inquired the meaning of the firing at Hanover.

I explained hurriedly, as some of his neighbors meantime gathered around me. They asked if I was not a soldier in the Yankee army, and as I rode away, followed me suspiciously with their eyes and wagged their heads. To end the matter I spurred my pony and soon galloped out of sight. Henceforward I met only stern, surprised glances, and seemed to read "murder" in the faces of the inhabitants. A wide creek crossed the road about five miles further on, where I stopped to water my horse. The shades of night were gathering now; there was no moon; and for the first time I realized the loneliness of my position. Hitherto, adventure had laughed down fear; hereafter my mind was to be darkened like the gloaming, and peopled with ghastly shadows.

I was yet young in the experience of death, and the toppled corpse of the slain cavalry-man on the scout, somehow haunted me. I heard his hoof-falls chiming with my own, and imagined, with a cold thrill, that his steed was still following me; then, his white rigid face and uplifted arms menaced my way; and, at last, the ruffianly form of his slayer pursued him along the wood. They glided like shadows over the foliage, and flashed across the surfaces of pools and rivulets. I heard their steel ringing in the underbrush, and they flitted around me, pursuing and retreating, till my brain began to whirl with the motion. Suddenly my horse stumbled, and I reined him to a halt.

The cold drops were standing on my forehead. I found my knees a-quiver and my breathing convulsive. With an expletive upon my unmanliness, I touched the nag with my heel, and whistled encouragingly. Poor pony! Fifty miles of almost uninterrupted travel had broken his spirit. He leaped into his accustomed pace: but his legs were unsteady and he floundered at every bound. There were pools, ruts, and boughs across the way, with here and there stretches of slippery corduroy; but the thick blackness concealed these, and I expected momentarily to be thrown from the saddle. By and by he dropped from a canter into a rock; from a rock to an amble; then into a walk, and finally to a slow painful limp. I dismounted and took him perplexedly by the bit. A light shone from the window of a dwelling across some open fields to the left, and I thought of repairing thither; but some deep-mouthed dogs began to bay directly, and then the lamp went out. A tiny stream sang at the roadside, flowing toward some deeper tributary; lighting a cigar, I made out, by its fitful illuminings, to wash the limbs of the jaded nag. Then I led him for an hour, till my own limbs were weary, troubled all the time by weird imaginings, doubts, and regrets. When I resumed the saddle the horse had a firmer step and walked pleasantly. I ventured after a time to incite him to a trot, and was going nicely forward, when a deep voice, that almost took my breath, called from the gloom —

"Who comes there? Halt, or I fire! Guard, turn out!"

Directly the road was full of men, and a bull's-eye lantern flashed upon my face. A group of foot-soldiery, with drawn pistols and sabres, gathered around me, and I heard the neigh of steeds from some imperceptible vicinity. "Who is it, Sergeant?" said one. "Is there but one of 'em?" said another. "Cuss him!" said a third; "I was takin' a bully snooze." "Who are yeou?" said the Sergeant, sternly; "what are yeou deouin' aout at this hour o' the night? Are yeou a rebbil?"

"No!"' I answered, greatly relieved; "I am a newspaper correspondent of Smith's division, and there's my pass!"

I was taken over to a place in the woods, where some fagots were smouldering, and, stirring them to a blaze, the Sergeant read the document and pronounced it right.

"Yeou hain't got no business, nevertheless, to be roamin' araound outside o' picket; but seein' as it's yeou, I reckon yeou may trot along!"

I offered to exchange my information for a biscuit and a drop of coffee, for I was wellnigh worn out; while one of the privates produced a canteen more wholesome than cleanly, another gave me a lump of fat pork and a piece of corn bread. They gathered sleepily about me, while I told of the scout, and the Sergeant said that my individual ride was "game enough, but nothin' but darn nonsense." Then they fed my horse with a trifle of oats, and after awhile I

8*

climbed, stiff and bruised, to the saddle again, and bade
them good night.

I knew now that I was at "Putney's," a ford on the
Pamunkey, and an hour later I came in sight of the ship-
lights at White House, and heard the steaming of tugs and
draught-boats, going and coming by night.   I hitched my
horse to a tree, pilfered some hay and fodder from two or
three nags tied adjacent, and picked my way across a gang-
way, several barge-decks, and a floating landing, to the mail
steamer that lay outside.   Her deck and cabin were filled
with people, stretched lengthwise and crosswise, tangled,
grouped, and snoring, but all apparently fast asleep.   I
coolly took a blanket from a man that looked as though he
did not need it, and wrapped myself cosily under a bench
in a corner.   The cabin light flared dimly, half irradiating
the forms below, and the boat heaved a little on the river-
swells.   The night was cold, the floor hard, and I almost
dead with fatigue.   But what of that!   I felt the newspapers in my breast pocket, and knew that the mail could not
leave me in the morning.   Blessed be the news-gatherer's
sleep!   I think he earned it.

It was very pleasant, at dawn, to receive the congratula-
tions of our agent, with whom I breakfasted, and to whom
I consigned a hastily written letter and all the Richmond
papers of the preceding day.   He was a shrewd, sanguine,
middle-aged man, of large experience and good standing in
our establishment.   He was sent through the South at
the beginning of the Rebellion, and introduced into all public
bodies and social circles, that he might fathom the designs
of Secession, and comprehend its spirit.   Afterward he
accompanied the Hatteras and Port Royal expeditions, and
witnessed those celebrated bombardments.   Such a thorough
individual abnegation I never knew.   He was a part of the
establishment, body and soul.   He agreed with its politics,
adhered to all its policies, defended it, upheld it, revered it.
The Federal Government was, to his eye, merely an adjunct

of the paper.   Battles and sieges were simply occurrences for its columns.   Good men, brave men, bad men, died to give it obituaries.   The whole world was to him a Reporter's district, and all human mutations plain matters of news. I hardly think that any city, other than New York, contains such characters.   The journals there are full of fever, and the profession of journalism is a disease.

He cashed me a draft for a hundred dollars, and I filled my saddle-bags with smoking-tobacco, spirits, a meerschaum pipe, packages of sardines, a box of cigars, and some cheap publications.   Then we adjourned to the quay, where the steamer was taking in mails, freight and passengers.   The papers were in his side-pocket, and he was about to commit them to a steward for transmission to Fortress Monroe, when my name was called from the strand by a young mounted officer, connected with one of the staffs of my division.   I thought that he wished to exchange salutations or make some inquiries, and tripped to his side.

" General McClellan wants those newspapers that you obtained at Hanover yesterday ! "

A thunderbolt would not have more transfixed me.   I could not speak for a moment.   Finally, I stammered that they were out of my possession.

" Then, sir, I arrest you, by order of General McClellan. Get your horse ! "

" Stop ! " said I, agitatedly, " —it may not be too late. I can recover them yet.   Here is our agent,— I gave them to him."

I turned, at the word, to the landing where he stood a moment before.   To my dismay, he had disappeared.

" This is some frivolous pretext to escape," said the Lieutenant ; you correspondents are slippery fellows, but I shall take care that you do not play any pranks with me.   The General is irritated already, and if you prevaricate relative to those papers he may make a signal example of you."

I begged to be allowed to look for ——; but he answered

cunningly, that I had better mount and ride on. An acquaintance of mine here interfered, and testified to the existency of the agent and his probable connection with the journals. Pale, flurried, excited, I started to discover him, the Lieutenant following me closely meantime. We entered every booth and tent, went from craft to craft, sought among the thick clusters of people, and even at the Commissary's and Quartermaster's pounds, that lay some distance up the railroad.

"I am sorry for you, old fellow," said the Lieutenant, "but your accomplice has probably escaped. It's very sneaking of him, as it makes it harder for you; but I have no authority to deal with him, though I shall take care to report his conduct at head-quarters."

I found that the Lieutenant was greatly gratified with the duty entrusted to him. He had been at the cavalry quarters on the return of the scouting party, and had overheard the Major muttering something as to McClellan's displeasure at receiving no Richmond journals. The Major had added that one of the correspondents took them to White House, and, mentioning me by name, this young and aspiring satellite had blurted out that he knew me, and could doubtless overtake me at the mail-boat in the morning. The Commanding General authorized him to arrest me *with the papers*, and report at head-quarters. This was then a journey to recommend him to authority, and it involved no personal danger. I was not so intimidated that I failed to see how the Lieutenant would lose his gayest feather by failing to recover the journals, and I dexterously insinuated that it would be well to recommence the search. This time we were successful. The shrewd, sanguine, middle-aged man was coolly contemplating the river from an outside barge, concealed from the shore by piled boxes of ammunition. He was reading a phonetic pamphlet, and appeared to take his apprehension as a pleasant morning call. I caught one meaning glance, however, that satisfied me how clearly he understood the case.

"Ha! Townsend," said he, smilingly, "back already? I thought we had lost you. One of your military friends? Good-day, Lieutenant."

"I am under arrest, my boy," said I, "and you will much aggravate General McClellan, if you do not consign those Richmond journals to his deputy here."

"Under arrest? You surprise me! I am sorry, Lieutenant that you have had so fatiguing a ride, but the fact is, those papers have gone down the river. If the General is not in a great hurry, he will see their columns reproduced by us in a few days."

"How did they go?" said the Lieutenant, with an oath, "if by the mail-boat I will have General Van Vliet despatch a tug to overhaul her."

"I am very sorry again," said the bland civilian, smoothing his hands: "but they went by the *South America* at a much earlier hour."

I looked appealingly to him; the satellite stared down the river perplexedly, but suddenly his eye fell upon something that absorbed it; and he turned like a madman to ——

"By! —— sir, you are lying to me. There is the *South America* moored to a barge, and her steam is not up!"

"Those words are utterly uncalled for," said the agent, — "but you cannot irritate me, my dear sir! I know that youth is hot, — particularly military youth yet inexperienced; and therefore I pardon you. I made a mistake. It was not the *South America*, it was — it was — upon my word I cannot recall the name!"

"You do not mean to!" thundered the young Ajax, to whose vanity, ——'s speech had been gall; "my powers are discretionary: I arrest you in the name of General McClellan."

"Indeed! Be sure you understand your orders! It isn't probable that such a fiery blade is allowed much discretionary margin. The General himself would not assume such airs. Why don't you shoot me? It might contribute to your promotion, and that is, no doubt, your object. I know General McClellan very well. He is a personal friend of mine."

His manner was so self-possessed, his tone so cutting, that the young man of fustian — whose name was Kenty — fingered his sword hilt, and foamed at the lips.

"March on," said he, — "I will report this insolence word for word."

He motioned us to the quay; we preceded him. The sanguine gentleman keeping up a running fire of malevolent sarcasm.

"Stop!" said he quietly, as we reached his tent, — "I have not sent them at all. They are here. And you have made all this exhibition of yourself for nothing. I am the better soldier, you see. You are a drummer-boy, not an officer. Take off your shoulder-bars, and go to school again."

He disappeared a minute, returned with two journals, and looking at me, meaningly, turned to their titles.

"Let me see!" he said, smoothly, — "Richmond *Examiner*, May 28, Richmond *Enquirer*, May 22. There! You have them! Go in peace! Give my respects to General McClellan! Townsend, old fellow, you have done your full duty. Don't let this young person frighten you. Good by."

He gave me his hand, with a sinister glance, and left something in my palm when his own was withdrawn. I examined it hastily when I girt up my saddle. It said: "*Your budget got off safe, old fellow.*" He had given Kenty some old journals that were of no value to anybody. When we were mounted and about to start, the Lieutenant looked witheringly upon his persecutor —

"Allow me to say, sir," he exclaimed, "that you are the most unblushing liar I ever knew."

"Thank you, kindly," said ——, taking off his hat, "you do me honor!"

Our route was silent and weary enough. The young man at my side, unconscious of his wily antagonist's deception, boasted for some time that he had attained his purposes. As I could not undeceive him, I held my tongue; but feared that when this trick should be made manifest, the vengeance would fall on me alone. I heartily wished the unlucky papers at the bottom of the sea. To gratify an adventurous whim, and obtain a day's popularity at New York, I had exposed my life, crippled my nag, and was now to be disgraced and punished. What might or might not befall me, I gloomily debated. The least penalty would be expulsion from the army; but imprisonment till the close of the war, was a favorite amusement with the War Office. How my newspaper connection would be embarrassed was a more grievous inquiry. It stung me to think that I had blundered twice on the very threshold of my career. Was I not acquiring a reputation for rashness that would hinder all future promotion and cast me from the courts of the press. Here the iron entered into my soul; for be it known, I loved Bohemia! This roving commission, these vagabond habits, this life in the open air among the armies, the white tents, the cannon, and the drums, they were my elysium, my heart! But to be driven away, as one who had broken his trust, forfeited favor and confidence, and that too on the eve of grand events, was something that would embitter my existence.

We passed the familiar objects that I had so often buoyantly beheld, — deserted encampments, cross-roads, rills, farm-houses, fields, and at last came to Daker's. I called out to them, and explained my woful circumstances with rueful conciseness.

It was growing dark when we came to general headquarters, two miles beyond Gaines's Mill. The tents were scattered over the surface of a hill, and most of them were illumined by candles.

The Lieutenant gave our horses to an orderly, and led the way through two outer circles of wall-tents, between which and the inner circle, guards were pacing, to deny all vulgar ingress.

A staff officer took in our names, and directly returned with the reply of "Pass in!" We were now in the sacred enclosure, secured by flaming swords. Four tents stood in a row, allotted respectively to the Chief of Staff, the Adjutant-General, the telegraph operators, and the select staff officers. Just behind them, embowered by a covering of cedar boughs, stood the tent of General Mc-Clellan. Close by, from an open plot or area of ground, towered a pine trunk, floating the national flag. Lights burned in three of the tents : low voices, as of subdued conversation, were heard from the first.

A little flutter of my heart, a drawing aside of canvas, two steps, an uncovering, and a bow, — I stood at my tribunal ! A couple of candles were placed upon a table, whereat sat a fine specimen of man, with kindly features, dark, grayish, flowing hair, and slight marks of years upon his full, purplish face. He looked to be a well-to-do citizen, whose success had taught him sedentary convivialities. A fuming cigar lay before him ; some empty champagne bottles sat upon a pine desk ; tumblers and a decanter rested upon a camp-stool ; a bucket, filled with water and a great block of ice, was visible under the table. Five other gentlemen, each with a star in his shoulder-bar, were dispersed upon chairs and along a camp bedside. The tall, angular, dignified gentleman with compressed lips and a "character" nose, was General Barry, Chief of Artillery. The lithe, severe, gristly, sanguine person, whose eyes flashed even in repose, was General Stoneman, Chief of Cavalry. The large, sleepy-eyed, lymphatic, elderly man, clad in dark, civil gray, whose ears turned up habitually as from deafness, was Prince de Joinville, brother to Louis Philippe, King of France. The little man with red hair and beard, who moved quickly and who spoke sharply, was Seth Williams, Adjutant-General. The stout person with florid face, large, blue eyes, and white, straight hair, was General Van Vliet, Quartermaster-General. And the man at the table, was General Marcy, father-in-law to McClellan, and Executive officer of the army.

Maps, papers, books, and luggage lay around the room; all the gentlemen were smoking and wine sparkled in most of the glasses. Some swords were lying upon the floor, a pair of spurs glistened by the bed, and three of the officers had their feet in the air.

"What is it you wish, Lieutenant?" said General Marcy, gravely.

The boor in uniform at my side, related his errand and order, gave the particulars of my arrest, declaimed against our agent, and submitted the journals. He told his story stammeringly, and I heard one of the officers in the background mutter contemptuously when he had finished.

"Were you aware of the order prohibiting correspondents from keeping with the advance?" said the General, looking up.

"I had not been notified from head-quarters. I have been with the army only a week."

"You knew that you had no business upon scouts, forages, or reconnoissances; why did you go?"

"I went by invitation."

"Who invited you?"

"I would prefer not to state, since it would do him an injury."

Here the voices in the background muttered, as I thought, applaudingly. Gaining confidence as I proceeded, I spoke more boldly —

"I am sure I regret that I have disobeyed any order of General McClellan's; but there can nothing occur in the rear of an army. Obedience, in this case, would be indolence and incompetence; for only the reliable would stay

9

behind and the reckless go ahead.   If I am accredited here
as a correspondent, I must keep up with the events.   And
the rivalries of our tribe, General, are so many, that the
best of us sometimes forget what is right for what is expedient.   I hope that General McClellan will pass by this
offence."

He heard my rambling defence quietly, excused the Lieutenant, and whistled for an orderly.

" I don't think that you meant to offend General McClellan," he said, "but he wishes you to be detained.   Give
me your pass.   Orderly, take this gentleman to General
Porter, and tell him to treat him kindly.   Good night."

When we got outside of the tent, I slipped a silver half-
dollar into the orderly's hand, and asked him if he understood the General's final remark.   He said, in reply, that I
was directed to be treated with courtesy, kindness, and care,
and asked me, in conclusion, if there were any adjectives
that might intensify the recommendation.   When we came
to General Porter, the Provost-Marshal, however, he pooh-
poohed the qualifications, and said that *his* business was
merely to put me under surveillance.   This unamiable man
ordered me to be taken to Major Willard, the deputy Provost, whose tent we found after a long search.   The Major
was absent, but some young officers of his mess were taking supper at his table, and with these I at once engaged
in conversation.

I knew that if I was to be spared an immersion in the
common guardhouse, with drunkards, deserters, and prisoners of war, I must win the favor of these men.   I gave
them the story of my arrest, spoke lightly of the offence
and jestingly of the punishment, and, in fact, so improved
my cause that, when the Major appeared, and the Sergeant
consigned me to his custody, one of the young officers took
him aside, and, I am sure, said some good words in my
favor.

The Major was a bronzed, indurated gentleman, scrupulously attired, and courteously stern. He looked at me twice or thrice, to my confusion; for I was dusty, wan, and running over with perspiration. His first remark had, naturally, reference to the lavatory, and, so far as my face and hair were concerned, I was soon rejuvenated. I found on my return to the tent, a clean plate and a cup of steaming coffee placed for me, and I ate with a full heart though pleading covertly the while. When I had done, and the tent became deserted by all save him and me, he said, simply—

"What am I to do with you, Mr. Townsend?"

"Treat me as a gentleman I hope, Major."

"We have but one place of confinement," said he, "the guardhouse; but I am loth to send you there. Light your pipe, and I will think the matter over."

He took a turn in front, consulted with some of his associates, and directly returning, said that I was to be quartered in his office-tent, adjoining. A horror being thus lifted from my mind, I heard with sincere interest many revelations of his military career. He had been a common soldier in the Mexican war, and had fought his way, step by step, to repeated commissions. He had garrisoned Fort Yuma, and other posts on the far plains, and at the beginning of the war was tendered a volunteer brigade, which he modestly declined. His tastes were refined, and a warm fancy, approaching poetry, enhanced his personal reminiscences. His face softened, his eyes grew milder, his large, commanding mouth relaxed,—he was young again, living his adventures over. We talked thus till almost midnight, when two regulars appeared in front,—stiff, ramrodish figures, that came to a jerking "present," tapped their caps with two fingers, and said, explosively; "Sergeant of Guard, Number Five!"

The Major rose, gave me his hand, and said that I would find a candle in my tent, with waterproof and blankets on the ground. I was to give myself no concern about the nag, and might, if I chose, sit for an hour to write, but must, on no account, attempt to leave the canvas, for the guard would instantly shoot me down.   The guard in question had a *doppel-ganger*, — counterpart of himself in inflexibility, — and both were appendages of their muskets.   He was not probably a sentient being, certainly not a conversational one.   He knew the length of a stride, and the manual of bayonet-exercise, but was, during his natural life, a blind idolater of a deity, called "Orders."   The said "Orders," for the present evening, were walking, not talking, and he was dumb to all conciliatory words.   He took a position at one end of my tent, and his double at the other end.   They carried their muskets at "support arms," and paced up and down, measuredly, like two cloaked and solemn ghosts.   I wrapped myself in the damp blankets, and slept through the bangs of four or five court-martials and several executions. At three o'clock, they changed ramrods, — the old doppelgangers going away, and two new ones fulfilling their functions.

CHAPTER X.

AFTER THE VICTORY.

THE two ramrods were still pacing to and fro, when I aroused in the gray of the morning; but they looked very misty and moist, as if they were impalpables that were shortly to evaporate. The Major poked his head between the flaps at eight o'clock, and said that breakfast was ready; but the ramrod nearest me kept vigilantly alongside, and I thought he had been invited also. The other ramrod guarded the empty tent, and I think that he believed me a droppel-ganger likewise.

I wondered what was to be done with me, as the hours slipped rapidly by. The guards were relieved again at ten o'clock, and Quartermaster's men commenced to take down the tents. Camps were to be moved, and I inquired solicitously if I was to be moved also. The Major replied that prisoners were commonly made to walk along the road, escorted by horsemen, and I imagined, with dread, the companionship of negroes, estrays, ragged Confederates, and such folk, while the whole army should witness my degradation. Finally, all the tents were lifted and packed in wagons, as well as the furniture. I adhered to a stool, at which the teamster looked wistfully, and the implacable sentinels walked to and fro. A rumor became current among the private soldiers, that I was the nephew of the southern General Lee, whose wife had been meantime captured at Hanover Court House. Curious groups sauntered

9*   (101)

around me, and talked behind their hands.   One man was overheard to say that I had fought desperately, and covered myself with glory, and another thought that I favored my uncle somewhat, and might succeed to his military virtues.

"I guess I'll take that cheer, if you ain't got no objection," said the teamster, and he slung it into the wagon. What to do now troubled me materially; but one of the soldiers brought a piece of rail, and I "squatted" lugubriously on the turf.

"If you ever get to Richmond," said I, "you shall be considerately treated."   (Profound sensation.)

"Thankee!" replied the man, touching his cap; "but I'm werry well pleased *out* o' Richmond, Captain."

Here the Major was seen approaching, a humorous smile playing about his eyes.

"You are discharged," said he; "General Marcy will return your pass, and perhaps your papers."

I wrung his hand with indescribable relief, and he sent the "ramrod" on guard, to saddle my horse.   In a few minutes, I was mounted again, much to the surprise of the observers of young Lee, and directly I stood before the kindly Chief of Staff.   At my request, he wrote a note to the division commander, specifying my good behavior, and restoring to me all privileges and immunities.   He said nothing whatever as to the mistake in the papers, and told me that, on special occasions, I might keep with advances, by procuring an extraordinary pass at head-quarters.   In short, my arrest conduced greatly to my efficiency.   I invariably carried my Richmond despatches to General Marcy, thereafter, and, if there was information of a legitimate description, he gave me the benefit of it.

My own brigade lay at Dr. Gaines's house, during this time, and we did not lack for excitement.   Just behind the house lay several batteries of rifled guns, and these threw shells at hourly intervals, at certain Confederate batteries across the river. The distance was two miles or less; but the firing was generally wretched. Crowds of soldiers gathered around, to watch the practice, and they threw up their hats applaudingly at successful hits. Occasionally a great round shot would bound up the hill, and a boy, one day, seeing one of these spent balls rolling along the ground, put out his foot to stop it, but shattered his leg so dreadfully that it had to be amputated. Dr. Gaines was a rich, aristocratic, and indolent old Virginian, whose stables, summerhouses, orchards, and negro-quarters were the finest in their district. The shooting so annoyed him that he used to resort to the cellar; several shots passed through his roof, and one of the chimneys was knocked off. His family carriages were five in number, and as his stables were turned into hospitals, these were all hauled into his lawn, where their obsolete trimmings and queer shape constantly amused the soldiers. About this time I became acquainted with some officers of the 5th Maine regiment, and by permission, accompanied them to Mechanicsville. I was here, on the afternoon of Thursday, May 27, when the battle of Hanover Court House was fought. We heard the rapid growl of guns, and continuous volleys of musketry, though the place was fourteen miles distant. At evening, a report was current that the Federals had gained a great victory, and captured seven hundred prisoners. The truth of this was established next morning; for detachments of prisoners were from time to time brought in, and the ambulances came to camp, laden with the wounded. I took this opportunity of observing the Confederate soldiers, as they lay at the Provost quarters, in a roped pen, perhaps one hundred rods square.

It was evening, as I hitched my horse to a stake near-by, and pressed up to the receptacle for the unfortunates. Sentries enclosed the pen, walking to-and-fro with loaded muskets; a throng of officers and soldiers had assembled to gratify their curiosity; and new detachments of captives came in hourly, encircled by sabremen, the Southerners

being disarmed and on foot.   The scene within the area
was ludicrously moving.   It reminded me of the witch-scene
in Macbeth, or pictures of brigands or Bohemian gypsies at
rendezvous, not less than five hundred men, in motley,
ragged costumes, with long hair, and lean, wild, haggard
faces, were gathered in groups or in pairs, around some
fagot fires.   In the growing darkness their expressions
were imperfectly visible ; but I could see that most of them
were weary, and hungry, and all were depressed and
ashamed.   Some were wrapped in blankets of rag-carpet,
and others wore shoes of rough, untanned hide.   Others
were without either shoes or jackets, and their heads were
bound with red handkerchiefs.   Some appeared in red
shirts ; some in stiff beaver hats ; some were attired in
shreds and patches of cloth ; and a few wore the soiled
garments of citizen gentlemen ; but the mass adhered to
homespun suits of gray, or "butternut," and the coarse
blue kersey common to slaves.   In places I caught glimpses
of red Zouave breeches and leggings ; blue Federal caps,
Federal buttons, or Federal blouses ; these were the spoils
of anterior battles, and had been stripped from the slain.
Most of the captives were of the appearances denominated
"scraggy" or "knotty."   They were brown, brawny, and
wiry, and their countenances were intense, fierce, and animal.   They came from North Carolina, the poorest and
least enterprising Southern State, and ignorance, with its
attendant virtues, were the common facial manifestations.
Some lay on the bare ground, fast asleep ; others chatted
nervously as if doubtful of their future treatment ; a few
were boisterous, and anxious to beg tobacco or coffee from
idle. Federals ; the rest — and they comprehended the
greater number — were silent, sullen, and vindictive.   They
met curiosity with scorn, and spite with imprecations.   A
child — not more than four years of age, I think — sat
sleeping in a corner upon an older comrade's lap.   A gray-
bearded pard was staunching a gash in his cheek with the
tail of his coat.   A fine-looking young fellow sat with his

face in his hands, as if his heart were far off, and he wished to shut out this bitter scene. In a corner, lying morosely apart, were a Major, three Captains, and three Lieutenants, — young athletic fellows, dressed in rich gray cassimere, trimmed with black, and wearing soft black hats adorned with black ostrich-feathers. Their spurs were strapped upon elegantly fitting boots, and they looked as far above the needy, seedy privates, as lords above their vassals.

After a time, couples and squads of the prisoners were marched off to cut and carry some firewood, and water, for the use of their pen, and then each Confederate received coffee, pork, and crackers; they were obliged to prepare their own meals, but some were so hungry that they gnawed the raw pork, like beasts of prey. Those who were not provided with blankets, shivered through the night, though the rain was falling, and the succession of choking coughs that ran through the ranks, told how ill they could afford the exposure. Major Willard had charge of these men, and he sent a young officer to get me admittance to the pen, that I might speak with them.

"Good evening, Major," I said, to the ranking Confederate officer, and extended my hand. He shook it, embarrassedly, and ran me over with his eye, as if to learn my avocation. "Can I obtain any facts from you," I continued, "as to the battle of Hanover?"

"Fuh what puhpose?" he said, in his strong southern dialect.

"For publication, sir."

He sat up at once, and said that he should be happy to tell me anything that would not be a violation of military honor. I asked him, therefore, the Confederate Commandant at Hanover, the number of brigades, regiments, and batteries engaged, the disposition of forces, the character of the battle, and the losses, so far as he knew, upon his own side. Much of this he revealed, but unguardedly let out other matters, that direct inquiry could not have discovered. I took notes of the legitimate passages, trusting to memory for the rest; and think that I possessed his whole stock of information, in the course of an hour's manœuvring. It seemed that General Branch, formerly a member of the Federal congress, had been sent with some thousands of Carolina troops across the upper Chickahominy, to see if it would not be possible to turn the Federal right, and cut off one of its brigades; but a stronger Federal reconnoissance had gone northward the day before, and discovering Branch's camp-fires, sent, during the night, for reinforcements. In the end, the " North State " volunteers were routed, their cannon silenced or broken, and seven hundred of their number captured. The Federals lost a large number of men killed, and the wounded upon both sides, were numerous.

The Confederate Major was of the class referred to in polite American parlance, as a " blatherskite." He boasted after the manner of his fellow-citizens from the county of " Bunkum," but nevertheless feared and trembled, to the manifest disgust of one of the young Captains.

" Majuh ! " said this young man, " what you doin' thah ! That fellow's makin' notes of all your slack; keep your tongue ! aftah awhile you'll tell the nombah of the foces ! Don't you s'pose he'll prent it all ? "

The Major had, in fact, been telling me how many regiments the " old Nawth State, suh," had furnished to the " suhvice," and I had the names of some thirty colonels, in order. The young Captain gave me a sketch of General Branch, and was anxious that I should publish something in extenuation of North Carolina valor.

" We have lost mo' men," said he, " than any otha' Commonwealth ; but these Vuhginians, whose soil, by ———— ! suh, we defend suh ! Yes, suh ! whose soil we defend ; these Vuhginians, stigmatize us as cowads ! *We*, suh ! yes suh, *we*, that nevah wanted to leave the Union, — *we*

cowads! Look at ou' blood, suh, ou' blood! That's it,
by —— ! look at that! shed on every field of the ole Dominion, — killed, muhdud, captued, crippled! We *cowads!* I want you prent that!"

I was able to give each of the officers a drop of whiskey
from my flask, and I never saw men drink so thirstily.
Their hands and lips trembled as they took it, and their
eyes shone like lunacy, as the hot drops sank to the cold
vitals, and pricked the frozen blood. Mingling with the
privates, I stirred up some native specimens of patriotism,
that appeared to be in great doubt as to the causes and ends
of the war. They were very much in the political condition of a short, thick, sententious man, in blue drilling
breeches, who said —

"Damn the country! What's to be done with *us?*"

One person said that he enlisted for the honor of his
family, that "fit in the American Revolution;" and another
came out to "hev a squint et the fightin'." Several were
northern and foreign lads, that were working on Carolina
railroads, and could not leave the section, and some labored
under the impression that they were to have a "slice" of
land and a "nigger," in the event of Southern independence.
A few comprehended the spirit of the contest, and took up
arms from principle; a few, also, declared their enmity to
"Yankee institutions," and had seized the occasion to
"polish them off," and "give them a ropein' in;" but many
said it was "dull in our deestreeks, an' the niggers was
runnin' away, so I thought I'ud jine the foces." The
great mass said, that they never contemplated "this box,"
or "this fix," or "these suckemstances," and all wanted the
war to close, that they might return to their families.
Indeed, my romantic ideas of rebellion were ruthlessly
profaned and dissipated. I knew that there was much selfishness, peculation, and "Hessianism" in the Federal
lines, but I had imagined a lofty patriotism, a dignified
purpose, and an inflexible love of personal liberty among

the Confederates.   Yet here were men who knew little of
the principles for which they staked their lives; — who
enlisted from the commonest motives of convenience, whim,
pelf, adventure, and foray; and who repented, after their
first misfortune, with the salt rheum in their eyes.   I think
that all "great uprisings" resolve to this complexion.
With due reverence for my own ancestry, I think that they
sometimes stooped from greatness to littleness.   I must
confess that certain admissions in my revolutionary text-
book are much clearer, now that I have followed a campaign.   And if, as I had proposed, I could have witnessed
the further fortunes of the illustrious Garibaldi, I think that
some of his compatriots would have been found equally
inconsistent.   Let no man believe that the noblest cause is
fought out alone by the unerring motives of duty and devotion.   The masses are never so constant.   They cannot
appreciate an abstraction, however divine.   Any of the
gentlemen in question would have preferred their biscuit
and fat pork before the political enfranchisement of the
whole world!

I rode across the fields to the Hogan, Curtis, and Gaines
mansions; for some of the wounded had meantime been
deposited in each of them.   All the cow-houses, wagon-
sheds, hay-barracks, hen-coops, negro cabins, and barns
were turned into hospitals.   The floors were littered with
"corn-shucks" and fodder; and the maimed, gashed, and
dying lay confusedly together.   A few, slightly wounded,
stood at windows, relating incidents of the battle; but at
the doors sentries stood with crossed muskets, to keep out
idlers and gossips.   The mention of my vocation was an
"open sesame," and I went unrestrained, into all the largest hospitals.   In the first of these an amputation was being
performed, and at the door lay a little heap of human fingers, feet, legs, and arms.   I shall not soon forget the
bare-armed surgeons, with bloody instruments, that leaned
over the rigid and insensible figure, while the comrades of

the subject looked horrifiedly at the scene. The grating of the murderous saw drove me into the open air, but in the second hospital which I visited, a wounded man had just expired, and I encountered his body at the threshold. Within, the sickening smell of mortality was almost insupportable, but by degrees I became accustomed to it. The lanterns hanging around the room streamed fitfully upon the red eyes, and half-naked figures. All were looking up, and saying, in pleading monotone: "Is that you, doctor?" Men with their arms in slings went restlessly up and down, smarting with fever. Those who were wounded in the lower extremities, body, or head, lay upon their backs, tossing even in sleep. They listened peevishly to the wind whistling through the chinks of the barn. They followed one with their rolling eyes. They turned away from the lantern, for it seemed to sear them. Soldiers sat by the severely wounded, laving their sores with water. In many wounds the balls still remained, and the discolored flesh was swollen unnaturally. There were some who had been shot in the bowels, and now and then they were frightfully convulsed, breaking into shrieks and shouts. Some of them iterated a single word, as, "doctor," or "help," or "God," or "oh!" commencing with a loud spasmodic cry, and continuing the same word till it died away in cadence. The act of calling seemed to lull the pain. Many were unconscious and lethargic, moving their fingers and lips mechanically, but never more to open their eyes upon the light; they were already going through the valley and the shadow. I think, still, with a shudder, of the faces of those who were told mercifully that they could not live. The unutterable agony; the plea for somebody on whom to call; the longing eyes that poured out prayers; the looking on mortal as if its resources were infinite; the fearful looking to the immortal as if it were so far off, so implacable, that the dying appeal would be in vain; the open lips, through which one could almost look at the quaking heart below; the ghastli-

10

ness of brow and tangled hair; the closing pangs; the awful *quietus*. I thought of Parrhasius, in the poem, as I looked at these things : —

> "Gods !
> Could I but paint a dying groan ——."

And how the keen eye of West would have turned from the reeking cockpit of the *Victory*, or the tomb of the Dead Man Restored, to this old barn, peopled with horrors. I rambled in and out, learning to look at death, studying the manifestations of pain, — quivering and sickening at times, but plying my avocation, and jotting the names for my column of mortalities.

At eleven o'clock there was music along the high-road, and a general rushing from camps. The victorious regiments were returning from Hanover, under escort, and all the bands were pealing national airs. As they turned down the fields towards their old encampments, the several brigades stood under arms to welcome them, and the cheers were many and vigorous. But the solemn ambulances still followed after, and the red flag of the hospitals flaunted bloodily in the blue midnight.

Both the prisoners and the wounded were removed between midnight and morning to White House, and as I had despatches to forward by the mail-boat, I rode down in an ambulance, that contained six wounded men besides. The wounded were to be consigned to hospital boats, and forwarded to hospitals in northern cities, and the prisoners were to be placed in a transport, under guard, and conveyed to Fort Delaware, near Philadelphia.

Ambulances, it may be said, incidentally, are either two-wheeled or four-wheeled. Two-wheeled ambulances are commonly called "hop, step, and jumps." They are so constructed that the forepart is either very high or very low, and may be both at intervals. The wounded occupants may be compelled to ride for hours in these carriages, with their heels elevated above their heads, and may finally be shaken out, or have their bones broken by the terrible jolting. The four-wheeled ambulances are built in shelves, or compartments, but the wounded are in danger of being smothered in them. It was in one of these latter that I rode, sitting with the driver. We had four horses, but were thrice "swamped" on the road, and had to take out the wounded men once, till we could start the wheels. Two of these men were wounded in the face, one of them having his nose completely severed, and the other having a fragment of his jaw knocked out. A third had received a ball among the thews and muscles behind his knee, and his whole body appeared to be paralyzed. Two were wounded in the shoulders, and the sixth was shot in the breast, and was believed to be injured inwardly, as he spat blood, and suffered almost the pain of death. The ride with these men, over twenty miles of hilly, woody country, was like one of Dante's excursions into the Shades. In the awful stillness of the dark pines, their screams frightened the hooting owls, and the whirring insects in the leaves and tree-tops quieted their songs. They heard the gurgle of the rills, and called aloud for water to quench their insatiate thirst. One of them sang a shrill, fierce, fiendish ballad, in an interval of relief, but plunged, at a sudden relapse, in prayers and curses. We heard them groaning to themselves, as we sat in front, and one man, it seemed, was quite out of his mind. These were the outward manifestations; but what chords trembled and smarted within, we could only guess. What regrets for good resolves unfulfilled, and remorse for years misspent, made-hideous these sore and panting hearts? The moonlight pierced through the thick foliage of the wood, and streamed into our faces, like invitations to a better life. But the crippled and bleeding could not see or feel it, — buried in the shelves of the ambulance.

CHAPTER XI.

BALLOON BATTLES.

SOME days ago, as I was sitting in Central Park, under a tree no bigger than Jonah's gourd, broiling nicely brown, and seasoning the process by reading what the lesser weeklies said about me, I saw at the Park gate a great phantasm, like a distended sausage, swaying to and fro as if striving to burst, and directly the horrible thing blew upwards, spilling all the stuffing from the case.

I saw in a moment that the apparition was a balloon, and that the aeronaut was only emptying ballast.

Straight toward me the floating vessel came, so close to the ground that I could hear the silk crackle and the ropes creak, till, directly, a man leaned over the side and shouted —

" Is that you, Townsend ? "

" Hallo, Lowe ! "

" I want you to get on your feet and be spry about it: we have a literary party here, and wish you to write it up. I'll let one bag of ballast go, as we touch the grass, and you must leap in simultaneously. Thump ! "

Here the car collided with the ground, and in another instant, I found quantities of dirt spilled down my back, and two or three people lying beneath me. The world slid away, and the clouds opened to receive me. Lowe was opening a bottle of Heidsick, and three or four gentlemen with *heads sick* were unclosing the petals of their lips to get the afternoon dew.

These were the various critics and fugitive writers of the weekly and daily press. They looked as if they wanted to put each other over the side of the car, but smothered their invective at my advent, as if I were so much pearl-ash.

It was just seven o'clock, and the Park lay like a veined and mottled blood-stone in the red sunset. The city wilted to the littleness of a rare mosaic pin, its glittering point parting the blue scarf of the bay, and the white bosom of the ocean swelling afar, all draped with purple clouds like golden hair, in which the entangled gems were the sails of the white ships.

I said this aloud, and all the party drew their lead pencils. They forgot the occasion in my eloquence, and wanted to report me.

Just here, I drew a field-glass from the aeronaut, and reconnoitred the streets of the city. To my dismay there was nobody visible on Broadway but gentlemen. I called everybody's attention to the fact, and it was accounted for on the supposition that the late bank forgeries and defalcations, growing out of the extravagance of womankind, had prompted all the husbands to make of their homes nunneries.

We observed, however, close by every gentleman, something that resembled a black dog with his tail curled over his back.

" Stuff ! " said one, " they're hay wagons."

" No ! " cried Lowe, " they're nothing of the sort; they are waterfalls, and the ladies are, of course, invisible under them."

We accepted the explanation, and thought the trip very melancholy. No landscape is complete without a woman. Very soon we struck the great polar current, and passed Harlem river; the foliage of the trees, by some strange anomaly, began to ascend towards us, but Lowe caught two

10*

or three of the supposed leaves, and they proved to be green-backs.

There was at once a tremendous sensation in the car; we knew that we were on the track of Ketchum and his carpet-bag of bank-notes.

"Is there any reward out?" cried Lowe.

"Not yet!"

"Then we won't pursue him."

As we slowly drifted to the left, the Hudson shone through the trees, and before dusk we swept across Lake Mahopec. I heard a voice singing to the dip of oars, and had to be held down by five men to restrain an involuntary impulse to quit my company.

"Townsend," said Lowe, "have you the copy of that matter you printed about me in England? This is the time to call you to account for it. We are two or three miles above *terra firma*, and I might like to drop you for a parachute."

I felt Lowe's muscle, and knew myself secure. Then I unrolled the pages, which I fortunately carried with me, and told him the following news about himself: —

The aeronaut of the Army of the Potomac was Mr. S. T. C. Lowe; he had made seven thousand ascensions, and his army companion was invariably either an artist, a corre-spondent, or a telegrapher.

A minute insulated wire reached from the car to head-quarters, and McClellan was thus informed of all that could be seen within the Confederate works. Sometimes they re-mained aloft for hours, making observations with powerful glasses, and once or twice the enemy tested their distance with shell.

On the 13th of April, the Confederates sent up a balloon, the first they had employed, at which Lowe was infinitely amused. He said that it had neither shape nor buoyancy, and predicted that it would burst or fall apart after a week. It certainly occurred that, after a few fitful appearances, the stranger was seen no more, till, on the 28th of June, it floated, like a thing of omen, over the spires of Richmond. At that time the Federals were in full retreat, and all the acres were covered with their dead.

On the 11th of April, at five o'clock, an event at once amusing and thrilling occurred at our quarters. The commander-in-chief had appointed his personal and confidential friend, General Fitz John Porter, to conduct the siege of Yorktown. Porter was a polite, soldierly gentleman, and a native of New Hampshire, who had been in the regular army since early manhood. He fought gallantly in the Mexican war, being thrice promoted and once seriously wounded, and he was now forty years of age, — handsome, enthusiastic, ambitious, and popular. He made frequent ascensions with Lowe, and learned to go aloft alone. One day he ascended thrice, and finally seemed as cosily at home in the firmament as upon the solid earth. It is needless to say that he grew careless, and on this particular morning leaped into the car and demanded the cables to be let out with all speed. I saw with some surprise that the flurried assistants were sending up the great straining canvas with a single rope attached. The enormous bag was only partially inflated, and the loose folds opened and shut with a crack like that of a musket. Noisily, fitfully, the yellow mass rose into the sky, the basket rocking like a feather in the zephyr; and just as I turned aside to speak to a comrade, a sound came from overhead, like the explosion of a shell, and something striking me across the face laid me flat upon the ground.

Half blind and stunned, I staggered to my feet, but the air seemed full of cries and curses. Opening my eyes ruefully, I saw all faces turned upwards, and when I looked above, — the balloon was adrift.

The treacherous cable, rotted with vitriol, had snapped in twain; one fragment had been the cause of my downfall, and the other trailed, like a great entrail, from the receding car, where Fitz John Porter was bounding upward upon a Pegasus that he could neither check nor direct.

The whole army was agitated by the unwonted occurrence. From battery No. 1, on the brink of the York, to the mouth of Warwick river, every soldier and officer was absorbed. Far within the Confederate lines the confusion extended. We heard the enemy's alarm-guns, and directly the signal flags were waving up and down our front.

The General appeared directly over the edge of the car. He was tossing his hands frightenedly, and shouting something that we could not comprehend.

" O — pen — the — valve ! " called Lowe, in his shrill tones ; " climb — to — the — netting — and — reach — the — valve — rope."

" The valve ! — the valve ! " repeated a multitude of tongues, and all gazed with thrilling interest at the retreating hulk that still kept straight upward, swerving neither to the east nor the west.

It was a weird spectacle, — that frail, fading oval, gliding against the sky, floating in the serene azure, the little vessel swinging silently beneath, and a hundred thousand martial men watching the loss of their brother in arms, but powerless to relieve or recover him. Had Fitz John Porter been drifting down the rapids of Niagara, he could not have been so far from human assistance. But we saw him directly, no bigger than a child's toy, clambering up the netting and reaching for the cord.

" He can't do it," muttered a man beside me ; " the wind blows the valve-rope to and fro, and only a spry, cool-headed fellow can catch it."

We saw the General descend, and appearing again over the edge of the basket, he seemed to be motioning to the breathless hordes below, the story of his failure. Then he dropped out of sight, and when we next saw him, he was reconnoitring the Confederate works through a long black spy-glass. A great laugh went up and down the lines as this cool procedure was observed, and then a cheer of applause ran from group to group. For a moment it was doubtful that the balloon would float in either direction ; it seemed to falter, like an irresolute being, and moved reluctantly southeastward, towards Fortress Monroe. A huzza, half uttered, quivered on every lip. All eyes glistened, and some were dim with tears of joy. But the wayward canvas now turned due westward, and was blown rapidly toward the Confederate works. Its course was fitfully direct, and the wind seemed to veer often, as if contrary currents, conscious of the opportunity, were struggling for the possession of the daring navigator. The south wind held mastery for awhile, and the balloon passed the Federal front amid a howl of despair from the soldiery. It kept right on, over sharpshooters, rifle-pits, and outworks, and finally passed, as if to deliver up its freight, directly over the heights of Yorktown. The cool courage, either of heroism or despair, had seized upon Fitz John Porter. He turned his black glass upon the ramparts and masked cannon below, upon the remote camps, upon the beleaguered town, upon the guns of Gloucester Point, and upon distant Norfolk. Had he been reconnoitring from a secure perch at the tip of the moon, he could not have been more vigilant, and the Confederates probably thought this some Yankee device to peer into their sanctuary in despite of ball or shell. None of their great guns could be brought to bear upon the balloon ; but there were some discharges of musketry that appeared to have no effect, and finally even these demonstrations ceased. Both armies in solemn silence were gazing aloft, while the imperturbable mariner continued to spy out the land.

The sun was now rising behind us, and roseate rays struggled up to the zenith, like the arcs made by showery bombs. They threw a hazy atmosphere upon the balloon, and the light shone through the network like the sun through the ribs of the skeleton ship in the *Ancient Mariner*. Then, as all looked agape, the air-craft " plunged, and tacked, and veered," and drifted rapidly toward the Federal lines again.

The allelujah that now went up shook the spheres, and
when he had regained our camp limits, the General was
seen clambering up again to clutch the valve-rope. This
time he was successful, and the balloon fell like a stone, so
that all hearts once more leaped up, and the cheers were
hushed. Cavalry rode pell-mell from several directions, to
reach the place of descent, and the General's personal staff
galloped past me like the wind, to be the first at his de-
barkation. I followed the throng of soldiery with due
haste, and came up to the horsemen in a few minutes. The
balloon had struck a canvas tent with great violence, felling
it as by a bolt, and the General, unharmed, had disentan-
gled himself from innumerable folds of oiled canvas, and
was now the cynosure of an immense group of people.
While the officers shook his hands, the rabble bawled their
satisfaction in hurrahs, and a band of music marching up directly, the throng on foot and horse gave him a vociferous
escort to his quarters.

Five miles east of Richmond, in the middle of May, we
found the balloon already partially inflated, resting behind a
ploughed hill that formed one of a ridge or chain of hills,
bordering the Chickahominy. The stream was only a half-
mile distant, but the balloon was sheltered from observation
by reason of its position in the hollow.

Heretofore the ascensions had been made from remote
places, for there was good reason to believe that batteries
lined the opposite hills; but now, for the first time, Lowe
intended to make an ascent whereby he could look into
Richmond, count the forts encircling it, and note the number
and position of the camps that intervened. The balloon
was named the "Constitution," and looked like a semi-
distended boa-constrictor, as it flapped with a jerking sound,
and shook its oiled and painted folds. It was anchored to
the ground by stout ropes affixed to stakes, and also by
sand-bags which hooked to its netting. The basket lay
alongside; the generators were contained in blue wooden

wagons, marked "U. S.;" and the gas was fed to the balloon through rubber and metallic pipes. A tent or two, a quantity of vitriol in green and wicker carboys, some horses and transportation teams, and several men that assisted the inflation, were the only objects to be remarked. As some time was to transpire before the arrangements were completed, I resorted to one of the tents and took a comfortable nap. The "Professor" aroused me at three o'clock, when I found the canvas straining its bonds, and emitting a hollow sound, as of escaping gas. The basket was made fast directly, the telescopes tossed into place; the Professor climbed to the side, holding by the network; and I coiled up in a rope at the bottom.

"Stand by your cables," he said, and the bags of ballast were at once cut away. Twelve men took each a rope in hand, and played out slowly, letting us glide gently upward. The earth seemed to be falling away, and we poised motionless in the blue ether. The tree-tops sank downward, the hills dropped noiselessly through space, and directly the Chickahominy was visible beyond us, winding like a ribbon of silver through the ridgy landscape.

Far and wide stretched the Federal camps. We saw faces turned upwards gazing at our ascent, and heard clearly, as in a vacuum, the voices of soldiers. At every second the prospect widened, the belt of horizon enlarged, remote farmhouses came in view; the earth was like a perfectly flat surface, painted with blue woods, and streaked with pictures of roads, fields, fences, and streams. As we climbed higher, the river seemed directly beneath us, the farms on the opposite bank were plainly discernible, and Richmond lay only a little way off, enthroned on its many hills, with the James stretching white and sinuous from its feet to the horizon. We could see the streets, the suburbs, the bridges, the outlaying roads, nay, the moving masses of people. The Capitol sat white and colossal on Shockoe Hill, the dingy buildings of the Tredegar works blackened the river-side above, the hovels of rockets clustered at the hither limits, and one by one we made out familiar hotels, public edifices, and vicinities. The fortifications were revealed in part only, for they took the hue of the soil, and blended with it; but many camps were plainly discernible, and by means of the glasses we separated tent from tent, and hut from hut. The Confederates were seen running to the cover of the woods, that we might not discover their numbers, but we knew the location of their camp-fires by the smoke that curled toward us.

A panorama so beautiful would have been rare at any time, but this was thrice interesting from its past and coming associations. Across those plains the hordes at our feet were either to advance victoriously, or be driven eastward with dusty banners and dripping hands. Those white farm-houses were to be receptacles for the groaning and the mangled; thousands were to be received beneath the turf of those pasture fields; and no rod of ground on any side, should not, sooner or later, smoke with the blood of the slain.

"Guess I got 'em now, jest where I want 'em," said Lowe, with a gratified laugh; "jest keep still as you mind to, and squint your eye through my glass, while I make a sketch of the roads and the country. Hold hard there, and anchor fast!" he screamed to the people below. Then he fell imperturbably to work, sweeping the country with his hawk-eye, and escaping nothing that could contribute to the completeness of his jotting.

We had been but a few minutes thus poised, when close below, from the edge of a timber stretch, puffed a volume of white smoke. A second afterward, the air quivered with the peal of a cannon. A third, and we heard the splitting shriek of a shell, that passed a little to our left, but in exact range, and burst beyond us in the ploughed field, heaving up the clay as it exploded.

"Ha!" said Lowe, "they have got us foul! Haul in the cables — quick!" he shouted, in a fierce tone. .

At the same instant, the puff, the report, and the shriek were repeated ; but this time the shell burst to our right in mid-air, and scattered fragments around and below us.

" Another shot will do our business," said Lowe, between his teeth ; " it isn't a mile, and they have got the range."

Again the puff and the whizzing shock. I closed my eyes, and held my breath hard. The explosion was so close, that the pieces of shell seemed driven across my face, and my ears quivered with the sound. I looked at Lowe, to see if he was struck. He had sprung to his feet, and clutched the cordage frantically.

" Are you pulling in there, you men ? " he bellowed, with a loud imprecation.

" Puff ! bang ! whiz-z-z-z ! splutter ! " broke a third shell, and my heart was wedged in my throat.

I saw at a glimpse the whole bright landscape again. I heard the voices of soldiers below, and saw them running across fields, fences, and ditches, to reach our anchorage. I saw some drummer-boys digging in the field beneath for one of the buried shells. I saw the waving of signal flags, the commotion through the camps, — officers galloping their horses, teamsters whipping their mules, regiments turning out, drums beaten, and batteries limbered up. I remarked, last of all, the site of the battery that alarmed us, and, by a strange sharpness of sight and sense, believed that I saw the gunners swabbing, ramming, and aiming the pieces.

" Puff ! bang ! whiz-z-z-z ! splutter ! crash ! "
" Puff ! bang ! whiz-z-z-z ! splutter ! crash ! "

" My God ! " said Lowe, hissing the words slowly and terribly, " *they have opened upon us from another battery!* "

The scene seemed to dissolve. A cold dew broke from my forehead. I grew blind and deaf. I had fainted.

" Pitch some water in his face," said somebody. " He ain't used to it. Hallo ! there he comes to."

I staggered to my feet. There must have been a thousand men about us. They were looking curiously at the

11

aeronaut and me.   The balloon lay fuming and struggling on the clods.

"Three cheers for the Union bal-loon!" called a little fellow at my side.

"Hip, hip — hoorooar! hoorooar! hoorooar!"

"Tiger-r-r — yah! whoop!"

CHAPTER XII.

SEVEN PINES AND FAIROAKS.

RETURNING from White House on Saturday, May 29, I heard the cannon of "Seven Pines." The roar of artillery came faintly upon the ear in the dells and woods, but in the open stretches of country, or from cleared hill-tops, I could hear also the volleys of musketry. It was the battle sound that assured me of bloody work; for the musket, as I had learned by experience, was the only certain signification of battle. It is seldom brought into requisition but at close quarters, when results are intended; whereas, cannon may peal for a fortnight, and involve no other destruction than that of shell and powder. I do not think that any throb of my heart was unattended by some volley or discharge. Dull, hoarse, uninterrupted, the whole afternoon was shaken by the sound. It was with a shudder that I thought how every peal announced flesh and bone riven asunder. The country people, on the way, stood in their side yards, anxiously listening. Riders or teamsters coming from the field, were beset with inquiries; but in the main they knew nothing. As I stopped at Daker's for dinner, the concussion of the battle rattled our plates, and the girls entirely lost their appetites, so that Glumley, who listened and speculated, observed that the baby face was losing all the lines of art, and was quite flat and faded in color. Resuming our way, we encountered a sallow, shabby person, driving a covered wagon, who recognized me at once. It was the "Doctor" who had lightened the journey down the Chesapeake, by a discourse upon embalming. He pointed toward the field with a long bony finger, and called aloud, with a smirk upon his face —

"I have the apparatus here, you see. They will need me out yonder, you know. There's opportunity there for the development of the 'system.'"

I did not reach my own camp at Gaines's Farm, till late in the day. The firing had almost entirely ceased, but occasional discharges still broke the repose of evening, and at night signal rockets hissed and showered in every direction. Next day the contest recommenced; but although not farther in a direct line, than seven miles, from our encampment, I could not cross the Chickahominy, and was compelled to lie in my tent all day.

These two battles were offered by the Confederates, in the hope of capturing that portion of the Federal army that lay upon the Richmond side of the river. Some days previously, McClellan had ordered Keyes's corps, consisting of perhaps twelve thousand men, to cross Bottom Bridge, eight miles down the Chickahominy, and occupy an advanced position on the York River railroad, six miles east of Richmond. Keyes's two divisions, commanded by Generals Couch and Casey, were thus encamped in a belt of woods remote from the body of the army, and little more than a mile from the enemy's line. Heintzelman's corps was lying at the Bridge, several miles in their rear, and the three finest corps in the army were separated from them by a broad, rapid river, which could be crossed at two places only. The troops of Keyes were mainly inexperienced, undisciplined volunteers from the Middle States. When their adversaries advanced, therefore, in force, on the twenty-ninth instant, they made a fitful, irregular resistance, and at evening retired in panic and disorder. The victorious enemy followed them so closely, that many of the Federals were slain in their tents. During that night, the Chickahominy, swollen by rains, overflowed its banks, and swept away the bridges. The beaten and disorganized relic of the fight of "Seven Pines," was thus completely isolated, and apparently to be annihilated at daybreak. But during the night, twenty thousand fresh men of Sumner's corps, forded the river, carrying their artillery, piece by piece across, and at dawn they assumed the offensive, seconded by the encouraged columns of Keyes. The fight was one of desperation; at night the Federals reoccupied their old ground at Fairoaks, and the Confederates retired, leaving their dead and wounded on the field. They lost, among their prisoners, General Pettigrew, of South Carolina, who was severely wounded, and with whom I talked as he lay in bed at Gaines's Mansion. He appeared to be a chivalrous, gossipy old gentleman, and said that he was the last South Carolinian to stand by the Union.

On the succeeding day, Monday, June 2, I rode to "Grape-Vine Bridge," and attempted to force my horse through the swamp and stream; but the drowned mules that momentarily floated down the current, admonished me of the folly of the hazard. The bridge itself was a swimming mass of poles and logs, that yielded with every pressure; yet I saw many wounded men, who waded through the water, or stepped lightly from log to log, and so gained the shore, wet from head to foot. Long lines of supply teams and ambulances were wedged in the depth of the thick wood, bordering the river; but so narrow were the corduroy approaches to the bridge, and so fathomless the swamp on either hand, that they could neither go forward, nor return. The straggling troops brought the unwelcome intelligence, that their comrades on the other side were starving, as they had crossed with a single ration of food, and had long ago eaten their last morsels. While I was standing close by the bridge, General McClellan, and staff, rode through the swamp, and attempted to make the passage. The "young Napoleon," urged his horse upon the floating

11*

timber, and at once sank over neck and saddle. His staff dashed after him, floundering in the same way; and when they had splashed and shouted, till I believed them all drowned, they turned and came to shore, dripping and discomfited. There was another Napoleon, who, I am informed, slid down the Alps into Italy; the present descendant did not slide so far, and he shook himself, after the manner of a dog. I remarked with some surprise, that he was growing obese; whereas, the active labors of the campaign had reduced the dimensions of most of the Generals.

I secured my horse, and placed a drummer-boy beside him, to prevent abduction or mistake; then stripping from top to toe, and holding my garments above my head, I essayed the difficult passage; as a commencement, I dropped my watch, but the guard-hook caught in a log and held it fast. Afterward, I slipped from the smooth butt of a tree, and thoroughly soused myself and clothing; a lumber-man from Maine, beheld my ill luck, and kindly took my burden to the other side. An estuary of the Chickahominy again intervened, but a rough scow floated upon it, which the Captain of Engineers sent for me, with a soldier to man the oars. I neglected to "trim boat," I am sorry to add, although admonished to that effect repeatedly by the mariner; and we swamped in four feet of water. I resembled a being of one of the antediluvian eras, when I came to land, finally, and might have been taken for a slimy Iguanodon. I sacrificed some of my under clothing to the process of cleansing and drying, and so started with soaking boots, and a deficiency of dress, in the direction of Savage's. Passing the "bottom," or swamp-land, I ascended a hill, and following a lane, stopped after a half hour at a frame-mansion, unpainted, with some barns and negro-quarters contiguous, and a fine grove of young oaks, shading the porch. An elderly gentleman sat in the porch, sipping a julep, with his feet upon the railing, and conversing with a

stout, ruddy officer, of decidedly Milesian physiognomy.
When I approached, the latter hurriedly placed a chair between himself and me, and said, with a stare —

"Bloodanowns! And where have ye been? Among the
hogs, I think?" I assured him that I did not intend to
come to close quarters, and that it would be no object on
my part to contaminate him. The old gentleman called for
"William," a tall, consumptive servant, whose walk reminded
me of a stubborn convict's, in the treadmill, and ordered
him to scrape me, which was done, accordingly, with a case-
knife. The young officer proposed to dip me in the well
and wring me well out, but I demurred, mainly on the
ground that some time would be so consumed, and that my
horse was waiting on the other side. He at once said that
he would send for it, and called "Pat," a civilian servant, in
military blue, who was nursing a negro baby with an eye, it
seemed, to obtain favor with the mother. The willingness
of the man surprised me, but he said that it was a short cut
of four miles to the railroad bridge, which had been repaired
and floored, and that he could readily recover the animal
and return at three o'clock. My benefactor, the officer,
then mixed a julep, which brought a comfortable glow to
my face, and said, without parley —

"You're a reporter, on the ————"

He said further, that he had been Coroner's Surgeon in
New York for many years, and had learned to know the
representatives of newspapers, one from the other, by
generic manner and appearance. Three correspondents
rode by at the time, neither of whom he knew personally, but designated them promptly, with their precise con-
nections. In short, we became familiar directly, and he told
me that his name was O'Gamlon, Quartermaster of Meagher's
Irish brigade, Sumner's corps. He was established with
the elderly gentleman, — whose name was Michie, — and
had two horses in the stable, at hand. He proposed to send
me to the field, with a note of introduction to the General,

and another to Colonel Baker, of the New York 88th (Irish), who could show me the lines and relics of battle, and give me the lists of killed, wounded, and missing. I repaired to his room, and arrayed myself in a fatigue officer's suit, with clean underclothing, after which, descending, I climbed into his saddle, and dashed off, with a mettlesome, dapper pony. The railroad track was about a mile from the house, and the whole country, hereabout, was sappy, dank, and almost barren. Scrub pines covered much of the soil, and the cleared fields were dotted with charred stumps. The houses were small and rude ; the wild pigs ran like deer through the bushes and across my path ; vultures sailed by hundreds between me and the sky ; the lane was slippery and wound about slimy pools ; the tree-tops, in many places, were splintered by ball and shell. I crossed the railroad, cut by a high bridge, and saw below the depot, at Savage's, now the head-quarters of General Heintzelman. Above, in full view, were the commands at Peach Orchard and Fair-oaks, and to the south, a few furlongs distant, the Williams-burg and Richmond turnpike ran, parallel with the railway, toward the field of Seven Pines. The latter site, was simply the junction of the turnpike with a roundabout way to Richmond, called the " Nine Mile Road," and Fairoaks was the junction of the diverging road with the railroad. Toward the latter I proceeded, and soon came to the Irish brigade, located on both sides of the way, at Peach Orchard.

They occupied the site of the most desperate fight-ing.

A small farm hollowed in the swampy thicket and wood, was here divided by the track, and a little farm-house, with a barn, granary, and a couple of cabins, lay on the left side. In a hut to the right General Thomas Francis Meagher made his head-quarters, and a little beyond, in the edges of the swamp timber, lay his four regiments, under arms.

A guard admonished me, in curt, lithe speech, that my horse must come no further ; for the brigade held the advance post, and I was even now within easy musket range of the imperceptible enemy. An Irish boy volunteered to hold the rein, while I paid my respects to the Commander. I encountered him on the threshold of the hut, and he welcomed me in the richest and most musical of brogues. Large, corpulent, and powerful of body; plump and ruddy — or as some would say, bloated — of face; with resolute mouth and heavy animal jaws; expressive nose, and piercing blue-eyes; brown hair, mustache, and eyebrows; a fair forehead, and short sinewy neck, a man of apparently thirty years of age, stood in the doorway, smoking a cigar, and trotting his sword fretfully in the scabbard. He wore the regulation blue cap, but trimmed plentifully with gold lace, and his sleeves were slashed in the same manner. A star glistened in his oblong shoulder-bar; a delicate gold cord seamed his breeches from his Hessian boots to his red tasselled sword-sash; a seal-ring shone from the hand with which he grasped his gauntlets, and his spurs were set upon small aristocratic feet.

A tolerable physiognomist would have resolved his temperament to an intense sanguine. He was fitfully impulsive, as all his movements attested, and liable to fluctuations of peevishness, melancholy, and enthusiasm. This was " Meagher of the Sword," the stripling who made issue with the renowned O'Connell, and divided his applauses; the " revolutionist," who had outlived exile to become the darling of the " Young Ireland " populace in his adopted country; the partisan, whose fierce, impassioned oratory had wheeled his factious element of the Democracy into the war cause; and the soldier, whose gallant bearing at Bull Run had won him a brigadiership. He was, to my mind, a realization of the Knight of Gwynne, or any of the rash, impolitic, poetic personages in Lever and Griffin. Ambitious without a name; an adventurer without a definite cause; an orator without policy; a General without caution or experience, he had led the Irish brigade through the hottest battles, and associated them with the most brilliant episodes of the war.

Every adjunct of the place was strictly Hibernian. The emerald green standard entwined with the red, white, and blue ; the gilt eagles on the flag-poles held the Shamrock sprig in their beaks ; the soldiers lounging on guard, had " 69 " or " 88 " the numbers of their regiments, stamped on a green hat-band ; the brogue of every county from Down to Wexford fell upon the ear ; one might have supposed that the " year '98 " had been revived, and that these brawny Celts were again afield against their Saxon countrymen. The class of lads upon the staff of Meagher, was an odd contrast to the mass of staff officers in the "Grand Army." Fox-hunters they all seemed to me, and there was one, who wore a long, twisted, pomatumed moustache, who talked of steeple chases, all the while, and wanted to have "a healthy dash " of some kind. A class of Irish exquisites, they appeared to be, — good for a fight, a card-party, or a hurdle jumping, — but entirely too Quixotic for the sober requirements of Yankee warfare. When anything absurd, forlorn, or desperate was to be attempted, the Irish brigade was called upon. But, ordinarily, they were regarded, as a party of mad fellows, more ornamental than useful, and entirely too clannish and factious to be entrusted with power. Meagher himself seemed to be less erratic than his subordinates ; for he had married a New York lady, and had learned, by observation, the superiority of the pelfish, plodding native before his own fitful, impracticable race. His address was infatuating : but there was a certain airiness, indicative of vanity, that revealed his great characteristic. He loved applause, and to obtain it had frittered away his fine abilities, upon petty, splendid, momentary triumphs. He was generous to folly, and, I have no doubt, maintained his whole staff.

When I requested to be shown the field, and its relics, Meagher said, in his musical brogue, that I need only look around.

"From the edge of that wood," he said, "the Irish brigade charged across this field, and fell upon their faces in the railway cutting below. A regiment of Alabamians lay in the timber beyond, with other Southerners in their rear, and on both flanks. They thought that we were charging bayonets, and reserved their fire till we should approach within butchering distance. On the contrary, I ordered the boys to lie down, and load and fire at will. In the end, sir, we cut them to pieces, and five hundred of them were left along the swamp fence, that you see. There isn't fifty killed and wounded in the whole Irish brigade."

A young staff officer took me over the field. We visited first the cottage and barns across the road, and found the house occupied by some thirty wounded Federals. They lay in their blankets upon the floors, — pale, helpless, hollow-eyed, making low moans at every breath. Two or three were feverishly sleeping, and, as the flies revelled upon their gashes, they stirred uneasily and moved their hands to and fro. By the flatness of the covering at the extremities, I could see that several had only stumps of legs. They had lost the sweet enjoyment of walking afield, and were but fragments of men, to limp forever through a painful life. Such wrecks of power I never beheld. Broad, brawny, buoyant, a few hours ago, the loss of blood, and the nervous shock, attendant upon amputation, has wellnigh drained them to the last drop. Their faces were as white as the tidy ceiling ; they were whining like babies ; and only their rolling eyes distinguished them from mutilated corpses. Some seemed quite broken in spirit, and one, who could speak, observing my pitiful glances toward his severed thigh, drew up his mouth and chin, and wept as if with the loss of comeliness all his ambitions were frustrated. A few attendants were brushing off the insects with boughs of cedar, laving the sores, or administering cooling draughts. The second story of the dwelling was likewise occupied by wounded, but in a corner clustered the terrified farmer and his family, vainly attempting to turn their eyes from the horrible spectacle. The farmer's wife had a baby at her breast, and its little blue eyes were straying over the room, half wonderingly, half delightedly. I thought, with a shudder, of babyhood thus surrounded, and how, in the long future, its first recollections of existence should be of booming guns and dying soldiers! The cow-shed contained seven corpses, scarcely yet cold, lying upon their backs, in a row, and fast losing all resemblance to man. The farthest removed, seemed to be a diminutive boy, and I thought if he had a mother, that she might sometime like to speak with me. When I took their names, I thought what terrible agencies I was fulfilling. Beyond my record, falsely spelled, perhaps, they would have no history. And people call such deaths glorious!

Upon a pile of lumber and some heaps of fence-rails, close by, sat some dozens of wounded men, mainly Federals, with bandaged arms and faces, and torn clothing. There was one, shot in the foot, who howled at every effort to remove his boot; the blood leaked from a rent in the side, and at last, the leather was cut, piecemeal from the flesh. These ate voraciously, though in pain and fear; for a little soup and meat was being doled out to them.

The most horrible of all these scenes — which I have described perhaps too circumstantially — was presented in the stable or barn, on the premises, where a bare dingy floor — the planks of which tilted and shook, as one made his way over them — was strewn with suffering people. Just at the entrance sat a boy, totally blind, both eyes having been torn out by a minnie-ball, and the entire bridge of the nose shot away. He crouched against the gable, in darkness and agony, tremulously fingering his knees. Near at hand, sat another, who had been shot through the middle of the forehead, but singular to relate, he still lived, though lunatic, and evidently beyond hope. Death had drawn blue and yellow circles beneath his eyes, and he muttered incomprehensibly, wagging his head. Two men, perfectly naked, lay in the middle of the place, wounded in bowels and loins ; and at a niche in the weather-boarding, where some pale light peeped in, four mutilated wretches were gaming with cards. I was now led a little way down the railroad, to see the Confederates. The rain began to fall at this time, and the poor fellows shut their eyes to avoid the pelting of the drops. There was no shelter for them within a mile, and the mud absolutely reached half way up their bodies. Nearly one third had suffered amputation above the knee. There were about thirty at this spot, and I was told that they were being taken to Meadow Station on hand cars. As soon as the locomotive could pass the Chickahominy, they would be removed to White House, and comfortably quartered in the Sanitary and hospital boats. Some of them were fine, athletic, and youthful, and I was directed to one who had been married only three days before.

"Doctor," said one, feebly, "I feel very cold : do you think that this is death ? It seems to be creeping to my heart. I have no feeling in my feet, and my thighs are numb."

A Federal soldier came along with a bucket of soup, and proceeded to fill the canteens and plates. He appeared to be a relative of Mark Tapley, and possessed much of that estimable person's jollity —

"Come, pardner," he said, "drink yer sup ! now, old boy, this'ill warm ye ; sock it down and ye'll see yer sweetheart soon. You dead, Ally-bammy ? Go way, now. You'll live a hundred years, you will. That's wot you'll do. Won't he, lad ? What ? Not any ? Get out ! You'll be slap on your legs next week and hev another shot at me the week a'ter that. You know you will ! Oh ! you Rebil ! You, with the butternut trousers ! Say ! Wake up and take some o' this. Hello ! lad, pardner. Wake up ! "

He stirred him gently with his foot ; he bent down to

12

touch his face. A grimness came over his merriment. The man was stiff and dumb.

Colonel Baker, commanding the 88th New York, was a tall, martial Irishman, who opened his heart and bottle at the same welcome, and took me into the woods, where some of the slain still remained. He had slept not longer than an hour, continuously, for seventy hours, and during the past night had been called up by eight alarums. His men lay in the dark thickets, without fires or blankets, as they had crossed the Chickahominy in light marching order.

"Many a lad," said he, "will escape the bullet for a lingering consumption."

We had proceeded but a very little way, when we came to a trodden place beneath the pines, where a scalp lay in the leaves, and the imprint of a body was plainly visible. The bayonet scabbard lay at one side, the canteen at the other. We saw no corpses, however, as fatigue parties had been burying the slain, and the whole wood was dotted with heaps of clay, where the dead slept below in the oozy trenches. Quantities of cartridges were scattered here and there, dropped by the retreating Confederates. Some of the cartridge-pouches that I examined were completely filled, showing that their possessors had not fired a single round; others had but one cartridge missing. There were fragments of clothing, hair, blankets, murderous bowie and dirk knives, spurs, flasks, caps, and plumes, dropped all the way through the thicket, and the trees on every hand were riddled with balls. I came upon a squirrel, unwittingly shot during the fight. Not those alone who make the war must feel the war! At one of the mounds the burying party had just completed their work, and the men were throwing the last clods upon the remains. They had dug pits of not more than two feet depth, and dragged the bodies heedlessly to the edges, whence they were toppled down and scantily covered. Much of the interring had been done by night, and the flare of lanterns upon the discolored faces and dead eyes must have been hideously effective. The grave-diggers, however, were' practical personages, and had probably little care for dramatic effects. They leaned upon their spades, when the rites were finished, and a large, dry person, who appeared to be privileged upon all occasions, said, grinningly —

" Colonel, your honor, them boys 'ill niver stand forninst the Irish brigade again. If they'd ha' known it was us, sur, begorra ! they 'ud ha' brought coffins wid 'em."

" No, niver !." " They got their ticket for soup ! " " We kivered them, fait', will inough ! " shouted the other grave-diggers."

" Do ye belave, Colonel," said the dry person, again, " that thim ribals'll lave us a chance to catch them. Be me sowl ! I'm jist wishin to war-rum me hands wid rifle practice."

The others echoed loudly, that they were anxious to be ordered up, and some said that " Little Mac'll give 'em his big whack now." The presence of death seemed to have added no fear of death to these people. Having tasted blood, they now thirsted for it, and I asked myself, forebodingly, if a return to civil life would find them less ferocious.

I dined with Colonel Owen of the 69th Pennsylvania (Irish) volunteers. He had been a Philadelphia lawyer, and was, by all odds, the most consistent and intelligent soldier in the brigade. He had been also a schoolmaster for many years, but appeared to be in his element at the head of a regiment, and was generally admitted to be an efficient officer. He shared the prevailing antipathy to West Point graduates ; for at this time the arrogance of the regular officers, and the pride of the volunteers, had embittered each against the other. His theory of military education was, the establishment of State institutions, and the reorganization of citizenship upon a strict militia basis. After dinner, I rode to " Seven Pines," and examined some of the rifle pits used during the engagement. A portion of this ground only had been retaken, and I was warned to keep under cover ; for sharpshooters lay close by, in the underbrush.   A visit to the graves of some Federal soldiers completed the inspection.   Some of the regiments had interred their dead in trenches ; but the New Englanders were all buried separately, and smooth slabs were driven at the heads of the mounds, whereon were inscribed the names and ages of the deceased.   Some of the graves were freshly sodded, and enclosed by rails and logs. They evidenced the orderly, religious habits of the sons of the Puritans ; for, with all his hardness of manner and selfishness of purpose, I am inclined to think that the Yankee is the best manifestation of Northern character.   He loves his home, at least, and he reveres his deceased comrades.

When I returned to Michie's, at six o'clock, the man "Pat," with a glowing face, came out to the gate.

"That's a splendid baste of yours, sur," he said, — "and sich a boi to gallop."

"My horse doesn't generally gallop," I returned, doubtfully.

When I passed to the barn in the rear, I found to my astonishment, a sorrel stallion, magnificently accoutred. He thrust his foot at me savagely, as I stood behind him, and neighed till he frightened the spiders.

"Pat," said I, wrathfully, "you have stolen some Colonel's nag, and I shall be hanged for the theft."

"Fait, sur," said Pat, "my ligs was gone intirely, wid long walkin', and I sazed the furst iligant baste I come to."

CHAPTER XIII.

STUART'S RAID.

THE old Chickahominy bridges were soon repaired, and the whole of Franklin's corps crossed to the south side. McClellan moved his head-quarters to Dr. Trent's farm, a half-mile from Michie's, and the latter gentleman's fields and lawn were made white with tents. Among others, the Chief of Cavalry, Stoneman, pitched his canopy under the young oaks, and the whole reserve artillery was parked in the woods, close to the house. The engineer brigade encamped in the adjacent peach-orchard and corn-field, and the wheat was trampled by battery and team-horses. Smith's division now occupied the hills on the south side of the Chickahominy, and the Federal line stretched southeastward, through Fairoaks, to White Oak Swamp, seven miles away. Porter's corps still lay between Mechanicsville and New Bridge, on the north bank of the river, and my old acquaintances, the Pennsylvania Reserves, had joined the army, and now formed its extreme right wing. This odd arrangement of forces was a subject of frequent comment: for the right was thus four miles, and the left fourteen miles, from Richmond. The four corps at once commenced to entrench, and from Smith's redoubt on the river bluffs, to Casey's entrenched hill at White Oak, a continuous line of moderately strong earthworks extended. But Porter and the Reserves were not entrenched at all, and only a few horsemen were picketed across the long reach

12*   (137)

of country from Meadow Bridge to Hanover Court House. Both flanks, in fact, were open, and the left was a day's march from the right. We were, meantime, drawing our supplies from White House, twenty miles in the rear ; there were no railroad guards along the entire line, and about five companies protected the grand depot. Two gunboats lay in the river, however, and as the teams still went to and fro, a second depot was established at a place called Putney's or " Garlic," five miles above White House. I went often, and at all hours of the day and night, over this exposed and lonely route. My horse had been, meantime, returned to the Provost Quarters, and the rightful owner had obtained his stallion in exchange. I rode the said stallion but once, when he proceeded to walk sideways, and several times rivalled the renowned Pegasus in his aerial flights. The man named " Pat " essayed to show his paces one day, but the stallion took him straight into Stoneman's wall-tent, and that officer shook the Irishman blind. My little bobtailed brownie was thrice endeared to me by our separation ; but I warned the man " Pat " to keep clear of him thereafter. The man " Pat " was a very eccentric person, who slept on the porch at Michie's, and used to wake up the house in the small hours, with the story that somebody was taking the chickens and the horses. He was the most impulsive person that I ever knew, and when I entrusted despatches to him once, he put them on the hospital boat by mistake, and they got to New York at the close of the campaign.

Michie's soon became a correspondents' rendezvous, and we have had at one time, at dinner, twelve representatives of five journals. The Hon. Henry J. Raymond, Ex-Lieutenant Governor of New York, and proprietor of the *Times* newspaper, was one of our family for several weeks. He had been a New Hampshire lad, and, strolling to New York, took to journalism at the age of nineteen years. His industry and probity obtained him both means and credit, and, also, what few young journalists obtain, social position. He was the founder of Harper's Magazine, one of the most successful serials in America, and many English authors are indebted to him for a trans-Atlantic recognition of their works. He edited an American edition of *Jane Eyre* before it had attracted attention in England, and conducted the *Courier and Enquirer* with great success for many years. The *Times* is now the most reputable of the great New York dailies, and Mr. Raymond has made it influential both at home and abroad. He has retained, amidst his social and political successes, a predilection for "Bohemia," and became an indefatigable correspondent. I rode out with him sometimes, and heard, with interest, his accounts of the Italian war, whither he also went in furtherance of journalism. Among our quill cavalry-men was a fat gentleman from Philadelphia, who had great fear of death, and who used to "tear" to White House, if the man "Pat" shot a duck in the garden. He was a hearty, humorous person, however, and an adept at searching for news.

O'Ganlon rode with me several times to White House, and we have crossed the railroad bridge together, a hundred feet in the air, when the planks were slippery, the sides sloping, and the way so narrow that two horses could not pass abreast. He was a true Irishman, and leaped barricades and ditches without regard to his neck. He had, also, a partiality for by-roads that led through swamps and close timber. He discovered one day a cow-path between Daker's and an old Mill at Grapevine Bridge. The long arms of oaks and beech trees reached across it, and young Absalom might have been ensnared by the locks at every rod therein. Through this devious and dangerous way, O'Ganlon used to dash, whooping, guiding his horse with marvellous dexterity, and bantering me to follow. I so far forgot myself generally, as to behave quite as irrationally, and once returned to Michie's with a bump above my right eye, that rivalled my head in size. At other times I rode alone, and my favorite route was an unfrequented lane called the "Quaker Road," that extended from Despatch Station, on the line of rail, to Daker's, on the New Bridge Road. Much of this way was shut in by thick woods and dreary pine barrens ; but the road was hard and light, and a few quiet farms lay by the roadside. There was a mill, also, three miles from Daker's, where a turbulent creek crossed the route, and at an oak-wood, near by, I used to frighten the squirrels, so that they started up by pairs and families ; I have chased them in this way a full mile, and they seemed to know me after a time. We used to be on the best of terms, and they would, at length, stand their ground saucily, and chatter, the one with the other, flourishing their bushy appendages, like so many straggling "Bucktails." When I turned from the beaten road, where the ruts were like a ditch and parapet, and dead horses blackened the fields ; where teams went creaking day and night, and squads of sabremen drove pale, barefooted prisoners to and fro like swine or cattle, the silence and solitude of this by-lane were beautiful as sleep. Many of the old people living in this direction had not seen even a soldier or a sutler, save some mounted scouts that vanished in clouds of dust ; but they had listened with awe to the music of cannon, though they did not know either the place or the result of the fighting. If fate has ordained me to survive the Rebellion, I shall some day revisit these localities ; they are stamped legibly upon my mind, and I know almost every old couple in New Kent or Hanover counties. I have lunched at all the little springs on the road, and eaten corn-bread and bacon at most of the cabins. I have swam the Pamunkey at dozens of places, and when my finances were low, and my nag hungry, have organized myself into a company of foragers, and broken into the good people's granaries. I do not know any position that admitted of as much adventure and variety. There was always enough danger to make my journeys precariously pleasant, and, when wearied of the saddle, my friends at Daker's and Michie's had a savory julep and a comfortable bed always prepared. I had more liberty than General McClellan, and a great deal more comfort.

Mrs. Michie was a warm-hearted, impulsive Virginia lady, with almost New England industry, and from very scanty materials she contrived to spread a bountiful table. Her coffee was bubbling with rich cream, and her "yellow pone" was overrunning with butter. A cleanly black girl shook a fly-brush over our shoulders as we ate, and the curious custom was maintained of sending a julep to our bedrooms before we rose in the mornings. Our hostess was too hospitable to be a bitter partisan, and during five weeks of tenure at her residence, we never held an hour's controversy. She had troubles, but she endured them patiently. She saw, one by one, articles of property sacrificed or stolen; she heard the servants speaking impudently; and her daughters and son were in a remote part of the State. The young man was a Confederate Surgeon at Lynchburg, and the young ladies had taken refuge in Rockbridge County. The latter were, from all accounts, pretty and intelligent, and one day, as I examined some parcels of books in the parlors, I found a volume of amateur poems that some laboring bard had dedicated to the youngest of them. Mr. Michie was a fine old Virginia gentleman, who remembered Thomas Jefferson well, as he had been reared in that great statesman's village, Charlottesville. He told me many anecdotes of Patrick Henry, John Randolph, and other distinguished patriots.

I wrote in one of the absent daughter's albums the following lines : —

> Alas ! for the pleasant peace we knew,
>   In the happy summers of long ago,
> When the rivers were bright, and the skies were blue,
>   By the homes of Henrico :

We dreamed of wars that were far away,
   And read, as in fable, of blood that ran,
Where the James and Chickahominy stray,
   Through the groves of Powhattan.

'Tis a dream come true; for the afternoons
   Blow bugles of war, by our fields of grain,
And the sabres clink, as the dark dragoons
   Come galloping up the lane;
The pigeons have flown from the eves and tiles,
   The oat-blades have grown to blades of steel,
And the Huns swarm down the leafy aisles
   Of the grand old Commonweal.

They have torn the Indian fisher's nets,
   Where flows Pamunkey toward the sea,
And blood runs red in the rivulets,
   That babbled and brawled in glee;
The corpses are strewn in Fairoak glades,
   The hoarse guns thunder from Drury's Ridge,
The fishes that played in the cove, deep shades,
   Are frightened from Bottom Bridge.

I would that the year were blotted away,
   And the strawberry grew in the hedge again;
That the scythe might swing in the tangled hay,
   And the squirrel romp in the glen;
The walnut sprinkle the clover slopes,
   Where graze the sheep and the spotted steer;
And the winter restore the golden hopes,
   That were trampled in a year.

On Friday, June 13, I made one of my customary trips
to White House, in the company of O'Ganlon. The latter
individual, in the course of a "healthy dash" that he made
down the railroad ties, — whereby two shoes shied from his
mare's hoofs, — reined into a quicksand that threatened to
swallow his steed. He afterward left his sword at Summit
Station, and I, obligingly, rode back three miles to recover
it. We dined at Daker's, where Glumley sat beside the
baby-face, pursuant to his art-duties, and the plump, red-

cheeked miss sat beside me. O'Ganlon was entertained by the talkative daughter, who drove him quite mad ; so that, when we resumed our horses, he insisted upon a second " healthy dash," and disappeared through a strip of woods. I followed, rationally, and had come to a blacksmith's shop, at the corner of a diverging road, when I was made aware of some startling occurrence in my rear. A mounted officer dashed past me, shouting some unintelligible tidings, and he was followed in quick succession by a dozen cavalry-men, who rode as if the foul fiend was at their heels. Then came a teamster, bare-backed, whose rent harness trailed in the road, and directly some wagons that were halted before the blacksmith's, wheeled smartly, and rattled off towards White House.

" What is the matter, my man ? " I said to one of these lunatics, hurriedly.

" The Rebels are behind ! " he screamed, with white lips, and vanished.

I thought that it might be as well to take some other road, and so struck off, at a dapper pace, in the direction of the new landing at Putney's or " Garlic." At the same instant I heard the crack of carbines behind, and they had a magical influence upon my speed. I rode along a stretch of chestnut and oak wood, attached to the famous Webb estate, and when I came to a rill that passed by a little bridge, under the way, turned up its sandy bed and buried myself in the under-brush. A few breathless moments only had intervened, when the roadway seemed shaken by a hundred hoofs. The imperceptible horsemen yelled like a war-party of Camanches, and when they had passed, the carbines rang ahead, as if some bloody work was being done at every rod.

I remained a full hour under cover; but as no fresh approaches added to my mystery and fear, I sallied forth, and kept the route to Putney's, with ears erect and expect- ant pulses. I had gone but a quarter of a mile, when I discerned, through the gathering gloom, a black, misshapen object, standing in the middle of the road. As it seemed motionless, I ventured closer, when the thing resolved to a sutler's wagon, charred and broken, and still smoking from the incendiaries' torch. Further on, more of these burned wagons littered the way, and in one place two slain horses marked the roadside. When I emerged upon the Hanover road, sounds of shrieks and shot issued from the landing at "Garlic," and, in a moment, flames rose from the woody shores and reddened the evening. I knew by the gliding blaze that vessels had been fired and set adrift, and from my place could see the devouring element climbing rope and shroud. In a twinkling, a second light appeared behind the woods to my right, and the intelligence dawned upon me that the cars and houses at Tunstall's Station had been burned. By the fitful illumination, I rode tremulously to the old head-quarters at Black Creek, and as I conjectured, the depot and train were luridly consuming. The vicinity was marked by wrecked sutler's stores, the embers of wagons, and toppled steeds. Below Black Creek the ruin did not extend: but when I came to White House the greatest confusion existed. Sutlers were taking down their booths, transports were slipping their cables, steamers moving down the stream. Stuart had made the circuit of the Grand Army to show Lee where the infantry could follow.

CHAPTER XIV.

FEVER DREAMS IN WAR.

A SUBTLE enemy had of late joined the Confederate cause against the invaders. He was known as Pestilence, and his footsteps were so soft that neither scout nor picket could bar his entrance. His paths were subterranean, — through the tepid swamp water, the shallow graves of the dead; and aerial, — through the stench of rotting animals, the nightly miasms of bog and fen. His victims were not pierced, or crushed, or mangled, but their deaths were not less terrible, because more lingering. They seemed to wither and shrivel away; their eyes became at first very bright, and afterward lustreless; their skins grew hard and sallow; their lips faded to a dry whiteness; all the fluids of the body were consumed; and they crumbled to corruption before life had fairly gone from them.

This visitation has been, by common consent, dubbed "the Chickahominy fever," and some have called it the typhus fever. The troops called it the "camp fever," and it was frequently aggravated by affections of the bowels and throat. The number of persons that died with it was fabulous. Some have gone so far as to say that the army could have better afforded the slaughter of twenty thousand men, than the delay on the Chickahominy. The embalmers were now enjoying their millennium, and a steam coffin manufactory was erected at White House, where twenty men worked day and night, turning out hundreds of pine boxes. I had, occasion, in one of my visits to the depot, to repair to the tent of one of the embalmers. He was a sedate, grave person, and when I saw him, standing over the nude, hard corpse, he reminded me of the implacable vulture, looking into the eyes of Prometheus. His battery and tube were pulsing, like one's heart and lungs, and the subject was being drained at the neck. I compared the discolored body with the figure of *Ianthe*, as revealed in Queen Mab, but failed to see the beautifulness of death.

"If you could only make him breathe, Professor," said an officer standing by.

The dry skin of the embalmer broke into chalky dimples, and he grinned very much as a corpse might do : —

"Ah !" he said, "*then* there would be money made."

To hear these embalmers converse with each other was like listening to the witch sayings in Macbeth. It appeared that the arch-fiend of embalming was a Frenchman named Sonça, or something of that kind, and all these worthies professed to have purchased his "system." They told grisly anecdotes of "operations," and experimented with chemicals, and congratulated each other upon the fever. They would, I think, have piled the whole earth with catacombs of stony corpses, and we should have no more green graves, but keep our dead with us as household ornaments.

The negroes did not suffer with the fever, although their quarters were close and filthy. Their Elysium had come ; there was no more work. They slept and danced and grinned, and these three actions made up the sum of their existence. Such people to increase and multiply I never beheld. There were scores of new babies every day ; they appeared to be born by twins and triplets ; they learned to walk in twenty-four hours ; and their mothers were strong and hearty in less time. Such soulless, lost, degraded men and women did nowhere else exist. The divinity they never had ; the human they had forgotten ; they did no great wrongs, — thieving, quarrelling, deceiving, — but they failed to do any rights, and their worship was animal, and almost profane. They sang incongruous mixtures of hymns and field songs : —

" Oh! bruddern, watch an' pray, *watch* an' pray!
De harvest am a ripenin' our Lord an' Marser say!
Oh! ho! yo! dat ole coon, de serpent, ho! oh!
Watch an' pray! "

I have heard them sing such medleys with tears in their eyes, apparently fervid and rapt. A very gray old man would lead off, keeping time to the words with his head and hands ; the mass joining in at intervals, and raising a screaming alleluja. Directly they would all rise, link hands, and proceed to dance the accompaniment. The motion would be slow at first, and the method of singing maintained ; after a time they would move more rapidly, shouting the lines together ; and suddenly becoming convulsed with strange excitement, they would toss up their arms, leap, fall, groan, and, seemingly, lose consciousness. Their prayers were earnest and vehement, but often degenerated to mere howls and noises. Some of both sexes had grand voices, that rang like bugles, and the very impropriety of their music made it fascinating. It used to seem to me that any of the great composers might have borrowed advantageously some of those original negro airs. In many cases, their owners came within the lines, registered their allegiance, and recovered the negroes. These were often veritable Shylocks, that claimed their pounds of flesh, with unblushing reference to the law. The poor Africs went back cowed and tearful, and it is probable that they were afterward sent to the far South, that terrible *terra incognita* to a border slave.

Among the houses to which I resorted was that of a Mr. Hill, one mile from White House. He had a thousand acres of land and a valuable fishery on the Pamunkey. The latter was worth, in good seasons, two thousand dollars a year. He had fished and farmed with negroes; but these had leagued to run away, and he sent them across the river to a second farm that he owned in King William County. It was at Hill's house that the widow Custis was visiting when young Washington reined at the gate, on his road to Williamsburg. With reverent feelings I used to regard the old place, and Hill frequently stole away from his formidable military household, to talk with me on the front porch. Perhaps in the same moonlights, with the river shimmering at their feet, and the grapevine shadowing the creaky corners, — their voices softened, their chairs drawn very close, their hands touching with a thrill, — the young soldier and his affianced had made their courtship. I sometimes sat breathless, thinking that their figures had come back, and that I heard them whispering.

Hill was a Virginian, — large, hospitable, severe, proud, — and once I ventured to speak upon the policy of slavery, with a view to develop his own relation to the "institution." He said, with the swaggering manner of his class, that slavery was a "domestic" institution, and that therefore no political law could reach it. I insinuated, quietly, that no political law should therefore sustain it, and took exception to the idea that what was domestic was therefore without the province of legislation. When I exampled polygamy, Hill became passionate, and asked if I was an abolitionist. I opined that I was not, and he so far relented as to say that slavery was sanctioned by divine and human laws; that it was ultimately to be embraced by all white nationalities, and that the Caucasian was certain, in the end, to subjugate and possess every other race. He pointed, with some shrewdness, to the condition of the Chinese in California and Australia, and epitomized the gradual enslaving of the Mongol and Malay in various quarters of the world.

"As to our treatment of niggers," he said, curtly, "I never prevaricate, as some masters do, in that respect. I whip my niggers when they want it ! If they are saucy, or careless, or lazy, I have 'em flogged. About twice a year every nigger has to be punished. If they ain't roped over twice a year, they take on airs and want to be gentlemen. A nigger is bound by no sentiment of duty or affection. You must keep him in trim by fear."

Among the victims of the swamp fever, were Major Larrabee, and Lieutenant-Colonel Emory, of the Fifth Wisconsin regiment ; I had been indebted to them for many a meal and draught of spirits. I had talked with each of them, when the camps were darkened and the soldiery asleep. Larrabee was a soldier by nature, — adventurous, energetic, intrepid, aggressive. He had been a country Judge in Wisconsin, and afterwards a member of Congress. When the war commenced, he enlisted as a common soldier, but public sentiment forced the State Government to make him a Major. Emory was a mild, reflective, unimpassioned gentleman, — too modest to be eminent, too scrupulous to be ambitious. The men were opposites, but both capital companions, and they were seized with the fever about the same time. The Major was removed to White House, and I visited him one day in the hospital quarters. Surgeon General Watson, hospital commandant, took me through the quarters ; there was quite a town of sick men ; they lay in wall-tents — about twenty in a tent, — and there were daily deaths ; those that caught the fever, were afterwards unfit for duty, as they took relapses on resuming the field. The tents were pitched in a damp cornfield ; for the Federals so reverenced their national 'shrines, that they forbade White House and lawn to be used for hospital purposes. Under the best circumstances, a field hospital is a comfortless place ; but here the sun shone like a furnace upon the tents, and the rains drowned out the inmates. If a man can possibly avoid it, let him never go to the hospital : for he will be called a " skulker," or a " shyster," that desires to escape the impending battle. Twenty hot, feverish, tossing

13*

men, confined in a small tent, like an oven, and exposed to contumely and bad food, should get a wholesome horror of war and glory.

So far as I could observe and learn, the authorities at White House carried high heads, and covetous hands. In brief, they lived like princes, and behaved like knaves. There was one — whose conduct has never been investigated — who furnished one of the deserted mansions near by, and brought a lady from the North to keep it in order. He drove a span that rivalled anything in Broadway, and his wines were luscious. His establishment reminded me of that of Napoleon III. in the late Italian war, and yet, this man was receiving merely a Colonel's pay. My impression is that everybody at White House robbed the Government, and in the end, to cover their delinquencies, these scoundrels set fire to an immense quantity of stores, and squared their accounts thus: " Burned on the Pamunkey, June 28, commissary, quartermaster's, and hospital stores, one million dollars."

The time was now drawing to a close that I should pass amid the familiar scenes of this region. The good people at Daker's were still kindly; but having climbed into the great bed one night, I found my legs aching, my brain violently throbbing, my chest full of pain and my eyes weak. When I woke in the morning my lips were fevered, I could eat nothing, and when I reached my saddle, it seemed that I should faint. In a word, the Chickahominy fever had seized upon me. My ride to New Bridge was marked by great agony, and during much of the time I was quite blind. I turned off, at Gaines's Mill, to rest at Captain Kingwalt's; but the old gentleman was in the grip of the ague, and I forebore to trouble him with a statement of my grievances. Skyhiski made me a cup of tea, which I could not drink, and Fogg made me lie on his " poncho." It was like old times come back, to hear them all speak cheerfully, and the man Clover said that, if there " warn't " a battle soon, he knew what he'd do, he did! he'd go home, straight as a buck!

"Becoz," said the man Clover, flourishing his hands, "I volunteered to fight. To *fight*, sir! not to dig and drive team. Here we air, sir, stuck in the mud, burnin' with fever, livin' on hardtack. And thair's Richmond! Just thair! You can chuck a stone at it, if you mind to. A'ter awhile them rebbils'll pop out, and fix us. Why ain't we led up, sa-a-y?"

The man Clover represented common sentiment among the troops at this time; but I told him that in all probability he would soon be gratified with a battle. My prediction was so far correct, that when I met the man Clover on the James River, a week afterward, he said, with a rueful countenance —

"Sa-a-a-y! It never rains but it pours, does it?"

As I rode from the camp of the Pennsylvania Reserves, at noon, on the 21st of June, I seemed to feel a gloomy premonition of the calamities that were shortly to fall upon the "Army of the Potomac." I passed in front of Hogan house; through the wood above the mill; along Gaines's Lane, between his mansion and his barn; across a creek, tributary to the Chickahominy; and up the ploughed hills by a military road, toward Grapevine Bridge. Lieutenant-Colonel Heath, of the Fifth Maine Regiment, was riding with me, and we stopped at the tip of an elevated field to look back upon the scene. I was very sick and weary, and I lay my head upon the mane of my nag, while Heath threw a leg across his saddle pommel, and straightened his slight figure; we both gazed earnestly.

The river lay in the hollow or ravine to the left, and a few farm-houses sat among the trees on the hill-tops beyond. A battery was planted at each house, and we could see the lines of red-clay parapets marking the sites. From the roof of one of the houses floated a speck of canvas, — the revolutionary flag. A horseman or two moved shadow-like across a slope of yellow grain.   Before and back the woods belted the landscape, and some pickets of both sides paced the river brink : they did not fire upon each other.

Our side of the Chickahominy was not less peaceful.   A couple of batteries lay below us, in the meadows ; but the horses were dozing in the harness, and the gunners, standing bolt upright at the breech, seemed parts of their pieces ; the teamsters lay grouped in the long grass.   Immediately in front, Gaines's Mansion and outhouses spotted a hillside, and we could note beyond a few white tents shining through the trees.   The roof of the old mill crouched between a medley of wavy fields and woods, to our right, and just at our feet a tiny rill divided Gaines's Mill from our own.   Behind us, over the wilderness of swamp and bog-timber, rose Smith's redoubt, with the Federal flag flaunting from the rampart.

"Townsend," said Heath, as he swept the whole country with his keen eye, "do you know that we are standing upon historic ground?"

He had been a poet and an orator, and he seemed to feel the solemnity of the place.

"It may become historic to-morrow," I replied.

"It is so to-day," he said, earnestly ; "not from battle as yet ; *that* may or may not happen ; but in the pause before the storm there is something grand ; and this is the pause."

He took his soft beaver in his hand, and his short red hair stood pugnaciously back from his fine forehead.

"The men that have been here already," he added, "consecrated the place ; young McClellan, and bluff, bullheaded Franklin ; the one-armed devil, Kearney, and handsome Joe Hooker ; gray, gristly Heintzelman ; whitebearded, insane Sumner ; Stuart, Lee, Johnston, the Hills——"

"Why not," said I, laughingly, "Eric the red,—the redoubtable Heath!"

"Why not?" he said, with a flourish ; "Fate may have something in store for me, as well as for these."

I have thought, since, how terribly our light conversation found verification in fact.   If I had said to Heath, that, at the very moment, Jefferson Davis and his Commander-in-chief were sitting in the dwelling opposite, reconnoitring and consulting; that, even now, their telescopes were directed upon us; that the effect of their counsel was to be manifest in less than a week; that one of the bloodiest battles of modern times was to be fought beside and around us; that six days of the most terrible fighting known in history were to ensue; that my friend and comrade was standing upon the same clods which would be reddened, at his next coming, with his heart's blood; and that the trenches were to yawn beneath his hoofs, to swallow himself and his steed, — if I had foretold these things as they were to occur, I wonder if the " pause before the storm " would have been less awful, and our ride campward less sedate.   Poor Heath ! Gallant New Englander ! he called at my bedside, the sixth day following, as I lay full of pain, fear, and fever, and after he bade me good by, I heard his horse's hoofs ringing down the lane.   Ten minutes afterward he was shot through the head.

When I reached Michie's, at three o'clock, I had to be helped from the saddle, and the fever was raging in my whole body before nightfall.   My hands were flushed, my face hot, but my feet were quite cold, and I was seized with chills that seemed to shake my teeth from my head.   Mrs. Michie made me a bowl of scorching tea, and one of the black-girls bathed my limbs in boiling water.   The fever dreams came to me that night, in snatches of burning sleep, and toward morning I lay restlessly awake, moving from side to side, famishing for drink, but rejecting it, when they brought it to my lips.   The next day, my kind hostess gave me some nourishing soup, but after a vain effort to partake of it, I was compelled to put it aside.   O'Ganlon procured some pickled fruit and vegetables from a sutler, which I ate voraciously, quaffing the vinegar like wine.   Some of my

regimental friends heard of my illness, and they sent me
quiet luxuries, which gladdened me, though I did not eat.
During the day I had some moments of ease, when I tried to
read.   There was a copy of Wordsworth's poems in the house,
and I used to repeat stanzas from "Peter Bell," till they rang,
in eddies of rhyme, through my weak brain, and continued to
scan and jangle far into the nights.   Some of these fever-
dreams were like delusions in delirium : peopled with monsters, that grinned and growled.   Little black globules used
to leer from corners, and after a time they began to revolve
toward me, increasing as they came, and at length rolling
like mountains of surge.   I frequently woke with a
scream, and found my body in profuse perspiration.   There
were fiery snakes, also, that, at first, moved slowly around
me, and I followed them with red and terrified eyes.   After
awhile they flashed in circles of lightning, and hissed showers of sparks, until I became quite crazed with fear.   The
most horrible apparitions used to come to my bedside, and
if I dropped to sleep with any thought half formed or half
developed, the odd half of that thought became impregnated,
somehow, and straightway loomed up a goblin, or a giant,
or a grotesque something, that proceeded to torture me,
like a sort of Frankenstein, for having made it.   Amid all
these ghastly things, there came beautiful glimpses of form,
scene, and sensation, that straightway changed to horrors.
I remember, for example, that I was gliding down a stream,
where the boughs overhead were as shady as the waters,
and there were holy eyes that seemed to cool my fever ;
but suddenly the stream became choked with corpses, that
entangled their dead limbs with mine, until I strangled and
called aloud,— waking up O'Ganlon and some reporters
who proposed to give me morphine, that I might not alarm
the house.

How the poor soldiers fared, in the hot hospitals, I shudder to think ; but a more merciful decree spared my life,
and kind treatment met me at every hand.   Otherwise, I be-

lieve, I should not be alive to-day to write this story; for the fever had seized me in its severest form, and I had almost tutored myself to look upon my end, far from my home and on the very eve of my manhood.

O'Ganlon, at last, resolved to send me to White House, and started thither one day, to obtain a berth for me upon a Sanitary steamer. The next day an ambulance came to the door. I tried to sit up in bed, and succeeded; I feebly robed myself and staggered to the stairs. I crawled, rather than walked, to the hall below; but when I took a chair, and felt the cool breeze from the oaks fanning my hair, I seemed to know that I should get well.

"Boom! Boom! Boom!" pealed some cannon at the moment, and all the windows shook with the concussion.

Directly we heard volleys of musketry, and then the camps were astir. Horses went hither and thither; signal flags flashed to-and-fro; a battery of the Reserve Artillery dashed down the lane.

I felt my strength coming back with the excitement; I even smiled feebly as the guns thundered past.

"Take away your ambulance, old fellow," I said, "I shan't go home till I see a battle."

CHAPTER XV.

TWO DAYS OF BATTLE.

THE Confederates had been waiting two months for McClellan's advance. Emboldened by his delay they had gathered the whole of their available strength from remote Tennessee, from the Mississippi, and from the coast, until, confident and powerful, they crossed Meadow Bridge on the 26th of June, 1862, and drove in our right wing at Mechanicsville. The reserves of Gen. McCall were stationed here; they made a wavering resistance, — wherein four companies of Bucktails were captured bodily, — and fell back at nightfall upon Porter's Corps, at Gaines's Mill. Fitz John Porter commanded the brigades of Gens. Sykes and Morrell, — the former made up solely of regulars. He appeared to have been ignorant of the strength of the attacking party, and he telegraphed to McClellan, early on Thursday evening, that he required no reinforcements, and that he could hold his ground. The next morning he was attacked in front and flank; Stewart's cavalry fell on his right, and turned it at Old Church. He formed at noon in new line of battle, from Gaines's House, along the Mill Road to New Coal Harbor; but stubbornly persisted in the belief that he could not be beaten. By three o'clock he had been driven back two miles, and all his energies were unavailing to recover a foot of ground. He hurled lancers and cavalry upon the masses of Jackson and the Hills, but the butternut infantry formed impenetrable squares, hemmed in with rods of steel, and as the horsemen galloped around them, searching for previous points, they were swept from their saddles with volleys of musketry. He directed the terrible fire of his artillery upon them, but though the gray footmen fell in heaps, they steadily advanced, closing up the gaps, and their lines were like long stretches of blaze and ball. Their fire never slackened nor abated. They loaded and moved forward, column on column, like so many immortals that could not be vanquished. The scene from the balloon, as Lowe informed me, was awful beyond all comparison, — of puffing shells and shrieking shrapnel, with volleys that shattered the hills and filled the air with deathly whispers. Infantry, artillery, and horse turned the Federal right from time to time, and to preserve their order of battle the whole line fell back toward Grapevine Bridge. At five o'clock Slocum's Division of volunteers crossed the creek from the south side, and made a desperate dash upon the solid columns of the Confederates. At the same time Toombs's Georgia Brigade charged Smith's redoubt from the south side, and there was a probability of the whole of both armies engaging before dark.

My fever of body had so much relinquished to my fever of mind, that at three o'clock I called for my horse, and determined to cross the bridge, that I might witness the battle.

It was with difficulty that I could make my way along the narrow corduroy, for hundreds of wounded were limping from the field to the safe side, and ammunition wagons were passing the other way, driven by reckless drivers who should have been blown up momentarily. Before I had reached the north side of the creek, an immense throng of panic-stricken people came surging down the slippery bridge. A few carried muskets, but I saw several wantonly throw their pieces into the flood, and as the mass were unarmed, I inferred that they had made similar dispositions. Fear, anguish, cowardice, despair, disgust, were the predom-

14

inant expressions of the upturned faces. The gaunt trees, towering from the current, cast a solemn shadow upon the moving throng, and as the evening dimness was falling around them, it almost seemed that they were engulfed in some cataract. I reined my horse close to the side of a team, that I might not be borne backward by the crowd; but some of the lawless fugitives seized him by the bridle, and others attempted to pull me from the saddle.

"Gi' up that hoss!" said one, "what business you got wi' a hoss?"

"That's my critter, and I am in for a ride; so you get off!" said another.

I spurred my pony vigorously with the left foot, and with the right struck the man at the bridle under the chin. The thick column parted left and right, and though a howl of hate pursued me, I kept straight to the bank, cleared the swamp, and took the military route parallel with the creek, toward the nearest eminence. At every step of the way I met wounded persons. A horseman rode past me, leaning over his pommel, with blood streaming from his mouth and hanging in gouts from his saturated beard. The day had been intensely hot and black boys were besetting the wounded with buckets of cool lemonade. It was a common occurrence for the couples that carried the wounded on stretchers to stop on the way, purchase a glass of the beverage, and drink it. Sometimes the blankets on the stretchers were closely folded, and then I knew that the man within was dead. A little fellow, who used his sword for a cane, stopped me on the road, and said —

"See yer! This is the ball that jes' fell out o' my boot."

He handed me a lump of lead as big as my thumb, and pointed to a rent in his pantaloons, whence the drops rolled down his boots.

"I wouldn't part with that for suthin' handsome," he said; "it'll be nice to hev to hum."

As I cantered away he shouted after me —

"Be sure you spell my name right! it's Smith, with an 'E' — S-M-I-T-H-E."

In one place I met five drunken men escorting a wounded sergeant; the latter had been shot in the jaw, and when he attempted to speak, the blood choked his articulation.

"You let go him, pardner," said one of the staggering brutes, "he's not your sergeant. Go 'way!"

"Now, sergeant," said the other, idiotically, "I'll see you all right, sergeant. Come, Bill, fetch him over to the corn-crib and we'll give him a drink."

Here the first speaker struck the second, and the sergeant, in wrath, knocked them both down. All this time the enemy's cannon were booming close at hand.

I came to an officer of rank, whose shoulder-emblem I could not distinguish, riding upon a limping field-horse. Four men held him to his seat, and a fifth led the animal. The officer was evidently wounded, though he did not seem to be bleeding, and the dust of battle had settled upon his blanched, stiffening face, like grave-mould upon a corpse. He was swaying in the saddle, and his hair — for he was bare-headed — shook across his white eyeballs. He reminded me of the famous Cid, whose body was sent forth to scare the Saracens.

A mile or more from Grapevine Bridge, on a hill-top, lay a frame farm-house, with cherry trees encircling it, and along the declivity of the hill were some cabins, corn-sheds, and corn-bins. The house was now a Surgeon's headquarters, and the wounded lay in the yard and lane, under the shade, waiting their turns to be hacked and maimed. I caught a glimpse through the door, of the butchers and their victims; some curious people were peeping through the windows at the operation. As the processions of freshly wounded went by, the poor fellows, lying on their backs, looked mutely at me, and their great eyes smote my heart.

Something has been written in the course of the war

upon straggling from the ranks, during battle. But I have seen nothing that conveys an adequate idea of the number of cowards and idlers that so stroll off. In this instance, I met squads, companies, almost regiments of them. Some came boldly along the road ; others skulked in woods, and made long detours to escape detection ; a few were composedly playing cards, or heating their coffee, or discussing the order and consequences of the fight. The rolling drums, the constant clatter of file and volley-firing,— nothing could remind them of the requirements of the time and their own infamy. Their appreciation of duty and honor seemed to have been forgotten ; neither hate, ambition, nor patriotism could force them back ; but when the columns of mounted provosts charged upon them, they sullenly resumed their muskets and returned to the field. At the foot of the hill to which I have referred the ammunition wagons lay in long lines, with the horses' heads turned from the fight. A little beyond stood the ambulances ; and between both sets of vehicles, fatigue-parties were going and returning to and from the field. At the top of the next hill sat many of the Federal batteries, and I was admonished by the shriek of shells that passed over my head and burst far behind me, that I was again to look upon carnage and share the perils of the soldier.

The question at once occurred to me : Can I stand fire ? Having for some months penned daily paragraphs relative to death, courage, and victory, I was surprised to find that those words were now unusually significant. "Death" was a syllable to me before ; it was a whole dictionary now. "Courage" was natural to every man a week ago ; it was rarer than genius to-day. "Victory" was the first word in the lexicon of youth yesterday noon ; "discretion" and "safety" were at present of infinitely more consequence. I resolved, notwithstanding these qualms, to venture to the hill-top : but at every step flitting projectiles took my breath. The music of the battle-field, I have often thought, should be introduced in opera. Not the drum, the bugle, or the fife, though these are thrilling, after their fashion ; but the music of modern ordnance and projectile, the beautiful whistle of the minie-ball, the howl of shell that makes unearthly havoc with the air, the whiz-z-z of solid shot, the chirp of bullets, the scream of grape and canister, the yell of immense conical cylinders, that fall like redhot stoves and spout burning coals.

All these passed over, beside, beneath, before, behind me. I seemed to be an invulnerable something at whom some cunning juggler was tossing steel, with an intent to impinge upon, not to strike him. I rode like one with his life in his hand, and, so far as I remember, seemed to think of nothing. No fear, *per se ;* no regret ; no adventure ; only expectancy. It was the expectancy of a shot, a choking, a loud cry, a stiffening, a dead, dull tumble, a quiver, and — blindness. But with this was mingled a sort of enjoyment, like that of the daring gamester, who has played his soul and is waiting for the decision of the cards. I felt all his suspense, *more* than his hope ; and withal, there was excitement in the play. Now a whistling ball seemed to pass just under my ear, and before I commenced to congratulate myself upon the escape, a shell, with a showery and revolving fuse, appeared to take the top off my head. Then my heart expanded and contracted, and somehow I found myself conning rhymes. At each clipping ball,— for I could hear them coming,— a sort of coldness and paleness rose to the very roots of my hair, and was then replaced by a hot flush. I caught myself laughing, syllabically, and shrugging my shoulders, fitfully. Once, the rhyme that came to my lips — for I am sure there was no mind in the iteration — was the simple nursery prayer —

"Now I lay me down to sleep,"
14*

and I continued to say "down to sleep," "down to sleep," "down to sleep," till I discovered myself, when I ceased. Then a shell, apparently just in range, dashed toward me, and the words spasmodically leaped up: "Now's your time. This is your billet." With the same insane pertinacity I continued to repeat "Now's your time, now's your time," and "billet, billet, billet," till at last I came up to the nearest battery, where I could look over the crest of the hill; and as if I had looked into the crater of a volcano, or down the fabled abyss into hell, the whole grand horror of a battle burst upon my sight. For a moment I could neither feel nor think. I scarcely beheld, or beholding did not understand or perceive. Only the roar of guns, the blaze that flashed along a zigzag line and was straightway smothered in smoke, the creek lying glassily beneath me, the gathering twilight, and the brownish blue of woods! I only knew that some thousands of fiends, were playing with fire and tossing brands at heaven,— that some pleasant slopes, dells, and highlands were lit as if the conflagration of universes had commenced. There is a passage of Holy Writ that comes to my mind as I write, which explains the sensation of the time better than I can do : —

"*He opened the bottomless pit ; and there arose a smoke out of the pit, as the smoke of a great furnace ; and the sun and the air were darkened by reason of the smoke of the pit.*

"*And there came out of the smoke locusts upon the earth.*" — Revelation, ix. 2, 3.

In a few moments, when I was able to compose myself, the veil of cloud blew away or dissolved, and I could see fragments of the long columns of infantry. Then from the far end of the lines puffed smoke, and from man to man the puff ran down each line, enveloping the columns again, so that they were alternately visible and invisible. At points between the masses of infantry lay field-pieces, throbbing with rapid deliveries, and emitting volumes of white steam. Now and then the firing slackened for a short time, when I could remark the Federal line, fringed with bayonets, stretching from the low meadow on the left, up the slope, over the ridge, up and down the crest, until its right disappeared in the gloaming of wood and distance. Standards flapped here and there above the column, and I knew, from the fact that the line became momentarily more distinct, that the Federals were falling stubbornly back. At times a battery would dash a hundred yards forward, unlimber, and fire a score of times, and directly would return two hundred yards and blaze again. I saw a regiment of lancers gather at the foot of a protecting swell of field ; the bugle rang thrice, the red pennons went upward like so many song birds, the mass turned the crest and disappeared, then the whole artillery belched and bellowed. In twenty minutes a broken, straggling, feeble group of horsemen returned ; the red pennons still fluttered, but I knew that they were redder for the blood that dyed them. Finally, the Federal infantry fell back to the foot of the hill on which I stood ; all the batteries were clustering around me, and suddenly a column of men shot up from the long sweep of the abandoned hill, with batteries on the left and right. Their muskets were turned towards us, a crash and a whiff of smoke swept from flank to flank, and the air around me rained buck, slug, bullet, and ball !

The incidents that now occurred in rapid succession were so thrilling and absorbing that my solicitude was lost in their grandeur. I sat like one dumb, with my soul in my eyes and my ears stunned, watching the terrible column of Confederates. Each party was now straining every energy, — the one for victory, the other against annihilation. The darkness was closing in, and neither cared to prolong the contest after night. The Confederates, therefore, aimed to finish their success with the rout or capture of the Federals, and the Federals aimed to maintain their ground till nightfall. The musketry was close, accurate, and uninterrupted. Every second was marked by a discharge, —

the one firing, the other replying promply. No attempt was now made to remove the wounded ; the coolness of the fight had gone by, and we witnessed only its fury. The stragglers seemed to appreciate the desperate emergency, and came voluntarily back to relieve their comrades. The cavalry was massed, and collected for another grand charge. Like a black shadow gliding up the darkening hillside, they precipitated themselves upon the columns : the musketry ceased for the time, and shrieks, steel strokes, the crack of carbines and revolvers succeeded. Shattered, humiliated, sullen, the horse wheeled and returned. Then the guns thundered again, and by the blaze of the pieces, the clods and turf were revealed, fitfully strewn with men and horses.

The vicinity of my position now exhibited traces of the battle. A caisson burst close by, and I heard the howl of dying wretches, as the fires flashed like meteors. A solid shot struck a field-carriage not thirty yards from my feet, and one of the flying splinters spitted a gunner as if he had been pierced by an arrow. An artillery-man was standing with folded arms so near that I could have reached to touch him ; a whistle and a thumping shock and he fell beneath my nag's head. I wonder, as I calmly recall these episodes now, how I escaped the death that played about me, chilled me, thrilled me, — but spared me ! " They are fixing bay-onets for a charge. My God !` See them come down the hill.''

In the gathering darkness, through the thick smoke, I saw or seemed to see the interminable column roll steadily downward. I fancied that I beheld great gaps cut in their ranks though closing solidly up, like the imperishable Gorgon. I may have heard some of this next day, and so confounded the testimonies of eye and ear. But I knew that there was a charge, and that the drivers were ordered to stand by their saddles, to run off the guns at any moment. The descent and bottom below me, were now all ablaze, and directly above the din of cannon, rifle, and pistol, I heard a great cheer, as of some salvation achieved.

" The Rebels are repulsed ! We have saved the guns ! "

A cheer greeted this announcement from the battery-men around me. They reloaded, rammed, swabbed, and fired, with naked arms, and drops of sweat furrowed the powder-stains upon their faces. The horses stood motionless, quivering not half so much as the pieces. The gristly officers held to their match-strings, smothering the excitement of the time. All at once there was a running hither and thither, a pause in the thunder, a quick consultation—

" 'Sdeath ! They have flanked us again."

In an instant I seemed overwhelmed with men. For a moment I thought the enemy had surrounded us.

" It's all up," said one ; " I shall cross the river."

I wheeled my horse, fell in with the stream of fugitives, and was borne swiftly through field and lane and trampled fence to the swampy margin of the Chickahominy. At every step the shell fell in and among the fugitives, adding to their panic. I saw officers who had forgotten their regiments or had been deserted by them, wending with the mass. The wounded fell and were trodden upon. Personal exhibitions of valor and determination there were ; but the main body had lost heart, and were weary and hungry.

As we approached the bridge, there was confusion and altercation ahead. The people were borne back upon me. Curses and threats ensued.

" It is the Provost-guard," said a fugitive, " driving back the boys."

" Go back ! " called a voice ahead. " I'll blow you to h—ll, if you don't go back ! Not a man shall cross the bridge without orders ! "

The stragglers were variously affected by this intelligence. Some cursed and threatened ; some of the wounded blubbered as they leaned languidly upon the shoulders of their comrades. Others stoically threw themselves on the

ground and tried to sleep. One man called aloud that the
" boys " were stronger than the Provosts, and that, therefore, the " boys " ought to " go in and win."

"Where's the man that wants to mutiny?" said the
voice ahead; "let me see him!"

The man slipped away; for the Provost officer spoke as
though he meant all he said.

"Nobody wants to mutiny!" called others.

"Three cheers for the Union."

The wounded and well threw up their hats together, and
made a sickly hurrah. The grim officer relented, and he
shouted stentoriously that he would take the responsibility
of passing the wounded. These gathered themselves up
and pushed through the throng; but many skulkers plead
injuries, and so escaped. When I attempted to follow, on
horseback, hands were laid upon me and I was refused exit.
In that hour of terror and sadness, there were yet jests and
loud laughter. However keenly I felt these things, I had
learned that modesty amounted to little in the army; so I
pushed my nag steadily forward and scattered the camp
vernacular, in the shape of imprecations, left and right.

"Colonel," I called to the officer in command, as the line
of bayonets edged me in, "may I pass out? I am a civilian!"

"No!" said the Colonel, wrathfully. "This is no place
for a civilian."

"That's why I want to get away."

"Pass out!"

I followed the winding of the woods to Woodbury's
Bridge,—the next above Grapevine Bridge. The approaches were clogged with wagons and field-pieces, and I
understood that some panic-stricken people had pulled up
some of the timbers to prevent a fancied pursuit. Along
the sides of the bridge many of the wounded were washing
their wounds in the water, and the cries of the teamsters
echoed weirdly through the trees that grew in the river.

At nine o'clock, we got under way, — horsemen, batteries, ambulances, ammunition teams, infantry, and finally some great siege 32s. that had been hauled from Gaines's House. One of these pieces broke down the timbers again, and my impression is that it was cast into the current. When we emerged from the swamp timber, the hills before us were found brilliantly illuminated with burning camps. I made toward head-quarters, in one of Trent's fields; but all the tents save one had been taken down, and lines of white-covered wagons stretched southward until they were lost in the shadows. The tent of General McClellan alone remained, and beneath an arbor of pine boughs, close at hand, he sat, with his Corps Commanders and Aides, holding a council of war. A ruddy fire lit up the historical group, and I thought at the time, as I have said a hundred times since, that the consultation might be selected for a grand national painting. The crisis, the hour, the adjuncts, the renowned participants, peculiarly fit it for pictorial commemoration.

The young commander sat in a chair, in full uniform, uncovered. Heintzelman was kneeling upon a fagot, earnestly speaking. De Joinville sat apart, by the fire, examining a map. Fitz John Porter was standing back of McClellan, leaning upon his chair. Keyes, Franklin, and Sumner, were listening attentively. Some sentries paced to and fro, to keep out vulgar curiosity. Suddenly, there was a nodding of heads, as of some policy decided; they threw themselves upon their steeds, and galloped off toward Michie's.

As I reined at Michie's porch, at ten o'clock, the bridges behind me were blown up, with a flare that seemed a blazing of the Northern Lights. The family were sitting upon the porch, and Mrs. Michie was greatly alarmed with the idea that a battle would be fought round her house next day.

O'Ganlon, of Meagher's staff, had taken the fever, and sent anxiously for me, to compare our symptoms.

I bade the good people adieu before I went to bed, and gave the man " Pat " a dollar to stand by my horse while I slept, and to awake me at any disturbance, that I might be ready to scamper. The man " Pat," I am bound to say, woke me up thrice by the exclamation of —·

" Sure, yer honor, there's — well — to pay in the yard ! I think ye and the Doctor had better ride off."

On each of those occasions, I found that the man Pat had been lonesome, and wanted somebody to speak to.

What a sleep was mine that night ! I forgot my fever. But another and a hotter fever burned my temples, — the fearful excitement of the time ! Whither were we to go, cut off from the York, beaten before Richmond, — perhaps even now surrounded, — and to be butchered to-morrow, till the clouds should rain blood ? Were we to retreat one hundred miles down the hostile Peninsula, — a battle at every rod, a grave at every footstep ? Then I remembered the wounded heaped at Gaines's Mill, and how they were groaning without remedy, ebbing at every pulse, counting the flashing drops, calling for water, for mercy, for death. So I found heart ; for I was not buried yet. And somehow I felt that fate was to take me, as the great poet took Dante, through other and greater horrors.

CHAPTER XVI.

M'CLELLAN'S RETREAT.

THE scene presented in Michie's lawn and oak grove, on Saturday morning, was terribly picturesque, and characteristic of the calamity of war. The well was beset by crowds of wounded men, perishing of thirst, who made frantic efforts to reach the bucket, but were borne back by the stronger desperadoes. The kitchen was swarming with hungry soldiers who begged corn-bread and half-cooked dough from the negroes. The shady side-yard was dotted with pale, bruised, and bleeding people, who slept out their weariness upon the damp grass, forgetful, for the moment, of their sores. Ambulances poured through the lane, in solemn procession, and now and then, couples of privates bore by some wounded officer, upon a canvas "stretcher." The lane proving too narrow, at length, for the passing vehicles, the gate-posts and fence were torn up, and finally, the soldiers made a footway of the hall of the dwelling.

The retreat had been in progress all night, as I had heard the wagons through my open windows. By daylight the whole army was acquainted with the facts, that we were to resign our depot at White House, relinquish the North bank of the river, and retire precipitately to the shores of the James. A rumor — indignantly denied, but as often repeated — prevailed among the teamsters, surgeons, and drivers, that the wounded were to be left in the enemy's hands. It shortly transpired that we were already cut off from the Pamunkey. A train had departed for White House at dawn, and had delivered its cargo of mortality safely ; but a second train, attempting the passage, at seven o'clock had been fired into, and compelled to return. A tremendous explosion, and a shaft of white smoke that flashed to the zenith, informed us, soon afterward, that the railroad bridge had been blown up.

About the same time, the roar of artillery recommenced in front, and regiments that had not slept for twenty hours, were hurried past us, to take position at the entrenchments. A universal fear now found expression, and helpless people asked of each other, with pale lips —

" How far have we to walk to reach the James ? "

It was doubtful, at this time, that any one knew the route to that river. A few members of the signal corps had adventured thither to open communication with the gunboats, and a small cavalry party of Casey's division had made a foray to New Market and Charles City Court House. But it was rumored that Wise's brigade of Confederates was now posted at Malvern Hills, closing up the avenue of escape, and that the whole right wing of the Confederate army was pushing toward Charles City. Malvern Hills, the nearest point that could be gained, was about twenty miles distant, and Harrison's Landing — presumed to be our final destination — was thirty miles away. To retreat over this distance, encumbered with baggage, the wounded and the sick, was discarded as involving pursuit, and certain calamity. Cavalry might fall upon us at every turning, since the greater portion of our own horse had been scouting between White House and Hanover, when the bridges were destroyed, and was therefore separated from the main army. At eight o'clock — weak with fever and scarcely able to keep in the saddle — I joined Mr. Anderson of the *Herald*, and rode toward the front, that I might discover the whereabouts of the new engagement. Wind-

ing through a cart-track in Michie's Woods, we came upon
fully one third of the whole army, or the remnant of all that
portion engaged at Gaines's Mill ;— the Reserves, Porter's
Corps, Slocum's division, and Meagher's brigade,—perhaps thirty-thousand men.   They covered the whole of
Tent's farm, and were drawn up in line, heavily equipped,
with their colors in position, field officers dismounted, and
detachments from each regiment preparing hot coffee at
certain fires.   A very few wagons — and these containing only ammunition — stood harnessed beside each regiment.   In many cases the men lay or knelt upon the
ground.   Such hot, hungry, weary wretches, I never
beheld.   During the whole night long they had been crossing the Chickahominy, and the little sleep vouchsafed
them had been taken in snatches upon the bare clay.   Travelling from place to place, I saw the surviving heroes of the
defeat : Meagher looking very yellow and prosaic ; Slocum, — small, indomitable, active ; Newton, — a little gray,
a trifle proud, very mercurial, and curiously enough, a
Virginian ; Meade, — lithe, spectacled, sanguine ; and finally General McCall, as grave, kindly odd and absent, as I
had found him four months before.   The latter worthy was
one of the first of the Federal Generals to visit Richmond.
He was taken prisoner the second day afterward, and the
half of his command was slain or disabled.

I went to and fro, obtaining the names of killed, wounded and missing, with incidents of the battle as well as its
general plan.   These I scrawled upon bits of newspaper,
upon envelopes, upon the lining of my hat, and finally upon
my shirt wristbands.   I was literally filled with notes before
noon, and if I had been shot at that time, endeavors to obtain my name would have been extremely difficult.   I
should have had more titles than some of the Chinese princes ; some parts of me would have been found fatally
wounded, and others italicized for gallant behavior.   Indeed, I should have been shot in every part, taken prisoner

at every place, killed outright in every skirmish, and marvellously saved through every peril. My tombstone would have been some hundreds of muster-rolls and my obituary a fortune to a newspaper. I recollect, with some amusement, the credit that each regiment took upon itself for distinguished behavior. There were few Colonels that did not claim all the honors. I fell in with a New Jersey brigade, that had been decimated of nearly half its *quota*, and a spruce young Major attempted to convey an idea of the battle to me. He said, in brief, that the New Jersey brigade, composed mainly of himself and his regiment, and some few organizations of little consequence, — although numbering ten thousand odd soldiers, — had received the whole shock of a quantity of " Rebels." The said " Rebels " appeared to make up one fourth part of the population of the globe. There was no end to them. They seemed to be several miles deep, longer and more crooked than the Pamunkey, and stood with their rear against Richmond, so that they couldn't fall back, even if they wanted to. In vain did the New Jersey brigade and his regiment attack them with ball and bayonet. How the " Rebels " ever withstood the celebrated charge of his regiment was altogether inexplicable.

In the language of the Major, — " the New Jersey brigade, — and my regiment, — fit, and fit, and fit, and give 'em ' get out!' But sir, may I be ——, well there (expression inadequate), we couldn't budge 'em. No, sir! (very violently,) not budge 'em, sir! *I* told the boys to walk at 'em with cold steel. Says I: ' Boys, steel'ill fetch 'em, or nothin' under heaven!' Well, sir, at 'em we went, — me and the boys. There ain't been no sich charge in the whole war! Not in the whole war, sir! (intensely fervid ;) leave it to any impartial observer if there has been ! We went up the hill, square in the face of all their artillery, musketry, cavalry, sharpshooters, riflemen, — everything, sir! Everything! (energetically.) One o' my men over-

heard the Rebel General say, as we came up : says he, —
'that's the gamest thing I ever see.' Well! we butchered
'em frightful. We must a killed a thousand or two of 'em,
don't you think so, Adjutant? But, sir, — it was all in
vain. No go, sir! no, sir, no go! (impressively.) And the
New Jersey brigade and my regiment fell back, inch by
inch, with our feet to the foe (rhetorically.) Is that so,
boys?"

The "boys," who had meantime gathered around, exclaimed loudly, that it was "true as preachin," and the Major added, in an undertone that his name was spelled * * *.

"But where were Porter's columns?" said I, "and the
Pennsylvania Reserves?"

"I didn't see 'em," said the Major: "I don't think
they was there. If they had a been, why wa'n't they on
hand to save my regiment, and the New Jersey brigade?"

It would be wrong to infer from these vauntings, that
the Federals did not fight bravely and endure defeat un-
shrinkingly. On the contrary, I have never read of higher
exemplifications of personal and moral courage, than I witnessed during this memorable retreat. And the young
Major's boasting did not a whit reduce my estimate of his
efficiency. For in America, swaggering does not necessarily
indicate cowardice. I knew a Captain of artillery in Smith's
division, who was wordier than Gratiano, and who exaggerated like Falstaff. But he was a lion in action, and at
Lee's Mills and Williamsburg his battery was handled with
consummate skill.

From Trent's farm the roadway led by a strip of corduroy,
through sloppy, swampy woods, to an open place, beyond
a brook, where Smith's division lay. The firing had almost
entirely ceased, and we heard loud cheers running up and
down the lines, as we again ventured within cannon range.
On this spot, for the second time, the Federals had won a
decided success. And in so far as a cosmopolitan could
feel elated, I was proud, for a moment, of the valor of my

15*

division. The victors had given me meals and a bed, and they had fed my pony when both of us were hungry. But the sight of the prisoners and the collected dead, saddened me somewhat.

These two engagements have received the name of the First and Second battles of Golding's Farm. They resulted from an effort of Toombs's Georgia brigade to carry the redoubt and breastworks of General Smith. Toombs was a civilian, and formerly a senator from Georgia. He had no military ability, and his troops were driven back with great slaughter, both on Friday and Saturday. Among the prisoners taken was Colonel Lamar of (I think) the 7th Georgia regiment. He passed me, in a litter, wounded, as I rode toward the redoubt.

Lamar was a beautiful man, shaped like a woman, and his hair was long, glossy, and wavy with ringlets. He was a tiger, in his love of blood, and in character self-willed and vehement. He was of that remarkable class of Southern men, of which the noted "Filibuster" Walker was the great exponent. I think I may call him an apostle of slavery. He believed it to be the destiny of our pale race to subdue all the dusky tribes of the earth, and to evangelize, with the sword, the whole Western continent, to the uses of master and man. Such people were called disciples of "manifest destiny." He threw his whole heart into the war; but when I saw him, bloodless, panting, quivering, I thought how little the wrath of man availed against the justice of God. From Smith's on the right, I kept along a military road, in the woods, to Sedgwick's and Richardson's divisions, at Fairoaks. Richardson was subsequently slain, at the second battle of Bull Run. He was called "Fighting Dick," and on this particular morning was talking composedly to his wife, as she was about to climb to the saddle. His tent had been taken down, and soldiers were placing his furniture in a wagon. A greater contrast I never remarked, than the ungainly, awkward, and rough

General, with his slight, trim, pretty companion. She had come to visit him and had remained until commanded to retire. I fancied, though I was separated some distance, that the little woman wept, as she kissed him good by, and he followed her, with frequent gestures of good-hap, till she disappeared behind the woods. I do not know that such prosaic old soldiers are influenced by the blandishments of love ; but "Fighting Dick" never wooed death so recklessly as in the succeeding engagements of New Market and Malvern Hills.

From Seven Pines to the right of Richardson's head-quarters, ran a line of alternate breastwork, redoubt, and stockade. The best of these redoubts was held by Captain Petit, with a New York Volunteer battery. I had often talked with Petit, for he embodied, as well as any man in the army, the martial qualifications of a volunteer. He despised order. Nobody cared less for dress and dirt. I have seen him, sitting in a hole that he hollowed with his hands, tossing pebbles and dust over his head, like another Job. He had profound contempt for any man and any system that was not "American." I remember asking him, one day, the meaning of the gold lace upon the staff hats of the Irish brigade.

"Means run like shell !" said Petit, covering me with dirt.

"Don't the Irish make the best soldiers ? " I ventured.

"No ! " said Petit, raining pebbles, "I had rather have one American than ten Irishmen."

The fighting of Petit was contrary to all rule ; but I think that he was a splendid artillery-man. He generally mounted the rampart, shook his fist at the enemy, flung up his hat, jumped down, sighted the guns himself, threw shells with wonderful accuracy, screamed at the gunners, mounted the rampart again, halloed, and, in short, managed to do more execution, make more noise, attract more attention and throw more dirt than anybody in the army. His redoubt was small, but beautifully constructed, and the parapet was heaped with double rows of sandbags. It mounted rifled field-pieces, and, at most times, the gunners were lying under the pieces, asleep. Not any of the entrenched posts among the frontier Indians were more enveloped in wilderness than this. The trees had been felled in front to give the cannon play, but behind and on each side belts of dense, dwarf timber covered the boggy soil. To the left of Petit, on the old field of Seven Pines, lay the divisions of Hooker and Kearney, and thither I journeyed, after leaving the redoubtable volunteer. Hooker was a New Englander, reputed to be the handsomest man in the army. He fought bravely in the Mexican war, and afterwards retired to San Francisco, where he passed a Bohemian existence at the Union Club House. He disliked McClellan, was beloved by his men, and was generally known as "Old Joe." He has been one of the most successful Federal leaders, and seems to hold a charmed life. In all probability he will become Commander-in-chief of one of the grand armies.

Kearney has passed away since the date of which I speak. He was known as the "one-armed Devil," and was, by odds, the best educated of all the Federal military chiefs. But, singularly enough, he departed from all tactics, when hotly afield. His personal energy and courage have given him renown, and he loved to lead forlorn hopes, or head storming-parties, or ride upon desperate adventures. He was rich from childhood, and spent much of his life in Europe. For a part of this time he served as a cavalry-man with the French, in Algiers. In private life he was equally reckless, but his tastes were scholarly, and he was generous to a fault. Both Kearney and Hooker were kind to the reporters, and I owe the dead man many a favor. General Daniel Sickles commanded a brigade in this corps. To the left, and in the rear of Heintzelman's corps, lay the divisions of Casey and Couch, that had relapsed into silence since their disgrace at Seven Pines. General Casey was a thin-haired old gentleman, too gracious to be a soldier, although I believe that he is still in the service. His division comprised the extreme left of the Grand Army, and bordered upon a deep, impenetrable bog called "White Oak Swamp." It was the purpose of McClellan to place this swamp between him and the enemy, and defend its passage till his baggage and siege artillery had obtained the shelter of the gunboats, on the shores of the James. I rode along this whole line, to renew my impressions of the position, and found that sharp skirmishing was going on at every point. When I returned to Savage's, where McClellan's headquarters had temporarily been pitched, I found the last of the wagons creaking across the track, and filing slowly southward. The wounded lay in the out-houses, in the trains of cars, beside the hedge, and in shade of the trees about the dwelling. A little back, beside a wood, lay Lowe's balloon traps, and the infantry "guard," and cavalry "escort" of the Commander-in-chief were encamped close to the new provost quarters, in a field beyond the orchard. An ambulance passed me, as I rode into the lane; it was filled with sufferers, and two men with bloody feet, crouched in the trail. From the roof of Savage's house floated the red hospital flag. Savage himself was a quiet Virginia farmer, and a magistrate. His name is now coupled with a grand battle.

I felt very hungry, at four o'clock, but my weak stomach revolted at coarse soldier fare, and I determined to ride back to Michie's. I was counselled to beware; but having learned little discretion afield, I cantered off, through a trampled tillage of wheat, and an interminable woods. In a half hour I rode into the familiar yard; but the place was so ruined that I hardly recognized it. Not a panel of fence remained : the lawn was a great pool of slime; the windlass had been wrenched from the well; a few gashed and expiring soldiers lay motionless beneath the oaks, the fields were littered with the remains of camps, and the old dwelling stood like a haunted thing upon a blighted plain. The idlers, the teamsters, and the tents were gone, — all was silence, — and in the little front porch sat Mrs. Michie, weeping ; the old gentleman stared at the desolation with a working face, and two small yellow lads lay dolorously upon the steps. They all seemed to brighten up as I appeared at the gate, and when I staggered from my horse, both of them took my hands. I think that tears came into all our eyes at once, and the little Ethiops fairly bellowed.

"My friends," I said, falteringly, "I see how you have suffered, and sympathize with you, from my heart."

"Our beautiful property is ruined," said Mrs. Michie, welling up.

"Yer's five years of labor, — my children's heritage, — the home of our old age, — look at it !"

The old gentleman stood up gravely, and cast his eyes mournfully around.

"I have nobody to accuse," he said ; "my grief is too deep for any hate. This is war !"

"What will the girls say when they come back ? " was the mother's next sob; "they loved the place : do you think they will know it ? "

I did not know how to reply. They retained my hands, and for a moment none of us spoke.

"Don't think, Mr. Townsend," said the chivalrous old gentleman again, "that we like you less because some of your country people have stripped us. Mother, where is the gruel you made for him ? "

The good lady, expecting my return, had prepared some nourishing chicken soup, and directly she produced it. I think she took heart when I ate so plentifully, and we all spoke hopefully again. Their kindness so touched me, that as the evening came quietly about us, lengthening the shadows, and I knew that I must depart, I took both their hands again, doubtful what to say.

"My friends, — may I say, almost my parents ? for you

have been as kind, — good by ! In a day, perhaps, you will be with your children again. Richmond will be open to you. You may freely go and come. Be comforted by these assurances. And when the war is over, — God speed the time ! — we may see each other under happier auspices."

"Good by !" said Mr. Michie; "if I have a house at that time, you shall be welcome."

"Good by," said Mrs. Michie; "tell your mother that a strange lady in Virginia took good care of you when you were sick."

I waved a final adieu, vaulted down the lane, and the wood gathered its solemn darkness about me. When I emerged upon Savage's fields, a succession of terrible explosions shook the night, and then the flames flared up, at points along the railroad. They were blowing up the locomotives and burning the cars. At the same hour, though I could not see it, White House was wrapped in fire, and the last sutler, teamster, and cavalry-man had disappeared from the shores of the Pamunkey.

I tossed through another night of fever, in the captain's tent of the Sturgis Rifles, — McClellan's body guard. And somehow, again, I dreamed fitfully of the unburied corpses on the field of Gaines's Mill.

CHAPTER XVII.

A BATTLE SUNDAY.

IN the dim of the morning of our Lord's Sabbath, the twenty-ninth of June, 1862, I sat in my saddle at Savage's. The gloom was very cheerless. A feeling of hopeless vagabondism oppressed me. I remembered the Disinherited Knight, the Wandering Jew, Robinson Crusoe, and other poor errants in the wide world, and wondered if any of them ever looked so ruefully as I, when the last wagon of the Grand Army disappeared through the shadow.

The tent had been taken down at midnight. I had been dozing in the saddle, with parched lips and throbbing temples, waiting for my comrade. Head-quarters had been intending to move, without doing it, for four hours, and he informed me that it was well to stay with the Commanding General, as the Commanding General kept out of danger, and also kept in provisions. I was sick and petulant, and finally quarrelled with my friend. He told me, quietly, that I would regret my harshness when I should be well again. I set off for White Oak, but repented at "Burnt Chimneys," and turned back. In the misty dawn I saw the maimed still lying on the ground, wrapped in relics of blankets, and in one of the outhouses a grim embalmer stood amid a family of nude corpses. He dealt with the bodies of high officers only; for, said he —

"I used to be glad to prepare private soldiers. They were wuth a five dollar bill apiece. 'But, Lord bless you, a

Colonel pays a hundred, and a Brigadier-General two hundred. There's lots of them now, and I have cut the acquaintance of everything below a Major. I might," he added, " as a great favor, do a Captain, but he must pay a Major's price. I insist upon that! Such windfalls don't come every day. There won't be another such killing for a century."

A few horsemen of the escort loitered around head-quarters. All the tents but one had been removed, and the staff crouched sleepily upon the refuse straw. The rain began to drizzle at this time, and I unbuckled a blanket to wrap about my shoulders. Several people were lying upon dry places, here and there, and espying some planks a little remote, I tied my horse to a peach-tree, and stretched myself languidly upon my back. The bridal couch or the throne were never so soft as those knotty planks, and the drops that fell upon my forehead seemed to cool my fever.

I had passed into a sort of cognizant sleep when a harsh, loud, cruel voice awakened me, and I seemed to see a great Polyphemus, stretching his hands into the clouds, and gaping like an earthquake.

"Boy," I heard him say, to a slight figure, near at hand, " boy, what are you standing there for? What in ———— do you want?"

"Nothing!"

"Take it, and go, ———— ———— you! Take it, and go!"

I peeped timorously from my place, and recognized the Provost-General of the Grand Army. He had been sleeping upon a camp chest, and did not appear to be refreshed thereby.

"I feel sulky as ————!" he said to an officer adjoining; "I feel ———— bad-humored! Orderly!"

"General!"

"Whose horses are these?"

"I don't know, General!"

"Cut every ———— ———— one of 'em loose. Wake up these

16

——— ——— loafers with the point of your sabre! Every
——— ——— one of 'em! That's what I call ——— ———
boldness!"

He strutted off like the great Bomba or the Czar, and I
thought I never beheld a more exceptional person in any
high position.

With a last look at Savage's white house, the abandoned
wretches in the lawn, the blood-red hospital flag, the torn
track and smouldering cars, I turned my face southward,
crossed some bare plains, that had once been fields, and at
eight o'clock passed down the Williamsburg road, toward
Bottom Bridge. The original roadway was now a bottomless
stretch of sand, full of stranded wheels, dead horses, shreds
of blankets, discarded haversacks, and mounds of spilled
crackers. Other routes for wagons had been opened across
fields, over bluffs, around pits and bogs, and through thickets and woods. The whole country was crossed with
deeply-rutted roads, as if some immense city had been lifted
away, and only its interminably sinuous streets remained.
Near Burnt Chimneys, a creek crossing the road made a ravine,
and here I overtook the hindmost of the wagons. They had
been stalled in the gorge, and a provost guard was hurrying
the laggard teamsters. The creek was muddy beyond
comparison, and at the next hill-top I passed "Burnt Chimneys," a few dumb witnesses that pointed to heaven. A
mile or two further, I came to some of the retreating regiments, and also to five of the siege thirty-twos with which
Richmond was to have been bombarded. The main army
still lay back at their entrenchments to cover the retreat,
and at ten o'clock I heard the roar of field guns; the pursuit had commenced, and the Confederates were pouring
over the ramparts at Fairoaks. I did not go back; battles
were of no consequence to me. I wanted some breakfast.
If I could only obtain a cup of warm coffee and a fragment
of meat, I thought that I might recover strength. But
nothing could be obtained anywhere, for money or charity.

The soldiers' that I passed looked worn and hungry, for their predecessors had swept the country like herds of locusts; but one cheerful fellow, whom I addressed, produced a lump of fat pork that I tried to eat, but made a signal failure. All my baggage had been left at Michie's, where it remains to this moment. None cared to be hospitable to correspondents at this despondent hour, and a horrible idea of starvation took possession of my mind. A mile from White Oak Swamp, some distance back of the road, lay the Engineer Brigade. They were now on the eve of breaking camp, and when I reached Colonel McCloud Murphy's, his chests were packed, and all his provisions had gone ahead. He gave me, however, a couple of hard crackers and a draught of whiskey and quinine, whereby I rallied for a moment. At General Woodbury's I observed a middle-aged lady, making her toilet by a looking-glass hung against the tent-pole. She seemed as careful of her personal appearance, in this trying time, as if she had been at some luxurious court. There were several women on the retreat, and though the guns thundered steadily behind, they were never flurried, but could have received company, or accepted offers of marriage, with the utmost complacency. If there was any one that rouged, I am sure that no personal danger would have disturbed her while she heightened her roses; and she would have tied up her back hair in defiance of shell or grape.

At Casey's ancient head-quarters, on the bluff facing White Oak Swamp, I found five correspondents. We fraternized immediately, and they all pooh-poohed the battle, as such an old story that it would be absurd to ride back to the field. We knew, however, that it was occurring at Peach Orchard, on a part of the old ground at Fairoaks. These gentlemen were in rather despondent moods, and there was one who opined that we were all to be made prisoners of war. In his own expressive way of putting it, we were to be "gobbled up." This person was stout and

inclined to panting and perspiration.   He wore glasses upon
a most pugnacious nose, and his large, round head was covered with short, bristly, jetty hair.

"I promised my wife," said this person, who may be
called Cindrey, "to stay at home after the Burnside business.   The Burnside job was very nearly enough for me.
In fact I should have quite starved on the Burnside job, if I
hadn't took the fever.   And the fever kept me so busy that
I forgot how hungry I was.   So I lived over that."

At this point he took off his glasses and wiped his face ;
the water was running down his cheeks like a miniature
cataract, and his great neck seemed to emit jets of perspiration.

"Well," he continued, "the Burnside job wasn't enough
for me ; I must come out again.   I must follow the young
Napoleon.   And the young Napoleon has made a pretty
mess of it.   I never expect to get home any more ; I know
I shall be gobbled up !"

A youngish, oldish, oddish fellow, whom they called
"Pop," here told Mr. Cindrey to keep his pulse up and take
a drink.   A tall, large person, in semi-quaker garb, who
did not look unlike George Fox, run to seed, said, with a
flourish, that these battles were nothing to Shiloh.   He was
attached to the provincial press, and had been with the
army of the West until recently.   Without any exception,
he was the "fussiest," most impertinent, most disagreea-
ble man that I ever knew.   He always made a hero of himself in his reports, and if I remember rightly, their headings
ran after this fashion : —

Tremendous Battle at ROANOKE ! *The Correspondent of*
THE BLUNDERBUSS *hoists the* NATIONAL FLAG *above the* REBEL
RAMPARTS ! ! !" or again — *Grand Victory at* SHILOH !
Mr. Twaddle, our Special Correspondent, TAKEN PRIS-
ONER ! ! ! *He* ESCAPES ! ! !   *He is* FIRED UPON ! ! ! *He wrig-
gles through* FOUR SWAMPS *and* SEVEN HOSTILE CAMPS !
He is AGAIN CAPTURED ! *He STRANGLES the sentry ! He*

drinks the Rebel Commander, Philpot, BLIND! Philpot gives him THE PASSWORD!! ☞ *Philpot compliments the Blunderbuss.* ☞ OUR *Correspondent gains the Gunboats! He is* TAKEN ABOARD! *His welcome! Description of* HIS BOOTS! *Remarks, etc.,* ETC., ETC!!!"

This man was anxious to regulate not only his own newspaper, but he aspired to control the entire press. And his self adulation was incessant. He rung all the changes upon Shiloh. Every remark suggested some incident of Shiloh. He was a thorough Shilohite, and I regretted in my heart that the "Rebels" had not shut him away at Shiloh, that he might have enjoyed it to the end of his days.

The man "Pop" produced some apple whiskey, and we repaired to a spring, at the foot of the hill, where the man "Pop" mixed a cold punch, and we drank in rotation. I don't think that Cindrey enjoyed his draught, for it filtered through his neck as if he had sprung aleak there ; but the man Twaddle might have taken a tun, and, as the man "Pop" said, the effect would have been that of "pouring whiskey through a knot-hole." It was arranged among our own reporters, that I, being sick, should be the first of the staff to go to New York. The man "Pop" said jocosely, that I might be allowed to die in the bosom of my family. The others gave me their notes and lists, but none could give me what I most needed, — a morsel of food. At eleven o'clock our little party crossed White Oak Creek. There was a corduroy bridge upon which the teams travelled, and a log bridge of perilous unsteadiness for foot passengers. But the soldiers were fording the stream in great numbers, and I plunged my horse into the current so that he spattered a group of fellows, and one of them lunged at me with a bayonet. Beyond the creek and swamp, on the hillsides, baggage wagons and batteries were parked in immense numbers. The troops were taking positions along the edge of the bottom, to oppose incursions of the enemy,

16*

when they attempted pursuit, and I was told that the line extended several miles westward, to New Market Cross Roads, where, it was thought, the Confederates would march out from Richmond to offer battle. The roadway, beyond the swamp, was densely massed with horse, foot, cannon, and teams. The latter still kept toward the James, but the nags suffered greatly from lack of corn. Only indispensable material had been hauled from the Chickahominy, and the soldiers who fought the ensuing protracted battles were exhausted from hunger. Everything had an uncomfortable, transient, expectant appearance, and the feeble people that limped toward the *ultima thule* looked fagged and wretched.

There were some with balls in the groin, thigh, leg, or ankle, that made the whole journey, dropping blood at every step. They were afraid to lie down, as the wounded limbs might then grow rigid and stop their progress. While I pitied these maimed persons, I held the sick in greater sympathy. The troubles of the one were local; the others were pained in every bone. Bullets are fearful tenants, but fevers are worse. And some of the flushed, staggering folk, that reeled along the roadside, were literally out of their minds. They muttered and talked incoherently, and shouted ribald songs till my blood curdled to see them. At the first house on the right of the road, a half-mile past the Creek, I noticed many idle soldiers climbing the white palings, to watch something that lay in the yard. A gray-haired man was expiring, under the coolness of a spreading tree, and he was even now in the closing pangs. A comrade at his side bathed his brow with cool water, but I saw that he would shortly be with Lazarus or Dives. His hands were stretched stiffly by his sides, his feet were rigidly extended, and death was hardening into his bleached face. The white eyeballs glared sightlessly upward: he was looking into the other world.

The heat at this time was so intolerable that our party,

in *lieu* of any other place of resort, resolved to go to the woods. The sun set in heaven like a fiery furnace, and we sweat at every pore. I was afraid, momentarily, of sunstroke, and my horse was bathed in foam. Some companies of cavalry were sheltered in the edges of the woods, and, having secured our nags, we penetrated the depths, and spread out our blankets that we might lie down. But no breath of air stirred the foliage. The "hot and copper sky" found counterpart in the burning earth, and innumerable flies and insects fastened their fangs in our flesh. Cindrey was upon the rack, and it seemed to me that he possessed a sort of capillary perspiration, for the drops stood at tips of each separate bristle. He appeared to be passing from the solid to the fluid state, and I said, ungenerously, that the existing temperature was his liquifying point.

"Then," said the man "Pop," with a youngish, oldish smile, "we may as well liquor up."

"I don't drink!" said Twaddle, with a flourish. "During all the perilous hours of Shiloh, I abstained. But I am willing to admit, in respect to heat, that Shiloh is nowhere at present. And, therefore, I drink with a protest."

"No man can drink from my bottle, with a protest," said "Pop." "It isn't regular, and implies coercion. Now I don't coerce anybody, particularly you."

"Oh!" said Twaddle, drinking like a fish, or, as "Pop" remarked, enough to float a gunboat; "oh! we often chaffed each other at Shiloh."

"If you persist in reminding me of Shiloh," blurted Cindrey, "you'll be the ruin of me, — you and the heat and the flies. You'll have me dissolving into a dew."

Here he wiped his forehead, and killed a large blue fly, that was probing his ear. We all resolved to go to sleep, and Twaddle said that *he* slept like a top, in the heat of action, at Shiloh. "Pop" asked him, youngishly, to be kind enough to capture no redoubts while we slumbered, and not to raise the national flag over any ramparts for fifteen minutes. Then he grinned oldishly, and commenced to snore, with his flask in his bosom. I am certain that nobody ever felt a tithe of the pain, hunger, heat, and weariness, which agonized me, when I awoke from a half-hour's sweltering nap. My clothing was soaking with water; I was almost blind; somebody seemed to be sawing a section out of my head; my throat was hot and crackling; my stomach knew all the pangs of emptiness; I had scarcely strength to motion away the pertinacious insects. A soldier gave me a trifle of boiling water from his canteen; but I gasped for air; we were living in a vacuum. Sahara could not have been so fierce and burning. Two of us started off to find a spring. We made our way from shade to shade, expiring at every step, and finally, at the base of the hill, on the brink of the swamp, discovered a rill of tepid water, that evaporated before it had trickled a hundred yards. If a sleek and venomous water-snake — for there were thousands of them hereabout — had coiled in the channel, I would still have sucked the draught, bending down as I did. Then I bethought me of my pony. He had neither been fed nor watered for twenty hours, and I hastened to obtain him from his place along the woodside. To my terror, he was gone. Forgetful of my weakness, I passed rapidly, hither and thither, inquiring of cavalry-men, and entertaining suspicions of every person in the vicinity. Finally, I espied him in charge of a rough, thievish sabreman, who affected not to see me. I went up to the animal, and pulled the reins from his shoulder, to discover the brand mark, — " U. S." As I surmised, he had not been branded, and I turned indignantly upon the fellow : —

" My friend, how came you by this horse ? "

" Quartermaster ! " said the man, guiltily.

" No sir ! He belongs to me. Take off that cavalry-saddle, and find mine, immediately."

" Not if the court knows itself," said the man — " and it thinks it do ! "

" Then," said I, white with rage, " I shall report you at once, for theft."

" You may, if you want to," replied the man, carelessly.

I struck off at once for the new Provost Quarters, at a farm-house, close by. The possible failure to regain my animal, filled me with rueful thoughts. How was I, so dismounted, to reach the distant river? I should die, or starve, on the way. I thought I should faint, when I came to the end of the first field, and leaned, tremblingly, against a tree. I caught myself sobbing, directly, like a girl, and my mind ran upon the coolness of my home with my own breezy bedroom, soft paintings, and pleasant books. These themes tortured me with a consciousness of my folly. I had forsaken them for the wickednesses of this unhappy campaign. And my body was to blacken by the road-side, — the sable birds of prey were to be my mourners.

But, looking through my tears, a moving something passed between me and the sky. A brownish bay pony, trailing a fence-rail by his halter, and browsing upon patches of oats. I whistled thrice and the faithful animal trotted to my feet, and extended his great nose to be rubbed. I believe that this horse was the only living thing in the army that sympathized with me. He knew that I was sick, and I thought once, that, like the great dogs of Saint Bernard, he was about to get upon his knees, that I might the more readily climb upon his back. He did, however, stand quietly, while I mounted, and I gave him a drink at the foot of the hill. Returning, I saw the soldier, wrongfully accused, eyeing me from his haunt beneath the trees. I at once rode over to him, and apologized for my mistake.

" Never mind," said the man, complacently. " You was all right. I might a done the same thing. Fact is," he added, " I did hook this hoss, but I knew you wan't the party."

During the rest of the day I travelled disconsolately, up and down the road, winding in and out of the lines of teams.

I was assured that it would be impossible to get to the James till next day, as no portion of that army had yet advanced so far. The moody minutes of that afternoon made the longest part of my life, while the cannon at Peach Orchard and Savage's, roared and growled incessantly. Toward the close of the day I fell in with Captain Hill, of the New York Saratoga regiment, who gave me the outline of the fight.

The Confederates had discovered that we were falling back, by means of a balloon, of home manufacture, — the first they had been able to employ during the entire war. They appeared at our entrenchments on Sunday morning, and finding them deserted, commenced an irregular pursuit, whereby, they received terrible volleys of musketry from ambuscaded regiments, and retired, in disorder, to the ramparts. This was the battle of "Peach Orchard," and was disastrous to the Southerners. In the afternoon, they again essayed to advance, but more cautiously. The Federals, meantime, lay in order of battle upon Savage's, Dudley's, and Crouch's farms, their right resting on the Chickahominy, their centre on the railroad, and their left beyond the Williamsburg turnpike. For a time, an artillery contest ensued, and the hospitals at Savage's, where the wounded lay, were thrice fired upon. The Confederates finally penetrated the dense woods that belted this country, and the battle, at nightfall, became fervid and sanguinary. The Federals held their ground obstinately, and fell back, covered by artillery, at midnight. The woods were set on fire, in the darkness, and conflagration painted fiery terrors on the sky. The dead, littered all the fields and woods. The retreating army had marked its route with corpses. This was the battle of "Savage's," and neither party has called it a victory.

During the rest of the night the weary fugitives were crossing White Oak Creek and Swamp. Toward daybreak, the last battery had accomplished the passage ; the bridge was destroyed ; and preparations were made to dispute the pursuit in the morning.

I noted these particulars and added to my lists of dead and captured. At dusk I was about to sleep, supperless, upon the bare ground, when my patron, Colonel Murphy, again came in sight, and invited me to occupy a shelter-tent, on the brow of the hill at White Oak. To my great joy, he was able to offer me some stewed beef, bread and butter, and hot coffee. I ate voraciously, seizing the food in my naked fingers, and rending it like a beast.

The regiment of Colonel Murphy was composed of laborers, and artificers of every possible description. There were blacksmiths, moulders, masons, carpenters, boat-builders, joiners, miners, machinists, riggers, and rope-makers. They could have bridged the Mississippi, rebuilt the Tredegar works, finished the Tower of Babel, drained the Chesapeake, constructed the Great Eastern, paved Broadway, replaced the Grand Trunk railroad, or tunnelled the Straits of Dover. I have often thought that the real greatness of the Northern army lay in its ingenuity and industry, not in its military qualifications.

Our conversation turned upon these matters, as we sat before the Colonel's tent in the evening, and a Chaplain represented the feelings of the North in this manner : " We must whip them. We have got more money, more men, more ships, more ingenuity. They are bound to knuckle at last. If we have to lose man for man with them, their host will die out before ours. And we wont give up the Union, — not a piece of it big enough for a bird or a bee to cover, — though we reduce these thirty millions one half, and leave only the women and children to inherit the land." The heart of the army was now cast down, though a large portion of the soldiers did not know why we were falling back. I heard moody, despondent, accusing mutterings, around the camp-fires, and my own mind was full of grief and bitterness. It seemed that our old flag had descended to a degenerate people. It was not now, as formerly, a proud recollection that I was an American. If I survived the retreat, it would become my mission to herald the evil tidings through the length and breadth of the land. If I fainted in their pursuit, a loathsome prison, or a grave in the trenches, were to be my awards. When I lay down in a shelter-tent, rolling from side to side, I remembered that this was the Sabbath day. A battle Sabbath! How this din and slaughter contrasted with my dear old Lord's days in the prayerful parsonage! The chimes in the white spire, where the pigeons cooed in the hush of the singing, were changed to cannon peals; and the boys that dozed in the "Amen corner," were asleep forever in the trampled grain-fields. The good parson, whose clauses were not less truthful, because spoken through his nose, now blew the loud trumpet for the babes he had baptized, to join the Captains of fifties and thousands; and while the feeble old women in the side pews made tremulous responses to the prayer for "thy soldiers fighting in thy cause," the banners of the Republic were craped, dusty, and bloody, and the scattered regiments were resting upon their arms for the shock of the coming dawn.

Thus I thought, tossing and talking through the long watches, and toward morning, when sleep brought fever-dreams, a monstrous something leered at me from the blackness, saying, in a sort of music —

"Gobbled up! Gobbled up!"

CHAPTER XVIII.

BY THE RIVERSIDE.

A CRASH and a stunning shock, as of a falling sphere, aroused me at nine o'clock. A shell had burst in front of our tent, and the enemy's artillery was thundering from Casey's old hill, beyond the swamp. As I hastily drew on my boots,—for I had not otherwise undressed,—I had opportunity to remark one of those unaccountable panics which develop among civilian soldiers. The camps were plunged into disorder. As the shells dropped here and there, among the tents and teams, the wildest and most fearful deeds were enacted. Here a caisson blew up, tearing the horses to pieces, and whirling a cannoneer among the clouds. There an ammunition wagon exploded, and the air seemed to be filled with fragments of wood, iron, and flesh. A boy stood at one of the fires, combing out his matted hair; suddenly his head flew off, spattering the brains, and the shell — which we could not see — exploded in a piece of woods, mutilating the trees. The effect upon the people around me was instantaneous and appalling. Some, that were partially dressed, took to their heels, hugging a medley of clothing. The teamsters climbed into the saddles, and shouted to their nags, whipping them the while. If the heavy wheels hesitated to revolve, they left horses and vehicles to their fate, taking themselves to the woods; or, as in some cases, cut traces and harness, and galloped away like madmen. In a twinkling our camps

17   (193)

were almost deserted, and the fields, woods, and roads were alive with fugitives, rushing, swearing, falling, and trampling, while the fierce bolts fell momentarily among them, making havoc at every rod.

To join this flying, dying mass was my first impulse ; but after-thought reminded me that it would be better to remain. I must not leave my horse, for I could not walk the whole long way to the James, and the fever had so reduced me that I hardly cared to keep the little life remaining. I almost marvelled at my coolness ; since, in the fulness of strength and health, I should have been one of the first of the fugitives ; whereas, I now looked interestedly upon the exciting spectacle, and wished that it could be daguerreotyped.

Before our artillery could be brought to play, the enemy, emboldened at his success, pushed a column of infantry down the hill, to cross the creek, and engage us on our camping-ground. For a time I believed that he would be successful, and in that event, confusion and ruin would have overtaken the Unionists. The gray and butternut lines appeared over the brow of the hill, — they wound at double quick through the narrow defile, — they poured a volley into our camps when half-way down, and under cover of the smoke they dashed forward impetuously, with a loud huzza. The artillery beyond them kept up a steady fire, raining shell, grape, and canister over their heads, and ploughing the ground on our side, into zigzag furrows, — rending the trees, shattering the ambulances, tearing the tents to tatters, slaying the horses, butchering the men. Directly Captain Mott's battery was brought to bear ; but before he could open fire, a solid shot struck one of his twelve-pounders, breaking the trunnion and splintering the wheels. In like manner one of his caissons blew up, and I do not think that he was able to make any practise whatever. A division of infantry was now marched forward, to engage the Confederates at the creek side ; but two of the regiments — and I think that one was the 20th New York — turned bodily, and could not be rallied. The moment was full of significance, and I beheld these failures with breathless suspense. In five minutes the pursuers would gain the creek, and in ten, drive our dismayed battalions, like chaff before the wind. I hurried to my horse, that I might be ready to escape. The shell and ball still made music around me. I buckled up my saddle with tremulous fingers, and put my foot upon the stirrup. But a cheer recalled me and a great clapping of hands, as at some clever performance in the amphitheatre. I looked again. A battery from our position across the road, had opened upon the Confederate infantry, as they reached the very brink of the swamp. For a moment the bayonets tossed wildly, the dense column staggered like a drunken man, the flags rose and fell, and then the line fell back disorderly. At that instant a body of Federal infantry, that I had not seen, appeared, as by invocation ; their steel fell flashingly, a column of smoke enveloped them, the hills and skies seemed to split asunder with the shock, — and when I looked again, the road was strewn with the dying and dead ; the pass had been defended.

As the batteries still continued to play, and as the prospect of uninterrupted battle during the day was not a whit abated, I decided to resume my saddle, and, if possible, make my way to the James. The geography of the country, as I had deciphered it, satisfied me that I must pass "New Market," before I could rely upon my personal safety. New Market was a paltry cross-road's hamlet, some miles ahead, but as near to Richmond as White Oak Creek. The probabilities were, that the Confederates would endeavor to intercept us at this point, and so attack us in flank and rear. As I did not witness either of these battles, though I heard the discharge of every musket, it may be as well to state, in brief, that June 30 was marked by the bloodiest of all the Richmond struggles, excepting, possibly,

Gaines's Mill.   While the Southern artillery engaged Franklin's corps, at White Oak Crossing, and their left made several unavailing attemps to ford the creek with infantry, — their entire right and centre, marched out the Charles City Road, and gave impetuous battle at New Market.   The accounts and the results indicate that the Federals won the day at New Market, sheerly by good fighting.   They were parching with thirst, weak with hunger, and it might have been supposed that reverses had broken their spirit.   On the contrary they did not fall back a rod, during the whole day, and at evening Heintzelman's corps crowned their success by a grand charge, whereat the Confederates broke and were pursued three miles toward Richmond.   The gunboats Galena and Aroostook, lying in the James at Turkey Bend, opened fire at three o'clock, and killed promiscuously, Federals and Confederates.   But the Southern soldiers were superstitous as to gunboats, and they could not be made to approach within range of the Galena's monstrous projectiles.

I shall always recall my journey from White Oak to Harrison's Bar, as marked by constantly increasing beauties of scenery, and terrors of event.   At every hoof-fall I was leaving the low, boggy, sparsely settled Chickahominy region, for the high farm-lands of the James.   The dwellings, as I progressed, became handsome ; the negro quarters were less like huts and cattle-sheds ; the ripe wheat-fields stretched almost to the horizon ; the lawns and lanes were lined with ancient shade-trees ; there were picturesque gates and lodges ; the fences were straight and white-washed, there were orchards, heavy with crimson apples, where the pumpkins lay beneath, like globes of gold, in the rows of amber corn.   Into this patriarchal and luxuriant country, the retreating army wound like a great devouring serpent.   It was to me, the coming back of the beaten *jetters* through *Midgards*, or the repulse of the fallen angels from heaven, trampling down the river-sides of Eden.

They rode their team-horses into the wavy wheat, and in some places, where the reapers had been at work, they dragged the sheaves from the stacks, and rested upon them. Hearing of the coming of the army, the proprietors had vainly endeavored to gather their crops, but the negroes would not work, and they had not modern implements, whereby to mow the grain rapidly. The profanation of those glorious stretches of corn and rye were to me some of the most melancholy episodes of the war. No mind can realize how the grain-fields used to ripple, when the fresh breezes blew up and down the furrows, and the hot suns of that almost tropical climate, had yielded each separate head till the whole landscape was like a bright cloud, or a golden sea. The tall, shapely stalks seemed to reach out imploringly, like sunny-haired virgins, waiting to be gathered into the arms of the farmer. They were the Sabine women, on the eve of the bridal, when the insatiate Romans tore them away and trampled them. The Indian corn was yet green, but so tall that the tasselled tops showed how cunningly the young ears were ripening. There were melons in the corn-rows, that a week would have developed, but the soldiers dashed them open and sucked the sweet water. They threw clubs at the hanging apples till the ground was littered with them, and the hogs came afield to gorge; they slew the hogs and divided the fresh pork among themselves. As I saw, in one place, dozens of huge German cavalry-men, asleep upon bundles of wheat, I recalled their Frankish forefathers, swarming down the Apennines, upon Italy.

The air was so sultry during a part of the day, that one was constantly athirst. But there was a belt of country, four miles or more in width, where there seemed to be neither rills nor wells. Happily, the roads were, in great part, enveloped in stately timber, and the shade was very grateful to men and horses. The wounded still kept with us, and many that were fevered. They did not complain

17*

with words ; but their red eyes and painful pace told all the
story.   If we came to rivulets, they used to lie upon their
bellies, along the margins, with their heads in the flowing
water.   The nags were so stiff and hot, that, when they
were reined into creeks, they refused to go forward, and my
brown animal once dropped upon his knees, and quietly
surveyed me, as I pitched upon my hands, floundering in
the pool.   I remember a stone dairy, such as are found
upon Pennsylvania grazing farms, where I stopped to drink.
It lay up a lane, some distance from the road, and two enormous tulip poplar trees sheltered and half-concealed it.   A
tiny creek ran through the dairy, over. cool granite slabs,
and dozens of earthen milk-bowls lay in the water, with the
mould of the cream brimming at the surface.   A pewter
drinking-mug hung to a peg at the side, and there were
wooden spoons for skimming, straining pails, and great
ladles of gourd and cocoanut.   A cooler, tidier, trimmer
dairy, I had not seen, and I stretched out my body upon the
dry slabs, to drink from one of the milk-bowls.   The cream
was sweet, rich, and nourishing, and I was so absorbed directly, that I did not heed the footfalls of a tall, broad, vigorous man, who said in a quiet way, but with a deep, sonorous voice, and a decided Northern twang —

"Friend, you might take the mug.   Some of your comrades will want to drink from that bowl."

I begged his pardon hastily, and said that I supposed he
was the proprietor.

"I reckon that I must give over my ownership, while the
army hangs around here," said the man ;   "but I must endure what I can't cure."

Here he smiled grimly, and reached down the pewter
cup.   Then he bent over a fresh bowl, and dexterously
dipped the cup full of milk, without seeming to break the
cream.

"Drink that," he said ;   "and if there's any better milk
in these parts, I want to know the man."

He looked at me critically, while I emptied the vessel, and seemed to enjoy my heartiness.

"If you had been smart enough to come this way, victorious," added the man, straightforwardly, "instead of being out-generalled, whipped, and driven, I should enjoy the loss of my property a great deal more!"

There was an irresistible heartiness in his tone and manner. He had, evidently, resolved to bear the misfortunes of war bravely.

"You are a Northern man?" I said, inquiringly.

"How do you know?"

"There are no such dairies in Virginia; a Virginian never dipped a mug of milk after your fashion; you haven't the Virginia inflection, and very weak Virginia principles."

The man laughed dryly, and filled himself a cup, which he drank sedately.

"I reckon you are correct," he said; "pretty much correct, any way. I'm a New Yorker, from the Mohawk Valley, and I have been showing these folks how they can't farm. If there's anybody that farms better than I do, I want to know the man!"

He looked at the flowing water, the clean slabs and walls, the shining tins, and smacked his lips satisfactorily. I asked him if he farmed with negroes, and if the prejudices of the country affected either his social or industrial interests. He answered that he was obliged to employ negroes, as he had thrice tried the experiment of working with whites, but with ill success.

"*I* would have kept 'em," he added, in his great voice, closing a prodigious fist, "but the men would not stay. I couldn't make the neighbors respect them. There was nobody for 'em to associate with. They were looked upon as niggers, and they got to feel it after a while. So I have had only niggers latterly; but I get more work from them than any other man in these parts. If there's anybody that gets more work out of niggers than I do, I want to know the man!"

There was a sort of hard, hearty defiance about him, typical of his severe, angular race, and I studied his large limbs and grim, full face with curious admiration. He told me that he hired his negro hands from the surrounding slave-owners, and that he gave them premiums upon excess of work, approximating to wages. In this way they were encouraged to habits of economy, perseverance, and sprightliness.

" I don't own a nigger," he said, " not one ! But I don't think a nigger's much too good to be a slave. I won't be bothered with owning 'em. And I won't be conquered into ' the institution.' I said, when I commenced, that I should not buy niggers, and I won't buy niggers, because I said so ! As to social disadvantages, every Northern man has 'em here. They called me an abolitionist ; and a fellow at the hotel in Richmond did so to my face. I knocked him into a heap, and nobody has meddled with me since. " Of course," he said, after a moment, " it won't do to inflame these people. These people are like my bulls, and you mustn't shake a red stick at 'em. Besides, I'm not a fanatic. I never was. My wife's one of these people, and I let her think as she likes. But, if there's anybody in these parts that wants to interfere with me, I should like to know the man ! "

The contemptuous tone in which he mentioned " these people " amused me infinitely, and I believed that his resolute, indomitable manner would have made him popular in any society. He was shrewd, withal, and walked beside me to his gate. When the regiments halted to rest, by the wayside, he invited the field officers to the dairy, and so obtained guards to rid him of depredators. He would have escaped very handsomely, but the hand of war was not always so merciful, and a part of the battle of Malvern Hills was fought upon his property. I have no doubt that he submitted unflinchingly, and sat more stolidly amid the wreck than old Marius in battered Carthage.

Until two o'clock in the afternoon I rode leisurely south-ward, under a scorching sky, but still bearing up, though aflame with fever. The guns thundered continuously be-hind, and the narrow roads were filled, all the way, with hurrying teams, cavalry, cannon, and foot soldiers. I stopped, a while, by a white frame church, — primly, squarely built, — and read the inscriptions upon the tombs uninterestedly. Some of the soldiers had pried open the doors, and a wounded Zouave was delivering a mock ser-mon from the pulpit. Some of his comrades broke up the meeting by singing —

"John Brown's body lies a mouldering in the grave,"

and then a Major ordered them out, and put a guard upon the building. The guard played cards upon the door sills.

I was frequently obliged, by the crowded state of the roads, to turn aside into woods, fens, and fields, and so make precarious progress. Sometimes I strayed, unwit-tingly, a good way from the army, and recovered the route with difficulty. On one of these occasions, I was surprised by a person in civil dress, who seemed to shoot up out of the ground. He was the queerest, grimest, fearfulest man that I have ever known, and, at first, I thought that the arch fiend had appeared before me. The wood was very deep here, and there were no wayfarers but we two. It was quite still ; but now and then we heard the rumble of wagons, and the crack of teamster's whips. The man in question wore dead black beard, and his eyebrows were of the same intense, lustreless hue. So were his eyes and his hair ; but the latter formed a circle or cowl around his head. He had a pale skin, his fingers were long and bony, and he rode dexterously in and out, among the tree boles, with his hat in his hand. His horse was as black as himself, and, together, they made a half-brigandish, half-satanic appear-ance.

I reined in sharply, when I saw this person, and he looked at me like the evil-eye, through his great owlish orbs.

"Good day," he said, in profound basso, as low I think as "double G," and when he opened his mouth, I saw that his teeth were very white.

I saluted him gravely, and, not without a shudder, rode beside him. He proved to be a sort of Missionary, from the Evangelical religious denominations of the North, to inquire into the spiritual condition of the soldiers. Camps were full of such people, but I had not found any man who appeared to be less qualified for his vocation; to have such a figure at one's deathbed, would be like a foretaste of the great fiend. He had a fashion of working his scalp half way down to his eyes, as he spoke, and when he smiled, — though he never laughed aloud, — his eyelashes did not contract, as with most people, but rather expanded, till his eyeballs projected from his head. On such occasions, his white teeth were revealed like a row of fangs, and his leprous skin grew yet paler.

"The army has not even the form of godliness," said this man. In the course of his remarks, he had discovered that I was a correspondent, and at once turned the conversation into a politico-religious channel.

"The form of godliness is gone," said the man again in "double G." "This is a calamitous fact! I would it were not so! I grieve to state it! But inquiry into the fact, has satisfied me that the form of godliness does not exist. Ah!"

When the man said "Ah!" I thought that my horse would run away, and really, the tone was like the deep conjuration in Hamlet: "*swear-r-r-r!*"

"For example," said the man, who told me that his name was Dimpdin, — "I made some remarks to the 1st New Jersey, on Sabbath week. The field officers directed the men to attend; I opened divine service with a feeling hymn; a very feeling hymn! A long measure hymn! By

Montgomery! I commenced earnestly in prayer. In appropriate prayer! I spoke advisedly for a short hour. What were the results? The deplorable results? There were men, sir, in that assembly, who went to sleep. To sleep!"

He must have gone a great way below "double G," this time, and I did not see how he could get back. He drew his scalp quite down to the bridge of his nose, and, seeing that my horse pricked up his ears, timorously smiled like the idol of Baal.

"There were men, sir, who did worse. Not simply failing to be hearers of the word! But doers of evil! Men who played cards during the service. Played cards! Gambled! Gambled! And some, — abandoned wretches! — who mocked me! Lifted up their voices and mocked! Mockers, gamblers, slumberers!"

I never heard anything so awful as the man Dimpdin's voice, at the iteration of these three words. They seemed to come from the bowels of the earth, and rang through the wood like the growl of a lion. He told me that he was engaged upon a Memorial to the Evangelical Union, which should state the number of unconverted men in the ranks, and the number of castaways. He accredited the loss of the campaign to the prevailing wickedness, but was unwilling to admit that the Southern troops were more religious. His theory of reform, if I remember it, embraced the raising of Chaplains to the rank of Major, with proportionate pay and perquisites, the establishment of a military religious bureau, and a Chaplain-General with Aides. Each soldier, officer, teamster, and drummer-boy was to have a Testament in his knapsack, and services should be held on the eve of every battle, and at roll-call in the mornings. There was to be an inspection of Testaments as of muskets. For swearing, a certain sum should be subtracted from the soldier's pay, and conferred upon the Chaplains.

"In fact," said Dimpdin, tragically, — scalping himself

meanwhile, — the church must be recognized in every department, and if my Memorial be acted upon favorably, we shall have such victories, in three months, as will sweep Rebellion into the grave. Yes! Into the grave! The grave!"

I was obliged to say, here, that my horse could not stand these sepulchral noises, and that my nerves, being shattered by the fever, were inadequate to bear the shock. So the man Dimpdin smiled, like a window-mummy, and contented himself with looking like Apollyon. We reached a rill directly, and he produced a wicker flask, with a Britannia drinking-case.

"Young men love stimulating drinks," said Dimpdin, — strong drinks! alcholic drinks! Here is a portion of Monongahela! old Monongahela! We will refresh ourselves!"

He found a lemon, accidentally, in his saddle-bag, and contrived an informal punch, with wonderful dexterity. I took a draught modestly, and he emptied the rest, with an "Ah!" that shook the woods.

I wondered if the man Dimpdin would suggest the apportionment of flasks to soldiers, in his Evangelical report!

He left me, when we regained the road, to ride with a lithe, bronchial person, in white neckcloth and coat cut close at the collar. They looked like the fox and the fiend, in the fable, and I seemed to hear the man Dimpdin's voice for three succeeding weeks.

At three o'clock, I climbed a gentle hill, — and I was now very weary and weak, — and from the summit, looked upon the river James, flowing far off to the right, through woods, and bluffs, and grainfields, and reedy islands. At last, I had gained the haven. The bright waters below me seemed to cool my red, fiery eyes, and a sort of blessed blindness fell for a time upon me, so that, when I looked again my lashes were wet. The prospect was truly beautiful. Far to the west, standing out from the chalky bluffs, were scattered the white camps of Wise's Confederate brigade. Beyond, on the remote bank of the river, lay farm-lands, and stately mansions, and some one showed me, rising faintly in the distance, "Drury's Bluff," the site of Fort Darling, where the gunboats were repulsed in the middle of May. Below, in the river, lay the *Galena*, and a little way astern, the *Aroostook*. Signal-men, with flags, were elevated upon the masts of each, and the gunners stood upon the decks, as waiting some emergency. The vessels had steam up, and seemed to be ready for action at any moment. This was Grand Turkey Bend, and the rising ground on which I stood, was known as "Malvern Hills." A farm-house lay to my left, and repairing thither, I cast myself from the nag, and lay down in the shady yard, thankful that I had reached the haven, and only solicitous now to escape the further privations of McClellan's Peninsular Campaign.

CHAPTER XIX.

THE HOSPITAL TRANSPORT.

An earnest desire now took possession of me, to be the first of the correspondents to reach New York. The scenes just transpired had been unparalleled in the war, and if, through me, the —— should be the first to make them public, it would greatly redound to my credit. Perhaps no profession imparts an enthusiasm in any measure kindred to that of the American Newsgatherer. I was careless of the lost lives and imperilled interests, the suffering, the defeat: no emotions either of the patriot or the man influenced me. I only thought of the *eclat* of giving the story to the world, and nurtured an insane desire to make to Fortress Monroe, by some other than the common expedient. That this was a paltry ambition I know; but I write what happened, and to the completion of my sketch of a correspondent, this is necessary to be said. I found Glumley at the old mansion referred to, and stealthily suggested to him the seizing of an open boat, whereby we might row down to the Fortress. He rejected it as impracticable, but was willing to hazard a horseback ride down the Peninsula. I knew that this would not do, and after a short time I continued my journey down the riverside, hopeful of finding some transport or Despatch boat. I was now in Charles City County, and the river below me was dotted with woodland islands. I soon got upon the main road to Harrison's Point or Bar, and followed the stream of ambulances and supply teams for more than an hour. At last we reached a diverging lane, through which we passed to a landing, close to a fine dwelling, whose style of architecture I may denominate, the "Gothic run mad." An old cider-press was falling into rottenness on the lawn ; four soldiers were guarding the well, that the mob might not exhaust its precious contents, and between some negro-huts and the brink of the bluff, stood a cluster of broad-armed trees, beneath whose shade the ambulance-drivers were depositing the wounded.

I have made these chapters sufficiently hideous, without venturing to transcribe these new horrors. Suffice it to say that the men whom I now beheld had been freshly brought from the fight of New Market, and were suffering the first agonies of their wounds. One hour before, they had felt all the lustiness of life and adventure. Now, they were whining like babes, and some had expired in the ambulances. The act of lifting them to the ground so irritated their wounds that they howled dismally, and yet were so exhausted that after lying upon the ground awhile, they quietly passed into sleep. Such are the hardening results of war, that some soldiers, who were unhurt, actually refused to give a trifle of river water from their canteens to their expiring comrades. At one time a brutal wrangle occurred at the well, and the guard was compelled to seek reinforcement, or the thirsty people would have massacred them.

I was now momentarily adding to my notes of the battles, and the wounded men very readily gave me their names ; for they were anxious that the account of their misfortunes should reach their families, and I think also, that some martial vanity lingered, even among those who were shortly to crumble away. A longboat came in from the Galena, after a time, and General McClellan, who had ridden down to the pier, was taken aboard. He looked to be very hot and anxious, and while he remained aboard the vessel, his staff dispersed themselves around the banks and

talked over the issues of the contest. As the General re-
ceded from the strand, every sweep of the long oars was
responded to from the hoarse cannon of the battle-field, and
when he climbed upon deck, the steamer moved slowly up
the narrow channel, and the signal-man in the foretop flourished his crossed flag sturdily. Directly, the Galena opened
fire from her immense pieces of ordnance, and the roar was
so great that the explosions of field-guns were fairly
drowned. She fired altogether by the direction of the signals, as nothing could be seen of the battle-field from her
decks. I ascertained afterward that she played havoc
with our own columns as well as the enemy's, but she
brought hope to the one, and terror to the other. The very
name of gunboat affrighted the Confederates, and they were
assured, in this case, that the retreating invaders had at
length reached a haven. The Galena kept up a steady fire
till nightfall, and the Federals, taking courage, drove their
adversaries toward Richmond, at eve. Meanwhile the
Commanding General's escort and body-guard had encamped
around us, and during the night the teams and much of the
field cannon fell back. I obtained shelter and meals from
Quartermaster Le Duke of Iowa, whose canvas was pitched
a mile or more below, and as I tossed through the watches
I heard the splashing of water in the river beneath, where
the tired soldiers were washing away the powder of the
battle.

In the morning I retraced to head-quarters, and vainly
endeavored to learn something as to the means of going
down the river. Commanders are always anxious to grant
correspondents passes after a victory; but they wish to
defer the unwelcome publication of a defeat. I was advised
by Quartermaster-General Van Vliet, however, to proceed
to Harrison's Bar, and, as I passed thither, the last day's
encounters — those of "Malvern Hills" — occurred. The
scenes along the way were reiterations of terrors already
described, — creaking ambulances, staggering foot soldiers,

profane wagoners, skulking officers and privates, officious Provost guards, defiles, pools and steeps packed with teams and cannon, wayside houses beset with begging, gossiping, or malicious soldiers, and wavy fields of wheat and rye thrown open to man and beast. I was amused at one point, to see some soldiers attack a beehive that they might seize the honey. But the insects fastened themselves upon some of the marauders, and after indescribable cursing and struggling, the bright nectar and comb were relinquished by the toilers, and the ravishers gorged upon sweetness.

Harrison's Bar is simply a long wharf, extending into the river, close by the famous mansion, where William Henry Harrison, a President of the United States, was born, and where, for two centuries, the scions of a fine old Virginia family have made their homestead. The house had now become a hospital, and the wounded were being conveyed to the pier, whence they were delivered over to some Sanitary steamers, for passage to Northern cities. I tied my horse to the spokes of a wagon-wheel, and asked a soldier to watch him, while I repaired to the quay. A half drunken officer was guarding the wharf with a squad of men, and he denied me admittance, at first, but when I had said something in adulation of his regiment — a trick common to correspondents — he passed me readily. The ocean steamer *Daniel Webster* was about being cast adrift when I stepped on board, and Colonel Ingalls, Quartermaster in charge, who freely gave me permission to take passage in her, advised me not to risk returning to shore. So, reluctantly, I resigned my pony, endeared to me by a hundred adventures, and directly I was floating down the James, with the white teams and the tattered groups of men, receding from me, and each moment the guns of Malvern Hills growing fainter. Away! praised be a merciful God! away from the accursed din, and terror, and agony, of my second campaign, — away forever from the Chickahominy.

For awhile I sat meditatively in the bow of the boat, full
18*

of strange perplexities and thankfulness. I had escaped
the bullet, and fever, and captivity, and a great success in
my profession was about to be accorded to me, but there
was much work yet to be done.   The rough material I had
for a grand account of the closing of the campaign ; but
these fragmentary figures and notes must be wrought into
narrative, and to avail myself of their full significance, I
must lose no moment of application.   I found that I was
one of four correspondents on board, and we resolved to
district the boat, each correspondent taking one fourth of
the names of the sick and wounded.   The spacious saloons,
the clean deck, the stairways, the gangways, the hold, the
halls, — all were filled with victims.   They lay in rows upon
straw beds, they limped feverishly here and there ; some
were crazed from sunstroke, or gashes ; and one man that I
remember counted the rivets in the boilers over the whole
hundred miles of the journey, while another, — a teamster,
— whipped and cursed his horses as if he had mistaken the
motion of the boat for that of his vehicle.

The *Daniel Webster* was one of a series of transports
supplied for the uses of the wounded by a national committee of private citizens.   Her wood work was shining and
glossy, her steel shone like mirrors, and she was cool as
Paradise.   Out of the smoke, and turmoil, and suffocation
of battle these wretched men had emerged, to enjoy the
blessedness, unappreciated before, of shelter, and free air
and cleanliness.   There was ice in abundance on board,
and savory lemonade lay glassily around in great buckets.
Women flitted from group to group with jellies, *bonbons*,
cigars, and oranges, and the grateful eyes of the prostrate
people might have melted one to tears.   These women were
enthusiasts of all ages and degrees, who proffered themselves, at the beginning of the war, as stewardesses and
nurses.   From the fact that some of them were of mascu-
line natures, or, in the vocabulary of the times, " strong-
minded," they were the recipients of many coarse jests,

and imputations were made upon both their modesty and their virtue. But I would that any satirist had watched with me the good offices of these Florence Nightingales of the West, as they tripped upon merciful errands, like good angels, and left paths of sunshine behind them. The soldiers had seen none of their countrywomen for months, and they followed these ambassadors with looks half-idolatrous, half-downcast, as if consciously unworthy of so tender regard.

"If I could jest die, now," said one of the poor fellows to me, "with one prayer for my country, and one for that dear young lady!"

There was one of these daughters of the good Samaritan whose face was so full of coolness, and her robes so airy, flowing, and graceful, that it would have been no miracle had she transmuted herself to something divine. She was very handsome, and her features bore the imprint of that high enthusiasm which may have animated the maid of Arc. One of the more forward of the correspondents said to her, as she bore soothing delicacies to the invalids, that he missed the satisfaction of being wounded, at which she presented an orange and a cigar to each of us in turn. Among the females on board, I remarked one, very large, angular, and sanguine, who sat at a small table, dispensing luxuries with the manners of a despot and the charity of a child. She had a large vessel of boiling coffee, from which she drew spicy quantities at intervals; and when the troops thronged around eagerly, she rebuked the more forward, and called up some emaciated, bashful fellows, giving them the preference. Every soldier who accepted coffee was obliged to take a religious tract, and she gave them away with a grim satisfaction that was infinitely amusing and interesting. I ventured to ask this imperative person for a bottle of ink, and after some difficulty, — arising out of a mistaken notion on her part that I was dangerously wounded, — she vaulted over a chair, and disappeared into a state-room. When she returned, her arms were filled with a perfect wilderness of stationery, and having supplied each of us in turn, she addressed herself to me in the following sententious manner : —

"See here! You reporter! (There's ink!) I want to be put in the newspapers! Look at me! Now! Right straight! (Pens?) Here I am; thirteen months at work; been everywhere; done good; country; church; never noticed. Never!—Now! I want to be put in newspapers."

At this point the Imperatress was called off by some soldiers, who presumed to draw coffee without her consent. She slapped one of them soundly, and at once overpowered him with kindnesses, and tracts ; then she returned and gave me a photograph, representing herself with a basket of fruit, and a quantity of good books. I took note of her name, but unfortunately lost the memorandum, and unless she has been honored-by some more careful scribe, I fear that her labors are still unrecognized.

During much of the trip, I wrote material parts of my report, copied portions of my lists, and managed before dusk, to get fairly underway with my narrative. From the deck of the steamer I beheld at five o'clock, what I had long wished to see, — the famous island of Jamestown, celebrated in the early annals of the New World, as the home of John Smith, and of Nathaniel Bacon, and as the resort of the Indian Princess, Pocahontas. A single fragment of a tower, the remnant of the Colonial church, was the only ruin that I could see.

At seven o'clock we dropped anchor in Hampton Roads, and a boat let down from the davits. Some of my wily compeers endeavored to fill all the stern seats, that I might not be pulled to shore ; but I swung down by a rope, and made havoc with their shins, so that they gained nothing ; the surf beat so vehemently against the pier at Old Point, that we were compelled to beach the boat, and I ran rapidly through the ordnance yard to the " Hygeia House," where our agent boarded ; he had gone into the Fortress to pass the night, and when I attempted to follow him thither, a knot of anxious idlers, who knew that I had just returned from the battle-fields, attempted to detain me by sheer force. I dashed rapidly up the plank walk, reached the portal, and had just vaulted into the area, when the great gates swung to, and the tattoo beat ; at the same instant the sergeant of guard challenged me : —

" Who comes there ? Stand fast ! Guard prime ! "

A dozen bright musket-barrels were levelled upon me, and I heard the click of the cocks as the fingers were laid upon the triggers. When I had explained, I was shown the Commandant's room, and hastening in that direction, encountered Major Larrabee, my old patron of the fifth Wisconsin regiment. He took me to the barracks, where a German officer, commanding a battery, lodged, and the latter accommodated me with a camp bedstead. Here I related the incidents of the engagements, and before I concluded, the room was crowded with people. I think that I gave a sombre narration, and the hearts of those who heard me were cast down. Still, they lingered ; for the bloody story possessed a hideous fascination, and I was cross-examined so pertinaciously that my host finally arose, protesting that I needed rest, and turned the party out of the place. The old fever-dreams returned to me that night, and my brain spun round for hours before I could close my eyes.

CHAPTER XX.

ON FURLOUGH AWHILE.

COUNTER winds and tides had so delayed the *Adelaide*, on which I departed for New York with my despatches, that it became a doubtful question as to whether we could make connection with the early train for New York. The captain shook his head distrustfully when he had looked at his watch, and told me that he frequently failed to land his passengers in time. The bitterness of the doubt so troubled me, that I paced the decks, looking at the approaching city, and thinking that all my labor was to be disappointed in the end. I could not telegraph my narrative and lists, for Government controlled the wires; and moreover, the Associated Press regulations forbade any newspaper to telegraph exclusive news from any point but Washington. I half resolved to hire a special locomotive, but it was doubtful that the railway authorities could procure one, at so short notice. Unless I overtook the eight o'clock A. M. train, I could not get to New York before two o'clock next morning, — too late for the press. Besides, how did I know that some correspondent had not reached Washington, by way of one of the Potomac vessels, and so forestalled me? Here was an opportunity to be the first of all our correspondents to publish the incidents and results of six days' stupendous warfare, — but escaping at the very moment of realization. The seconds were hours as we swept past Fort Carroll, rounded Fort McHenry, and swung toward our moorings, under Fort Federal Hill.

"If we make a prompt landing," said the Captain, "you may barely get the train."

I stood with my bundles of notes upon the high deck, and signalled a cab-driver. He caught the precious manuscript, and bolted for his cab. In another second he was dashing like a runaway up the pier, over the bridge, through Pratt Street, and — out of sight. Slowly the great hulk turned awkwardly about; one turn of her paddles brought us close enough to fling a rope, a second drew her very near the shore; the distance was fearful, but I braced myself for the leap.

"Stand clear!" I called to the score of hackmen.

A little run, a spring, — and I fell upon my feet, rolled over upon my face, gathered myself to the arms of all the Jehus, and was carried off bodily by a man with a great knob on his forehead as big as the end of his whip-handle.

"G'lang! Who-o-o-oh! Swis-s-s!"

I think that I promised that man everything under the sun to catch the train. I recollect that the knob on his forehead grew black and bulging as he lashed his horse. I found myself standing up in the cab, screaming like the driver. We were both insane, and the horse must have been of the breed of *Pegasus*, for I could feel the vehicle gyrating in the air. Now we turned a lamp-post, and the glass splintered somewhere; a dog howled as we drove over his appendage; a woman with a baby gave a short scream and disappeared into the earth; a policeman gave chase, but we laughed him to scorn.

Huzza! Here we are! The train stands puffing at the long platform. "Your bundle, yer honor! Wasn't I the boy to make the keers?" "Didn't I projuce yer honor in good time, sur?" I only know that I flung a greenback to the two, — that I vainly besought the ticket agent to give me no change, but consign it to the first engineer who failed to make time, — that I wrote on the back of my hat for four hours, — that I devoured a chicken and as many eggs as she had laid in a lifetime, at Havre de Grace, — that I leaped upon the platform at Broad and Prime streets, Philadelphia, at noon, — that I plunged into a cab, and said, significantly —

" New York Ferry ! "

It chafed me to pass through the promenade street of my home-city, without a moment to spare for my family or friends.   The cab-horse slipped in Chestnut Street, and I went over the rest of the route on foot, at a dog-trot pace, passing in various quarters for a sportsman, a professional runner, and a lunatic.   I was greatly aggravated between Amboy and Camden, by persons making inquiries for brothers, sons, and acquaintances.   At last, when I attained the steamer, the Captain kindly shut me up in his office, and I went on with my narrative till my eyes were burning and my hands failed in their function.   Kill von Kull and its picturesque shores wept by ; we emerged into the beautiful bay, and winding among its buoys, harbor lights, and shipping, came to, at length, at the foot of Christopher Street. I repaired to the office at once, and wrote far into the night, refraining, finally, from sheer blindness and exhaustion, and dropped asleep in the carriage as I was taken toward the Metropolitan Hotel.

The next day was Friday, July 4, the anniversary of American Independence, and my version of the six-days' battles caused universal gloom and grief.   I had furnished five pages or forty columns of closely printed matter, and thousands of tremulous fingers were tracing out the names of their dead dear ones, while I sipped my wine and rehearsed for the hundredth time, the incidents of the retreat to a multitude of men.   Cards and letters came to me by the gross, from bereaved countrymen, and I was obliged, finally, to add a postscript to my account, and a protest that I knew no more, and could answer no interrogatories.   A bath, fresh clothing, and rich food so far improved my appearance in a few days, that I presented no other traces of sickness and travel than a sunburnt face, and a rheumatic walk.

With restoration came a revival of old desires, appetites, and attachments. It required one additional campaign to sober me in these respects, and I was not a little relieved, to receive an order on the fourth day, to proceed to Washington, and attach myself to the "Army of Virginia" at the head of which Major-General John Pope had just been placed. After two quieter days' enjoyment, in the Quaker City, I reported myself at the Capital, but was debarred from taking the field at once, owing to the tardiness of the new Commander. For two weeks or more, I loitered around Washington, and although the time passed monotonously, I saw many persons and events which have much to do with the history of the Rebellion. The story of "Washington During the War" has yet to be written in all its vividness of enterprise, devotion, and infamy. It has been, in periods of peace, a dull, dolorous town, of mammoth hotels, paltry dwellings, empty lots, prodigiously wide avenues, a fossil population, and a series of gigantic public buildings, which seemed dropped by accident into a fifth-rate backwoods settlement. During the sessions Washington was overrun with "Smartness" : Smart pages, smart messengers, smart cabmen, smart publicans, smart politicians, smart women, smart scoundrels! Greatness became commonplace here, and Mr. Douglas might drink at Willard's Bar, with none so poor to do him reverence, or General Winfield Scott strut like a colossus along "the Avenue," and the sleepy negroes upon their hacks would give him the attention of only one eye. It was interesting, to notice how rapidly provincial eminence lost caste here. Slipkins, who was "Honorable" at home, and of whom his county newspaper said that "this distinguished fellow citizen of ours will be heard from, among the greatest of the free," — Slipkins moved to and fro unnoticed, and voted

19

with his party, and drank much brandy and water, and left no other record at the Capital than some unpaid bills, and perhaps an unacknowledged heir. A gaping rustic and his new bride, or a strolling foreigner, marvelling and making notes at every turn, might be observed in the Patent Office examining General Washington's breeches, but these were at once called " greenies," and people put out their tongues and winked at them. The Secretaries' ladies gave parties now and then, attended by the folks who sold them horses, or carpets, or wines; the President gave a " levee," whereat a wonderfully Democratic horde gathered to pinch his hands and ogle his lady; the Marine band (in *red* coats), played twice a week in the Capital grounds, and Senators, Cyprians, Ethiops, and children rallied to enjoy; a theatre or two played time-honored dramas with Thespian companies; a couple of scholars lectured in the sombre Smithsonian Institution; an intrigue and a duel filled some most doleful hiatus; and a clerk absconded with half a million, or an Indian agent robbed the red men and fell back to the protection of his "party." A very dismal, a very dirty, and a very Democratic settlement was the American Capital, till the war came.

Even the war lost half its interest in Washington. A regiment marching down Broadway was something to see, but the same regiment in Pennsylvania Avenue looked mean and matter-of-fact. A General in the field, or riding uncovered through Boston or Baltimore, or even lounging at the bar of the Continental or the Astor House or the Tremont, was invested with an atmosphere half heroic, half poetic; but Generals in Washington may be counted by pairs, and I used to sit at dinner with eight or a dozen of them in my eye. There was the new Commander-in-Chief, Halleck, a short, countryfied person, whose blue coat was either threadbare or dusty, or lacked some buttons, and who picked his teeth walking up and down the halls at Willard's, and argued through a white, bilious eye and a huge mouth.

There was General Mitchel, also, who has since passed away; — a little, knotty gentleman, with stiff, gray, Jacksonian hair. And General Sturgis passed in and out perpetually, with impressive, individual Banks, or some less prominent person, all of them wearing the gold star upon their shoulders, and absolute masters of some thousands of souls. The town, in fact, was overrun with troops. Slovenly guards were planted on horseback at crossings, and now and then they dashed, as out of a profound sleep, to chase some galloping cavalier. Gin and Jews swarmed along the Avenue, and I have seen gangs of soldiers of rival regiments, but oftener of rival nationalities, pummelling each other in the highways, until they were marched 'off by the Provosts. The number of houses of ill-fame was very great, and I have been told that Generals and Lieutenants of the same organization often encountered and recognized each other in them. Contractors and "jobbers" used to besiege the offices of the Secretaries of War and Navy, and the venerable Welles (who reminded me of Abraham in the lithographs), and the barnacled Stanton, seldom appeared in public. Simple-minded, straightforward A. Lincoln, and his ambitious, clever lady, were often seen of afternoons in their barouche; the little old-fashioned Vice-President walked unconcernedly up and down; and when some of the Richmond captives came home to the Capital, immense meetings were held, where patriotism bawled itself hoarse. A dining hour at Willard's was often wondrously adapted for a historic picture, when accoutred officers, and their beautiful wives, — or otherwise, — sat at the *table d'-hôte*, and sumptuous dishes flitted here and there, while corks popped like so many Chinese crackers, and champagne bubbled up like blood. At night, the Provost Guard enacted the farce of coming by deputations to each public bar, which was at once closed, but reopened five minutes afterward. Congress water was in great demand for weak heads of mornings, and many a young lad, girt up for war, wasted his strength in dissipation here, so that he was worthless afield, and perhaps died in the hospital. The curse of civil war was apparent everywhere. One had but to turn his eye from the bare Heights of Arlington, where the soldiers of the Republic lay demoralized, to the fattening vultures who smoked and swore at the National, to see the true cause of the North's shortcomings, — its inherent and almost universal corruption. Human nature was here so depraved, that man lost faith in his kind. Death lurked behind ambuscades and fortifications over the river, but Sin, its mother, coquetted *here*, and as an American, I often went to bed, loathing the Capital, as but little better than Sodom, though its danger had called forth thousands of great hearts to throb out, in its defence. For every stone in the Capitol building, a man has laid down his life. For every ripple on the Potomac, some equivalent of blood has been shed.

I lodged for some time in Tenth Street, and took my meals at Willard's. The legitimate expenses of living in this manner were fourteen dollars a week ; but one could board at Kirkwood's or Brown's for seven or eight dollars, very handsomely. A favorite place of excursion, near the city, was "Crystal Spring," where some afternoon orgies were enacted, which should have made the sun go into eclipse. I repaired once to Mount Vernon, and looked dolorously at the tomb of the *Pater Patris*, and once to Annapolis, on the Chesapeake, which the war has elevated into a fine naval station.

At length Pope's forces were being massed along the line of the Rappahannock, below the Occoquan river, and upon the "Piedmont" highlands. "Piedmont" is the name applied to the fine table-lands of Northern Virginia, and the ensuing campaign has received the designation of the "Piedmont Campaign." Pope's army proper was composed of three corps, commanded respectively by Generals Irvin McDowell, Franz Siegel, and Nathaniel P. Banks. But a portion of General McClellan's peninsular army had meantime returned to the Potomac, and the corps of General Burnside was stationed at Fredericksburg, thirty miles or more below Pope's head-quarters at Warrenton.

I presented myself to General Pope on the 12th of July, at noon. His Washington quarters consisted of a quiet brick house, convenient to the War office, and the only tokens of its importance were some guards at the threshold, and a number of officers' horses, saddled in the shade of some trees at the curb. The lower floor of the dwelling was appropriated to quartermasters' and inspectors' clerks, before whom a number of people were constantly presenting themselves, with applications for passes ; — sutlers, in great quantities, idlers, relic-hunters, and adventurers in still greater ratio, and, last of all, citizens of Virginia, solicitous to return to their farms and families. The mass of these were rebuffed, as Pope had inaugurated his campaign with a show of severity, even threatening to drive all the non-combatants out of his lines, unless they took the Federal oath of allegiance. He gave me a pass willingly, and chatted pleasantly for a time. In person he was dark, martial, and handsome, — inclined to obesity, richly garbed in civil cloth, and possessing a fiery black eye, with luxuriant beard and hair. He smoked incessantly, and talked imprudently. Had he commenced his career more modestly, his final discomfiture would not have been so galling ; but his vanity was apparent to the most shallow observer, and although he was brave, clever, and educated, he inspired distrust by his much promising and general love of gossip and story-telling. He had all of Mr. Lincoln's garrulity (which I suspect to be the cause of their affinity), and none of that good old man's unassuming common sense.

The next morning, at seven o'clock, I embarked for Alexandria, and passed the better half of the forenoon in negotiating for a pony. At eleven o'clock, I took my seat in a bare, filthy car, and was soon whirled due southward, over the line of the Orange and Alexandria railroad. The

19*

country between Alexandria and Warrenton Junction, or, indeed, between Washington and Richmond, was not unlike those masterly descriptions of Gibbon, detailing the regions overrun by Hyder Ali. The towns stood like ruins in a vast desert, and one might write musing epitaphs at every wind-beaten dwelling, whence the wretched denizens had fled in cold and poverty to a doubtful hospitality in the far South. Fences there were none, nor any living animals save the braying hybrids which limped across the naked plains to eke out existence upon some secluded patches of grass. These had been discharged from the army, and they added rather than detracted from the lonesomeness of the wild. Their great mournful eyes and shaggy heads glared from copses, and in places where they had lain down beside the track to expire. If we sometimes pity these dumb beasts as they drag loaded wains, or heavy omnibuses, or sub-soil ploughs, we may also bestow a tender sentiment upon the army mules. Flogged by teamsters, cursed by quartermasters, ridiculed by roaring regiments of soldiers, strained and spavined by fearful draughts, stalled in bogs and fainting upon hillsides, — their bones will evidence the sites of armies, when the skeletons of men have crumbled and become reabsorbed. I have seen them die like martyrs, when the inquisitor, with his bloody lash, stood over them in the closing pangs, and their last tremulous howl has almost moved to tears. Some of the dwellings seemed to be occupied, but the tidiness of old times was gone. The women seemed sunburnt and hardened by toil. They looked from their thresholds upon the flying train, with their hair unbraided and their garters ungyved, — not a negro left to till the fields, nor a son or brother who had not travelled to the wars. They must be now hewers of wood, and drawers of water, and the fingers whereon diamonds used to sparkle, must clench the axe and the hoe.

At last we came to Bull Run, the dark and bloody ground

where the first grand armies fought and fled, and again to be consecrated by a baptism of fire. The railway crossed the gorge upon a tall trestle bridge, and for some distance the track followed the windings of the stream. A black, deep, turgid current, flowing between gaunt hills, lined with cedar and beech, crossed here and there by a ford, and vanishing, above and below, in the windings of wood and rock; while directly beyond, lie the wide plains of Manassas Junction, stretching in the far horizon, to the undulating boundary of the Blue Ridge. As the Junction remains to-day, the reader must imagine this splendid prospect, unbroken by fences, dwellings, or fields, as if intended primevally to be a place for the shock of columns, with redoubts to the left and right, and fragments of stockades, dry rifle pits, unfinished or fallen breastworks, and, close in the foreground, a medley of log huts for the winter quartering of troops. The woods to the north mark the course of Bull Run; a line of telegraph poles going westward points to Manassas Gap; while the Junction proper is simply a point where two single track railways unite, and a few frame "shanties" or sheds stand contiguous. These are, for example, the "New York Head-quarters," kept by a person with a hooked nose, who trades in cakes, lemonade, and (probably) whiskey, of the brand called "rotgut;" or the "Union Stores," where a person in semi-military dress deals in India-rubber overcoats, underclothing, and boots. As the train halts, lads and negroes propose to sell sandwiches to passengers, and soldiers ride up to take mail-bags and bundles for imperceptible camps. In the distance some teams are seen, and a solitary horseman, visiting vestiges of the battle; sidelings beside the track are packed with freight cars, and a small mountain of pork barrels towers near by; there are blackened remains of locomotives a little way off, but these have perhaps hauled regiments of Confederates to the Junction; and over all—men, idlers, ruins, railway, huts, entrenchments — floats the star-spangled banner from the roof of a plank depot.

The people in the train were rollicking and well-disposed, and black bottles circulated freely. I was invited to drink by many persons, but the beverage proffered was intolerably bad, and several convivials became stupidly drunk. A woman in search of her husband was one of the passengers; and those contiguous to her were as gentlemanly as they knew how to be. "A pretty woman, in war-time," said a Captain, aside, to me, "is not to be sneezed at." At "Catlett's," a station near Warrenton Junction, we narrowly escaped a collision with a train behind, and the occupants of our train, women included, leaped down an embankment with marvellous agility. Here we switched off to the right, and at four o'clock dismounted at the pleasant village of Warrenton.

CHAPTER XXI.

CAMPAIGNING WITH GENERAL POPE.

THE court-house village of Fauquier County contained a population of twelve or fifteen hundred at the commencement of the war. Its people embraced the revolutionary cause at the outstart, and furnished some companies of foot to the Confederate service, as well as a mounted company known as the "Black Horse Cavalry." The guns of Bull Run were heard here on the day of battle, and hundreds of the wounded came into town at nightfall. Thenceforward Warrenton became prominently identified with the struggle, and the churches and public buildings were transmuted to hospitals. After the Confederates retired from Manassas Junction, the vicinity of Warrenton was a sort of neutral ground. At one time the Southern cavalry would ride through the main street, and next day a body of mounted Federals would pounce upon the town, the inhabitants, meanwhile, being apprehensive of a sabre combat in the heart of the place. Some people were ruined by the war; some made fortunes. The Mayor of the village was named Bragg, and he was a trader in horses, as well as a wagon-builder. There were two taverns, denominated respectively, the "Warrenton Inn," and the "Warren Green Hotel." I obtained a room at the former. A young man named Dashiell kept it. He was a fair-complexioned, clever, high-strung Virginian, and managed to obtain a great deal of paper money from both republics. It is an encomium in America, to say that a man "Can keep a hotel," but what shall be said of the man who can keep a hotel in war-time? I observed young Dashiell's movements from day to day, and I am satisfied that his popularity arose from his fairness and frankness. He charged nine dollars a week for room, and "board," of three meals, but could, with difficulty, obtain meat and vegetables for the table. His mother and his brother-in-law lived in the house. The latter was a son of Mayor Bragg, and had been twice in the Confederate service. He was engaged both at Bull Run and at Fairfax Court House, and made no secret of his activity at either place. But he was treated considerately, though he vaunted intolerably. The "Inn" was a frame dwelling, with a first floor of stone, surrounded by a double portico. The first room (entering from the street) was the office, consisting of a bare floor, some creaking benches, some chairs with whittled and broken arms, a high desk, where accounts were kept, a row of bells, numbered, communicating with the rooms. Hand-bills were pinned to the walls, announcing that William Higgins was paying good prices for "likely" field hands, that Timothy Ingersoll's stock of dry goods was the finest in Piedmont, that James Mason's mulatto woman, named Rachel, had decamped on the night of Whitsuntide, and that one hundred dollars would be paid by the subscriber for her return. Most of these bills were out of date, but some recent ones were exhibited to me calling for volunteers, labelled, " Ho ! for winter-quarters in Washington ; " " Sons of the South arise ! " — "Liberty, glory, and no Yankeedom ! " A bell-cord hung against the " office " door, communicating with the stables, where a deaf hostler might *not* be rung up. In the back yard, suspended from a beam, and upright, hung a large bell, which called the boarders to meals. It commonly rung thrice, and I was told on inquiry, by the cook —

"De fust bell, sah, is to prepah to prepah for de table ; dat bell, when de fust cook don't miss it, is rung one hour

befo' meâltime.   De second bell, sah, is to *prepah* for de
table ; de last bell, to *come* to de table.''

I should have been better pleased with the ceremony, if
the food had been more cleanly, more wholesome, and more
abundant.   We used to clear the plates in a twinkling, and
if a person asked twice for beef, or butter, he was stared at
by the negroes, as if he had eaten an entire cow.   I soon
brought the head-waiter to terms by promising him a dollar
a week for extra attendance, and could even get ice after a
time, which was a luxury.   There was a bar upon the
premises, which opened stealthily, when there were liquors
to be sold.   Cider (called champaigne) could be purchased
for three dollars a bottle, and whiskey came to hand occasionally.   There were cigars in abundance, and I used to
sit on the upper porch of evenings, puffing long after midnight, and watching the sentinels below.

There was some female society in Warrenton, but the
blue-coats engrossed it all.   The young women were ardent
partisans, but also very pretty ; and treason, somehow,
heightened their beauty.   Disloyalty is always pardonable
in a woman, and these ladies appreciated the fact.   They
refused to walk under Federal flags, and stopped their ears
when the bands played national music ; but every evening
they walked through the main street, arm in arm with dashing Lieutenants and Captains.   Many flirtations ensued,
and a great deal of gossip was elicited.   In the end, some
of the misses fell out among themselves, and hated each
other more than the common enemy.   I overheard a young
lady talking in a low tone one evening, to a Captain in the
Ninth New York regiment.

"If you knew my brother,'' she said, "I am sure you
would not fire upon *him*.''

As there were plain, square, prim porches to all the
dwellings, the ladies commonly took positions therein of
evenings, and a grand promenade commenced of all the
young Federals in the town.   The streets were pleasantly

shaded, and a leafy coolness pervaded the days, though sometimes, of afternoons, the still heat was almost stifling. A jaunt after supper often took me far into the country, and the starlights were softer than one's peaceful thoughts. To be a civilian was a distinguished honor now, and I enjoyed the staring of the citizens, who pondered as to my purposes and pursuits, as only villagers can do. There is a quiet pleasure in being a strange person in a country town, and so far from objecting to the inquisitiveness of the folk, I father like it. One may be passing for a young duke, or tourist, or clergyman, or what not?

The Ninth New York (militia) regiment guarded Warrenton, and it was composed of clever, polite young fellows, who had taken to volunteering before there was any promise of war, and who turned out, pluckily, when the strife began. Perhaps public sentiment or pride of organization influenced them. They were all good-looking and tidy, and their dress-parades, held in the main street, were handsome affairs. I have never seen better disciplined columns, and the youthful faces of the soldiers, with the staid locality of the exhibition, — young women, negroes, dogs and babies, and old men looking on, — seemed to contradict the bloody mission of the troops. The old men, referred to, were villagers of such long standing that had the Court of Saint James, or the Vatican, or the battle of Waterloo been ʼmoved into their country, they would have still been villagers to the last. They met beside the Warrenton Inn, under the shade of the trees, at eleven o'clock every morning, and borrowed the New York papers of the latest date. One individual, slightly bald, would read aloud, and the rest crouched or stood about him, making grunts and remarks at intervals. They did not wish to believe the Federal reports, but they must needs read, and as most of them had sons in the other army, their pulses were constantly tremulous with anxiety. I think that Pope's resolve to transport these harmless old people beyond his lines was very barbarous, and the soldiers denounced it in similar terms. They spoke of Pope, as of some terrible despot, and wished to know when he was coming to town, as they had appointed a committee, and drafted a petition, asking his forbearance and charity. When these villagers found me out to be a Newspaper Correspondent, they regarded me with amusing interest, and marvelled what I would say of their town. A villager is very sensitive as to his place of residence, and these good people read the ——— daily, confounding me with all the paper, — editorial, correspondence, and, I verily believe, advertisements. One of them wished me to board at his residence, and I was, after a time, invited out to dinner and tea frequently.

The negroes remained in Warrenton, in great numbers, and held carnival of evenings when the bands played. "Contrabands" were coming daily into town, and idleness and vice soon characterized the mass of them. They were ignorant, degraded, animal beings, and many of them loved rum ; it was the last link that bound them to human kind. Servants could be hired for four dollars a month and "keep ; " but they were "shiftless" and unprofitable. The Provost-Marshal of the place was a Captain Hendrickson. His quarters were in the Court House building, and he kept a zealous eye upon sutlers and citizens. The former trespassed in the sales of liquors to soldiers, and the latter were accused of maintaining a contraband mail, and of conspiring to commit divers offences. There were a number of churches in the village, all of which served as hospitals, and in the quiet cemetery west of the town, two hundred slain soldiers were interred. A stake of white pine was driven at the head of each grave. Here lay some of the men who had helped to change the destinies of a continent. No public worship was held in the place. The Sundays were busy as other days : trains came and went, teams made dust in the streets, cavalry passed through the village, music arose from all the outlying camps ; parades and inspections were made, and all the preparations for killing

20

men were relentlessly forwarded. A pleasant entertainment occurred one evening, when a plot of ground adjoining the Warrenton Inn, was appropriated for a camp theatre. Candle footlights were arranged, and the stage was canopied with national flags. The citizens congregated, and the performers deferred to their prejudices by singing no Federal songs. The negroes climbed the trees to listen, and their gratified guffaws made the night quiver. The war lost half its bitterness at such times ; but I thought with a shudder of Stuart's thundering horsemen, charging into the village, and closing the night's mimicry with a horrible tragedy.

Some of the dwellings about the place were elegant and spacious, but many of these were closed and the owners removed. Two newspapers had been published here of old, and while ransacking the office of one of them, I discovered that the type had been buried under the floor. The planks were speedily torn away, and the cases dragged to light. I obtained some curious relics, in the shape of " cuts " of recruiting officers, runaway negroes, etc., as well as a column of a leader, in type, describing the first battle of Bull Run. For two weeks I had little to do, as the campaign had not yet fairly commenced, and I passed many hours every day reading. A young lawyer, in the Confederate service, had left an ample library behind him, and the books passed into the hands of every invader in the town.

Pope finally arrived at Warrenton, and as the troops seemed to be rapidly concentrating, I judged it expedient to procure a horse at once, and canvassed the country with that object. By paying a quartermaster the Government price ($130), I could select a steed from the pound, but inspection satisfied me that a good saddle nag could not be obtained in this way. After much parleying with Hebrews and chaffing with country people, I heard that Mayor Bragg kept some fair animals, and when I stated my purpose at his house, he commenced the business after a fashion immemorial at the South, by producing some whiskey.

When Mayor Bragg had asked me pertinently, if I knew much about the " pints of a hoss," and what " figger in the way of price " would suit me, he told an erudite negro named " Jeems " to trot out the black colt. The black colt made his appearance by vaulting over a gate, and playfully shivering a panel of fence with his " off" hoof. Then he executed a flourish with his tail, leaped thrice in the air, and bit savagely at the man " Jeems."

When I asked Mayor Bragg if the black colt was sufficiently gentle to stand fire, he replied that he was gentle as a lamb and offered to put me astride him. I had no sooner taken my seat, however, than the black colt backed, neighed, flourished, and stood erect, and finally ran away.

A second animal was produced, less mettlesome, but also black, finely strung, daintily hoofed, and as Mayor Bragg said, " just turned four year." The price of this charger was one hundred and ninety dollars ; but in consideration of my youth and pursuit, Mayor Bragg proposed to take one hundred and seventy-five ; we compromised upon a hundred and fifty dollars, Major Bragg throwing in a halter, and by good luck I procured a saddle the same evening, so that I rode triumphantly through the streets of Warrenton, and fancied that all the citizens were admiring my new purchase.

I was struck with the fact, that Mayor Bragg, though an ardent patriot, would accept of neither Confederate nor Virginia money ; he required payment for his animal, in Father Chase's " greenbacks."

Mounted anew, I fell into my former active habits, and made two journeys, to Sperryville and Little Washington, in one direction, to Madison in another ; each place was probably twenty miles distant ; the latter was merely a cavalry outpost, where Generals Hatch and Bayard were stationed, and the former villages were the head-quarters, respectively, of General Banks and General Siegel.

Madison was, at this time, a precarious place for a long tarrying. I went to sleep in the inn on the night of my arrival, and at that time the place was thronged with cavalry and artillery-men. Next morning, when I aroused, not a blue-coat could be seen. They had fallen back in the darkness, and prudently abstaining from breakfast, I galloped northward, as if the whole Confederate army was at my heels. These old turnpike roads were now marked by daily chases and rencontres. A few Virginians, fleetly mounted, would provoke pursuit from a squad of Federals, and the latter would be led into ambuscades. A quaint incident happened in this manner, near Madison.

Captain T. was chasing a party of Confederates one afternoon, when his company was suddenly fired upon from a wheatfield, parties rising up on both sides of the road, and discharging carbines through the fence rails. Three or four men, and as many horses were slain; but the ambushing body was outnumbered, and several of its members killed. Among others, a young lieutenant took deliberate aim at Captain T. at the distance of twelve yards; and, seeing that he had missed, threw up his carbine to surrender. The Captain had already drawn his revolver, and, amazed at the murderous purpose, he shot the assassin in the head, killing him instantly. Nobody blamed Captain T., but he was said to be a humane person, and the affair preyed so continually upon his mind, that he committed suicide one night in camp.

At Sperryville I saw and talked with Franz Siegel, the idol of the German Americans. He had been a lieutenant in his native country, but subsided, in St. Louis, to the rank of publican, keeping a beer saloon. When the war commenced, he was appointed to a colonelcy, in deference to the large German republican population of Missouri. His abilities were speedily manifested in a series of engagements which redeemed the Southern border, and he finally fought the terrible battle of Pea Ridge, Arkansas, which broke the spirit of the Confederates west of the Mississippi. The man who fought "mit Siegel" in those days, was always told in St. Louis: "Py tam! you pays not'ing for your lager." Siegel now commanded one of Pope's corps. He was a diminutive person, but well-knit, emaciated by his active career, feverish and sanguine of face, and, as it appeared to me, consuming with energy and ambition. As a General he was prompt to decide and do, and his manner of dealing with Confederate property was severer than that of any American. He battered the splendid mansion hotel of White Sulphur Springs to the ground, for example, when somebody discharged a rifle from its window. He preferred to fight by retreating, and if pursued, generally unmasked his guns and made massacre with the scattered opponents. Another German commander was Blenker, whose corps of Germans might have belonged to the free bands of the Black forest. They were the most lawless men in the Federal service, and what they did not steal they destroyed. Such volunteers were mercenaries, in every sense of the word. I have been told that they slaughtered sheep and cattle in pure wantonness, and the rats of Ehrenfels did not make a cleaner sweep of provisions. The Germans, as a rule, lacked the dash of the Irish troops and the tact of the Americans. They thought and fought in masses, had little individuality, and were thick-skulled ; but they were persevering and had their hearts in the cause.

General Banks was a fine representative of the higher order of Yankee. Originally a machinist in a small manufacturing town near Boston, he educated himself, and was elected successively Legislator, Governor, Congressman, and General of volunteers. His personal graces were equalled by his energy, and his ability was considerable. He has been very successful in the field, and has conducted a retreat unparalleled in the war ; these things being always reckoned among American successes. The country hereabout was mountainous, healthy, and well adapted for campaigning. Streams and springs were numerous, and there were fine sites for camps. The deserted toll-houses along

20*

the way glowered mournfully through the rent windows, and I fancied them, sometimes, as I rode at night, haunted by the shambling tollman.

> Ancient road that wind'st deserted,
>   Through the level of the vale, —
> Sweeping toward the crowded market,
>   Like a stream without a sail,
>
> Standing by thee, I look backward,
>   And, as in the light of dreams,
> See the years descend and vanish,
>   Like thy tented wains and teams. — T. B. READ.

To provide myself with thorough equipment for Pope's campaign, I returned to Washington, and purchased a patent camp-bed, which-strapped to my saddle, saddle bags of large capacity, India-rubber blankets, and a full suit of waterproof cloth, — hat, coat, *genoullieres*, and gauntlets. I had my horse newly shod, I drew upon my establishment for an ample sum of money, and, to properly inaugurate the campaign, I gave an entertainment in the parlor of the inn.

Pipes, cold ham, a keg of beer, and a demijohn of whiskey comprised the attractions of the night. The guests were three Captains, two Adjutants, two Majors, a Colonel, four Correspondents, several Lieutenants, and a signal officer. There was some jesting, and much laughing, considerable story-telling, and (toward the small hours) a great deal of singing. Much heroism was evolved ; all the guests were devoted to death and their country ; and there was one person who took off his coat to fight an imaginary something, but changed his mind, and dropped asleep directly. At length, a gallant Captain, to demonstrate his warlike propensities, fired a pistol through the front window ; and somebody blowing out the candles, the whole party retired to rest upon the floor. In this delightful way my third campaign commenced, and next evening I set off for the advance.

CHAPTER XXII.

ARMY MORALS.

SOME of General McDowell's aides had invited me to pass a night with them at Warrenton Springs. Fully equipped, I joined Captain Ball, of Cincinnati, and we rode southward, over a hard, picturesque turnpike, under a clear moonlight. The distance was seven miles, and a part of this route was enlivened by the fires, halloos, and the music of camps. Volunteers are fond of serenading their officers; and this particular evening was the occasion of much merry-making, since a majority of the brass bands were to be mustered out of the service to-morrow. We could hear the roll of drums from imperceptible localities, and the sharp winding of bugles broke upon the silence like the trumpet of the Archangel. Stalwart shapes of horsemen galloped past us, and their hoofs made monotone behind, till the cadence died so gradually away that we did not know when the sound ceased and when the silence began. The streams had a talk to themselves, as they strolled away into the meadow, and an owl or two challenged us, calling up a corporal hawk. This latter fellow bantered and blustered, and finally we fell into an ambush of wild pigs, which charged across the road and plunged into the woods. There were despatch stations at intervals, where horses stood saddled, and the couriers waited for hoof-beats, to be ready to ride fleetly toward head-quarters. Anon, we saw wizard lights, as of Arctic skies, where remote camps built conflagration;

(235)

and trudging wearily down the stony road, poor ragged, flying negroes, with their families and their worldly all, came and went— God help them!— and touched their hats so obsequiously that my heart was wrung, and I felt a nervous impulse to put them upon my steed and take their burdens upon my back. Little sable folk, asleep and ahungered, drawn to that barefoot woman's breast; and the tired boy, weeping as he held to his father's hand; and the father with the sweat of fatigue and doubt upon his forehead, — children of Ishmael all; war raging in the land, but God overhead! These are the "wandering Jews" of our day, hated North and South, because they are poor and blind, and do no harm; but out of their wrongs has arisen the abasement of their wrongers. Is there nothing over all?

We entered the beautiful lawn of the Springs' hotel, at ten o'clock, and a negro came up to take our horses. By the lamplight and moonlight I saw McDowell's tent, a sentry pacing up and down before it, and the thick, powerful figure of the General seated at a writing-table within. Irvin McDowell was one of the oldest officers in the service, and when the war commenced he became a leading commander in the Eastern army. At Bull Run he had a responsible place, and the ill success of that battle brought him into unpleasant notoriety. Though he retained a leading position he was still mistrusted and disliked. None bore ingratitude so stolidly. He may have flinched, but he never replied; and though ambitious, he tried to content himself with subordinate commands. Some called him a traitor, others an incompetent, others a plotter. If McClellan failed, McDowell was cursed. If Pope blundered, McDowell received half the contumely. But he loosened no cord of discipline to make good will. Implacable, dutiful, soldierly, rigorous in discipline, sententious, brave, — the most unpopular man in America went on his way, and I think that he is recovering public favor again. The General of a republic has a thorny path to tread, and almost every public man has been at one time disgraced during the civil war. McDowell, I think, has been treated worse than any other.

Our nags being removed, we repaired to one of the rustic cottages which bounded the lawn, and I was introduced to several members of the staff; among others, to a Count Saint Alb, an Austrian. He had been an officer in his native country ; but came to America, anxious for active service, and was appointed to Gen. McDowell's Staff with the rank of Captain. I understood that he was writing a book upon America. There are many such adventurers in the Federal service, but the present one was clever and amusing, and he spoke English fluently.

Our tea was plain but abundant, consisting of broiled beef, fresh bread, butter, and cheese ; and the inveterate whiskey was produced afterward, when we assembled on the piazza, so that the hours passed by pleasantly, if not profitably, and we retired at two o'clock.

In the morning I bathed in the clear, cold sulphur spring, where thousands of invalid people had come for healing waters. A canopy covered the spring, and a soldier stood on guard at the top of the descending steps, to preserve the property in its original cleanliness. This was one of the most famous medical springs on the American continent; the water was so densely impregnated that its peculiarly offensive smell could be detected at the distance of a mile. The place was going to ruin now. All the bathing-rooms were falling apart, the pipes had been carried off to be moulded into bullets, and the great hotel was desolate. I walked into the ball-room ; but the large gilded mirrors had been splintered, and lewd writings defaced the wall. Some idlers were asleep upon the piazzas, and the furniture was removed or broken. Some rustic cottages dotted the lawn, but these were now inhabited by officers and their servants. A few days were to finish the work of rapine, and a heap of ashes was to mark the scene of tournament, coquetry, and betrothal. I witnessed a review of troops in a field contiguous, at nine o'clock. The heat was so intense that many men fell out of line and were carried off to their camps. McDowell passed exactingly from man to man, examined muskets, clothing, and knapsacks, and the inspection was proceeding, when I bade my friends good by and set out for Culpepper.

I crossed the North Rappahannock, or Hedgemain river, upon a precarious bridge of planks. A new bridge for artillery was being constructed close by; for the river beneath had a swift, deep current, and could with difficulty be forded. Patches of wagons, squads of horse, and now and then a regiment of infantry, varied the monotony of the journey. The country was high, woody, and sparsely settled. At noon I overtook Tower's brigade, and observing the 94th N. Y. Regiment resting in the woods, I dismounted and made the acquaintance of its Colonel. He was at this juncture greatly enraged with some of his soldiers who had been plucking green apples.

"Boy," he said to one, "put down that fruit! Drop it, or I'll blow your head off! Directly you'll double up, pucker, and say that you have the "di-o-ree," and require an ambulance. Orderly!"

A sergeant came up and touched his cap.

"Take your musket," said the Colonel; "go out to that orchard, and order those men away. If they hesitate or object, shoot them!"

A few such colonels would marvellously improve the volunteer organization.

The Hazel or North Anne river, a branch of the Hedgemain, interposed a few miles further on, and passing through a covered bridge, I turned down the north bank, crossed some spongy fields, and at length came to a dry place in the edge of a woods, where I tied my nag, spread out my bed, and prepared to dine. A box of sardines, a lemon, and some fresh sandwiches constituted the repast, and being dusty and parched I stripped afterward and swam across the river. Seeing that my horse plunged and neighed, with swollen eyeballs, and every evidence of terror, I hastened toward him and discovered a black snake, six feet or more in length, which seemed about to coil itself around the nag's leg. The size and contiguity of the reptile at first appalled me, and my mind was not more composed when the serpent, at my approach, manifested an inclination to assume the offensive. Its folds were thicker than my arm, and it commenced to revolve rapidly, at length running up a sapling, suspending itself by the tail, and hissing vehemently. It belonged to the family of "racers," and was hideous and powerful beyond any specimen that I had seen. I blew it into halves at the second discharge of my pistol, and at once resumed my saddle, indisposed to remain longer amidst such acquaintances.

At four o'clock I saw Culpepper, a trim little village, lying in the hollow of several hills. A couple of steeples added to its picturesqueness, and a swift creek, crossed by a small bridge, interposed between myself and the main part of the place. It looked like Sunday when I rode through the principal street. The shutters were closed in the shop windows, the dwellings seemed tenantless, no citizens were abroad, no sutlers had invaded the country; only a few cavalry-men clustered about an ancient pump to water their nags, and some military idlers were sitting upon the long porch of a public house, called the Virginia Hotel. I tied my horse to a tree, the bole of which had been gnawed bare, and found the landlord to be an old gentleman named Paine, who appeared to be somewhat out of his head. Two days before the Confederate cavalry had vacated the village, and the army had been encamped about the town for many months. A sabre conflict had taken place in the streets; and these events, happening in rapid succession, combined with the insolence of some Federal outriders, had so agitated the host that his memory was quite gone, and he could not perform even the slightest function.   There is a panacea for all these things, which the faculty and philanthropy alike forbid, but which my experience in war-matters has invariably found unfailing.   I produced my flask, and gently insinuated it to the old gentleman's lips.   He possessed instinct sufficient to uncork and apply it, and the results were directly apparent, in a partial recovery of memory. He said that meals were one dollar each, board four dollars a day, or by the week twenty-five dollars.   These terms are unknown in America; but when Mr. Paine added that horse provender was one dollar per "feed," I looked aghast, and required some stimulant myself to appreciate the enormity of the reckoning.   I discovered, however, that the people of the village were almost starving; that beef had been fifty cents a pound during the whole winter, flour twenty-five dollars per barrel, coffee one dollar and a quarter a pound, and corn one dollar per bushel.   The army had swept the country like famine, and the citizens had pinched, pining faces, with little to eat to-day and nothing for tomorrow.

I acquiesced in the charge, as no choice remained, and asked to be shown to my room.   A burly negro, apparently suffering *delirium tremens*, seized my baggage with quaking hands, and lifting a pair of red eyes upon me, shuffled through a bare hall, up a stairway, and into a bedroom.   I never saw a more hideous being in my life, and when he had flung my luggage upon the floor, he sank into a chair, and glared wofully into my face, breathing like one about to expire.

"Young Moss," said he, "cant you give a po' soul a drop o' sperits? Do for de good Lord's sake! Do, Moss, fo' de po' nigga's life. Do! do! Moss."

I poured him out a little in a tumbler, less from charity than from fear; for he knew that I was provided with a bottle, and I seemed to read murder in his eyes.

He drank like one athirst and scant of breath, making a dry, chuckling noise with his throat. When he had finished, he leaned his powerful neck and head upon the bed and groaned terribly.

"Moss," he said again, "ain't you got no tobacco, Moss? I haint had none since Christmas. I's mos dead I'm po' sinful nigga'. Do give some tobacco to po' creature, do!"

I told him that I did not chew the weed, but gave him a crushed cigar, and he thrust it into his mouth, as if it was food and he was perishing. This wretched animal performed the duties of a chambermaid upon the premises; he made the beds, attended to the toilets, answered the bells, etc. He finally became so offensive that I forbade him my room, and he revenged himself by paltry thefts. There were two other servants, a woman with a baby, and a shrewd, dishonest mulatto man, who was the steward and carver. This fellow secreted provender in the kitchen and sold it stealthily to hungry soldiers. A public house so mismanaged I had nowhere met. Sometimes we could get no breakfast till noon, and finally the price of dinner went up to one dollar and a half, with nothing to eat. The table was protected from flies by a series of paper fans, pendant from the ceiling and connected by a cord, which an ebony boy pulled, at the foot of the room to keep them in motion. This boy being worked day and night, often fell asleep upon his stool, when the yellow man boxed his ears, or knocked him down; and then he would fan with such vigor that a perfect gale swept down the table. The landlord was a kindly old man, but he could not "keep a hotel," and the strong-minded part of the house consisted of his wife and four daughters. Gen. Ben Butler would have sent these young women to Ship Island, five times of a day. They were very bad-mannered and always sat apart at one end of the cloth, talking against the "Yankees." As there was no direct provocation to do so, this boldness was gratuitous,

21

and detracted rather than added to my estimate of the heroism of Southern women.   I have known them to burst into
the office, crowded with blue-coats, and scream —
    " Pop, Yankees thieving in garden ! " or, " Pop, drive
these Yankees out of parlor ! "
    Every afternoon when the pavement was unusually patron-
ized by young officers, these women would sally out, promenade in crinoline, silk stockings, and saucy hoods, and the
crowd would fall respectfully back to let them pass.   A
flag hung from a hospital over the sidewalk, and with a
pert flourish, the landlord's daughters filed off the pavement, around the ensign, and back again.   This was amusing, I thought, but not very clever, and rather immodest.
Had they been handsome, some romance might have attached to the act ; but being homely and not marriageable,
I smiled at the occurrence and entered it in my diary as
" patriotism run mad."   The stable arrangements were, if
possible, worse.   One had to be certain, from actual presence, that his horse was fed at all, and during the first three
days of my tenure, the black hostler lost me a breast strap,
a halter, a crupper strap, and finally emptied my saddle-
bags.
    Now and then a woman made her appearance at a front
window, stealthily peeping into the street, or a neighboring
farmer ventured into town upon a lean consumptive mule.
The very dogs were skinny and savage for want of sustenance, and when a long, cadaverous hog emerged from nowhere one day, and tottered up the main street, he was
chased, killed, and quartered so rapidly, that the famous
steam process seemed to have been applied to him, of being
dropped into a hopper, and tumbling out, a medley of hams,
ribs, lard, and penknives.   The stock of provisions at the
hotel finally gave out, and I was compelled to purchase
morsels of meat from the steward.   Dreadful visions of famishing ensued, but ultimately the railway was opened to
town, and a sutler started a shop in the village.   I lived

upon sardines and crackers for two days, and a Major Fifield, Superintendent of Military Railroads, gave me savory breakfasts of ham afterward. Troops were now concentrating in the neighborhood of Culpepper, and a bevy of camps encircled the little village. Crawford's Brigade, of Banks's Corps, garrisoned the place, and a Provost Marshal occupied the quaint Court House. Reconnoissances were made southward daily, and I joined one of these, which left the village on the second of August, at three o'clock, for Orange Court House, seventeen miles on the way to Richmond. Detachments of a Vermont and a New York cavalry regiment composed the reconnoitring party, and the whole was commanded by Gen. Crawford, a clever and unostentatious soldier. We bivouacked that night near Raccoon Ford, on the river Rapidan. No fires were built; for we knew that the enemy was all around us, and we slept coldly and imperfectly till the gray of Sunday morning. At daylight we galloped into the main street of Orange Court House, having first sent a squadron around the village, to ride in at the other end. At the very moment of our entry, a company or more of Confederate horse was also trotting into town. Both parties sounded the charge simultaneously, and the carbines exploded in the very heart of the village. For a minute or more a sabre fight ensued, alternated by the firing of revolvers; but the defenders were overmatched, and several of them having been slain, they turned to escape. At that moment, however, our other squadron charged upon them, effectually blocking up the street, and the whole party surrendered. A major, who exhibited some obstinacy, was felled from the saddle by a terrible cut, which clove his skull, and a very dexterous young fellow, who attempted to escape by a side street, dodged a bevy of pursuers and saved his head by the loss of both his ears. The disfigured corpses of those freshly slain were laid along the sidewalk in a row; and after some invasion of henroosts and private pantries, we remounted, and with fifty or more prisoners crossed the Rapidan, and were welcomed into Culpepper with cheers. The prisoners were lodged in the loft of the Court House, and their officers were paroled, and boarded among the neighbors. They complied with the terms of their parole very honorably, and bore testimony to the courtesy of their captors. I talked with them often upon the tavern porch, but an undue intimacy with any of them might have brought me into disrepute. Although the larders of the village were supposed to be empty, savory meals were nevertheless sent daily to these cavalry-men, and it was evident that the people on all hands sympathized with their soldiery.

The stringent orders of Pope, relative to removing the disaffected beyond his lines, were never enforced. I doubt if the veritable commander himself meant to do more than intimidate evil doers ; but I saw frequent evidences of scrupulous humanity on the part of his general officers.

One day, when I was negotiating with the Provost for the purchase of some port wine, stored upon the premises of a village druggist, a sergeant elbowed his way into the presence of the Marshal, and pushed forward two very dirty lads, who gave their ages respectively, as ten and thirteen years. They were of Hibernian parentage, and belonged to the class of newsboys trading with the different brigades. The younger lad was wiping his nose and eyes with a relic of a coat sleeve, and the elder was studying the points of the case, with a view to an elaborate defence. The sergeant produced a thick roll of bills and laid them upon the desk.

" Gineral Crawford," said he, "orders these boys to be locked up in the jail. They have been passing this stuff upon the country folks, and belong to a gang of young varmints who follers the 'lay.' The Gineral is going to have 'em brought up at the proper time and punished."

The bills were fair imitations of Confederate currency, and were openly sold in the streets of Northern cities at the rate of thousands of dollars for a penny. These lads probably purchased horses, swine, or fowls with them, or perhaps paid some impoverished widow for board in the worthless counterfeit.

The younger lad sobbed and howled when the order for his incarceration had been announced, but the elder made a stout remonstrance.

He didn't know the Gineral would arrest him. Everybody else passed the bills. He thought they wos good bills; some man gave 'em to him. They wan't passed, nohow, upon nobody but *Rebels!* He could prove that! He "know'd" a quartermaster that passed 'em. Wouldn't they let him and Sam off this wunst?

They were both sent to Coventry, despite their tears, and down to the last day of our tenure in Culpepper, I saw these wicked urchins peeping through the grates of the old brick jail, where they lay in the steam and vapor, among negroes, drunkards, and thieves,— an evidence of justice, which it is a pleasure to record, in this free narrative.

I joined a mess in the Ninth New York regiment finally, and contrived to exist till the fifth of the month, when Pope moved his head-quarters to a hill back of Culpepper, and thereafter I lived daintily for a little while. On the 8th of August, however, an event occurred, which disturbed the wisest calculations of the correspondent and the Generals, THE BATTLE OF CEDAR-MOUNTAIN.

21*

CHAPTER XXIII.

GOING INTO ACTION.

WHILE General Pope's army was concentrating between the Rappahannock and Rapidan rivers, the army of General Stonewall Jackson was lying upon the south bank of the Rapidan, and that renowned commander's head-quarters were at Gordonsville, about thirty miles from Culpepper. It was generally presumed that Jackson had fortified Gordonsville, intending to lie in wait there, or possibly to oppose the crossing of Pope upon the banks of the river. It was not believed that Jackson's force was very great, because the main body of the Confederates were held below Richmond, where McClellan's army still remained. The Southern capital seemed to be menaced both from the North and the South; but in reality, the Grand Army was re-embarking at Harrison's Bar, and sailing up the Chesapeake in detachments, to effect a junction with Pope on the plains of Piedmont. So important a movement could not be concealed from the Confederates, and they had resolved to annihilate Pope before McClellan's reinforcements could arrive. It was the work of two weeks to transport eighty or a hundred thousand men three hundred miles, and finding that Burnside's corps had already landed upon the Potomac, Stonewall Jackson determined to cross the Rapidan and cripple the fragment of Pope's forces stationed at Culpepper.

Stonewall Jackson is one of the many men whose ex-

(246)

traordinary military genius has been developed by the civil war. But unlike the mass who have become famous in a day, and lost their laurels in a week, Jackson's glory has steadily increased. He was first brought into notice at Winchester, where he fought a fierce battle with Banks, and derived the *sobriquet* which he has retained to the present time. Soon afterward, he chased Banks's army down the Shenandoah Valley, and across the Potomac. Afterward, he bore a conspicuous part in the engagement below Richmond, and was now to become prominent in the most daring episodes of the whole war. His excellence was *activity.* He scrupled at no fatigue, marched his troops over steep and circuitous roads, was everywhere when unexpected, and nowhere when sought, and his boldness was equal to his energy. He did not fear to attack overpowering numbers, if the situation demanded it. All that General Lee might plan, General Jackson would dare to execute; and he has been, above all others, the Soult of the Southern war, while Stuart was its Murat, and Lee its Napoleon.

We first had intimation of the advance of Jackson on the afternoon of the 7th of August. Two regiments of cavalry, picketed upon the Rapidan, rode pell-mell into Culpepper, reporting a large Southern force at the fords, and rapidly advancing. Pope at once ordered the whole of one of these regiments under arrest, and it was the opinion of the army that the approach was a feint, or, at most, a reconnoissance in force. Subsequent information satisfied the incredulous, however, that a considerable body of troops were marching northward, and their outriding scouts had been seen at Cedar Mountain, only six miles from Culpepper. The latter is one of the many woody knobs or heights that environ the village, but it is nearer than any other, and should have been occupied by Pope, simultaneously with his arrival. It is scarcely a mountain in elevation, but so high that the clouds often envelope its crest, and it commands a view of all the surrounding country. There are cleared patches up its sides, and the highest of these constitutes the farm of a clergyman, after whom the eminence is sometimes called "Slaughter's Mountain." At its base lie a few pleasant farms; and a shallow rivulet or creek, called Cedar Run, crosses the road between the mountain and Culpepper. Upon the mountain side Jackson had placed his batteries, and his infantry lay in dense thickets and belts of woods before the hill and on each side of it. The position was a powerful, though not an impregnable one; for batteries might readily be pushed up the slope, and our infantry had often ascended steeper eminences. But an opposing army scattered about the meadow lands below, would find its several components exposed to shot and shell, thrown from points three or four hundred feet above them.

When it had been discovered that the enemy had anticipated us in seizing this strong position, word was at once despatched to Banks and Siegel to bring up their columns without delay. The brigade of General Crawford was marched through Culpepper at noon on Friday; and that afternoon, foot-sore, but enthusiastic, regiments began to arrive in rapid succession.

I had been passing the morning of Friday with Colonel Bowman, a modest and capable gentleman, when the serenity of our converse was disturbed by a sergeant, who rode into camp with orders for a prompt advance in light marching order. In a twinkling all the camps in the vicinity were deserted, and the roads were so blocked with soldiers on my return, that I was obliged to ride through fields.

I trotted rapidly into the village, and witnessed a scene exciting and martial beyond anything which I had remarked with the Army of Virginia. Regiments were pouring by all the roads and lanes into the main street, and the spectacle of thousands of bayonets, extending as far as the eye could reach, was enhanced by the music of a score of bands, throbbing all at the same moment with wild music. The orders of officers rang out fitfully in the din, and when the steel shifted from shoulder to shoulder, it was like looking down a long sparkling wave. Above the confusion of the time, the various nativities of volunteers roared their national ballads. "St. Patrick's Day," intermingled with the weird refrain of "Bonnie Dundee," and snatches of German sword-songs were drowned by the thrilling chorus of the "Star-Spangled Banner." Then some stentor would strike a stave of—

"John Brown's body lies a mouldering in the grave,"

and the wild, mournful music would be caught up by all,—Germans, Celts, Saxons, till the little town rang with the thunder of voices, all uttering the name of the grim old Moloch, whom—more than any one save Hunter—Virginia hates. Suddenly, as if by rehearsal, all hats would go up, all bayonets toss and glisten, and huzzas would deafen the winds, while the horses reared upon their haunches and the sabres rose and fell. Then, column by column, the masses passed eastward, while the prisoners in the Court-House cupola looked down, and the citizens peeped in fear through crevices of windows.

Being unattached to the staff of any General at the time, and therefore at liberty as a mere spectator, I rode rapidly after the troops, passed the foremost regiments, and unwittingly kept to the left, which I did not discover in the excitement of the ride, till my horse was foaming and my face furrowed with heat drops. I saw that the way had been little travelled, and inquiry at a log farm-house, some distance further, satisfied me that I had mistaken the way. Two men in coarse brown suits, were chopping wood here, and they informed me, with an oath, that the last soldiers seen in the neighborhood, had been Confederate pickets. A by-road enabled me to recover the proper route, and from

the top of a hill overlooking Culpepper, I had a view of
the hamlet, nestling in its hollow ; the roads entering it,
black with troops, and all the slopes covered with wagon-
trains, whose white canopies seemed infinite.   The skies
were gorgeously dyed over the snug cottages and modest
spires ; some far woods were folded in a pleasant haze ;
and the blue mountains lifted their huge backs, voluming in
the distance, like some boundary for humanity, with a happier land beyond.   Here I might have stood, a few months
before, and heard the church bells ; and the trees around
me might have been musical with birds.   But now the par-
sons and the choristers were gone ; the scaffold was erected,
the axe bare, and with a good by glance at the world and
man, some hundreds of wretches were to drop into eternity.   We have all read of the guillotine in other lands ; it
was now before me in my own.

As I passed into the highway again, and riding through
narrow passages, grazing officers' knees, turning vicious
battery horses, winding in and out of woods, making detours through pasture fields, leaping ditches, and so making perilous progress, I passed many friends who hailed me
cheerfully, — here a brigadier-general who waved his hand,
or a colonel who saluted, or a staff officer who rode out and
exchanged inquiries or greetings, or a sergeant who winked
and laughed.   These were some of the men whose bodies
I was to stir to-morrow with my foot, when the eyes that
shone upon me now would be swollen and ghastly.

Some of the privates seeing me in plain clothes, as I had
joined the army merely as a visitor and with no idea of seeing immediate service there, mistook me for a newspaper
correspondent, which in one sense I was ; and I was greeted
with such cries as —

" Our Special Artist ! "

" Our Own Correspondent ! "

" Give our Captain a setting up, you sir ! "

" Puff our Colonel ! "

"Give me a good obituary!"

"Where's your pass, bub?"

"Halloo! Jenkins. Three cheers for Jenkins!"

I shall not soon forget one fellow, who planted himself in my path (his regiment had halted), and leaning upon his musket looked steadily into my eyes.

"Ef I had a warrant for the devil," he said, "I'd arrest that feller."

Many of the soldiers were pensive and thoughtful; but the mass were marching to their funerals with boyish outcries, apparently anxious to forget the responsibilities of the time.

"Let's sing, boys." "Oh! Get out, or I'll belt you over the snout." "Halloo! Pardner, is there water over there?" "Three groans for old Jeff!" "Hip-hip — hooroar! Hi! Hi!"

A continual explosion of small arms, in the shape of epithets, jests, imitations of the cries of sheep, cows, mules, and roosters, and snatches of songs, enlivened the march. If something interposed, or a halt was ordered, the men would throw themselves in the dust, wipe their foreheads, drink from their canteens, gossip, grin, and shout confusedly, and some sought opportunities to straggle off, so that the regiments were materially decimated before they reached the field. The leading officers maintained a dignity and a reserve, and reined their horses together in places, to confer. At one time, a private soldier came out to me, presenting a scrap of paper, and asked me to scrawl him a line, which he would dictate. It was as follows:—

"*My dear Mary, we are going into action soon, and I send you my love. Kiss baby, and if I am not killed I will write to you after the fight.*" The man asked me to mail the scrap at the first opportunity; but the same post which carried his simple billet, carried also his name among the rolls of the dead.

At five o'clock I overtook Crawford's brigade, drawn up

in front of a fine girdle of timber, in a grass field, and on the edge of Cedar Creek. Their ambulances had been unhitched, and ranged in a row against the woods and the soldiers were soon formed in line of battle, extending across the road, with their faces toward the mountain. In this order they moved through the creek, and disappeared behind the ridge of a cornfield. The hill towered in front, but with the naked eye I could distinguish only a speck of floating something above the roof of Slaughter's white house. This was said to be a flag, though I did not believe it; and as there were no evidences of any enemy, which I could determine, I turned my attention to the immediate necessities of myself and my horse. A granary lay at a little distance, and as I was hastening thither, a trooper came along with a blanket full of corn. Fortuitously, he dropped about a dozen ears, which I secured, and hitched my animal to a tree, where he munched until I had fallen asleep. The latter event happened in this wise.

I had observed a slight person in the uniform of a surgeon. He was dividing a large lump of pork at the time, and three great crackers lay before him. I approached and introduced myself, and in a few minutes I was a partial proprietor of the meat, and he a recipient of some drink. The same person directed me to occupy a shelf of the ambulance, and when we lay down together he narrated some of his experiences in Martinsburg, when the Confederates occupied the place after Banks's retreat. He had charge of a hospital at that time, and witnessed the entrance of the Confederate army. The wildness of the people was unbounded, he said, and all who had given so much as a drop of cold water to the invaders were pointed out and execrated. The properties of a few, said to be Unionists, were endangered; and ruffianly soldiers climbed to the windows of the hospital, hooting and taunting the sick. Not to be outdone in bitterness, the tenants flung up their crutches and cheered for the "Union,"— that darling idea, which has marshalled a million of men and filled hecatombs with its champions. In a few days the Federals took possession of the town anew, and the Southern element was in turn oppressed. This is Civil War,— more cruel than the excesses of hereditary enemies. A year before these people of the Shenandoah were fellow-countrymen of the soldiery they contemned.

22

CHAPTER XXIV.

CEDAR MOUNTAIN.

THERE being nothing to eat in the vicinity of the ambulances, I mounted anew at five o'clock and rode back toward Culpepper. No portion of the troops of Crawford were visible now, and only some gray smoke moved up the side of the mountain. A few stragglers were bathing their faces in Cedar Creek, and some miles in the rear lay several of McDowell's brigades under arms. Their muskets were stacked along the sides of the road, the men lay sleepily upon the ground, — company by company, each in its proper place, — the field-officers gossiping together, and the colors upright and unfurled. I was stopped, all the way along the lines, and interrogated as to what was happening in front.

"Any Reb-bils out yonder?" asked a grim, snappish Colonel.

"Guess they don't mean to fight before breakfast!" blurted a Captain.

"Wish they'd cut away, anyway, if they goin' to!" muttered a chorus of privates.

At the village there was nothing to be purchased, although some sutlers' stores lay at the depot, guarded by Provost officers. I persuaded a negro to give me a mess of almost raw pork, and a woman, with a child at the breast, cooked me some biscuit. There were many civilians and idle officers in the town, and the streets were lined with cavalry. Mr. Paine, the landlord, was losing the remnant of his wits, and the young ladies were playing the "Bonnie Blue Flag," and laughing satirically at some young officers who listened. The correspondents began to show themselves in force, and a young fellow whom I may call Chitty, representing a provincial journal, greatly amused me, with the expression of fears that there might be no engagement after all. Chitty was an attorney, who had forsaken a very moderate practice, for a press connection, and he informed me, in confidence, that he was gathering materials for a history of the war. By reason of his attention to this weighty project, he failed to do any reporting, and as his mind was not very well balanced, he was commonly taken to be a simpleton. As there was nobody else to talk to, I amused myself with Chitty during the forenoon, and he narrated to me some doubtful intrigues which had varied his career in Piedmont. But Chitty had mingled in no battles, and now that a contest was about to take place, his heart warmed in anticipation. He asked me if the hottest fighting would not probably occur on the right, and intimated, in that event, his desire to carry despatches through the thickest of the fray. Death was welcome to Chitty if he could so distinguish himself. Between Chitty and a nap in a wagon, I managed to loiter out the morning, and at three o'clock, a cannon peal, so close that it shook the houses, brought my horse upon his haunches. For awhile I did not leave the village. Cannon upon cannon exploded ; the young ladies ceased their mirth ; the landlord staggered with white lips into the air, and after a couple of hours, I heard the signal that I knew so well —— a volley of musketry. Full of all the old impulses, I climbed into the saddle, and spurred my horse towards the battle-field.

The ride over six miles of clay road was a capital school for my pony. Every hoof-fall brought him closer to the cannon, and the sound had become familiar when he reached the scene. At four o'clock, the musketry was close and

effective beyond anything I had known, and now and then
I could see, from secure places, the spurts of white cannon-
smoke far up the side of the mountain. The action was
commenced by emulous skirmishers, who crawled from the
woodsides, and annoyed each other from coverts of ridge,
stump, and stone heap. A large number of Southern rifle-
men then threw themselves into a corner of wood, considerably advanced from their main position. Their fire was
so destructive that General Banks felt it necessary to order
a charge. Two brigades, when the signal was given,
marched in line of battle, out of a wood, and charged across
a field of broken ground toward the projecting corner. As
soon as they appeared, sharpshooters darted up from a
stretch of scrub cedars on their right, and a battery mowed
them down by an oblique fire from the left. The guns up
the mountain side threw shells with beautiful exactness, and
the concealed rifle-men in front poured in deadly showers
of bullet and ball. As the men fell by dozens out of line,
the survivors closed up the gaps, and pressed forward gallantly. The ground was uneven, however, and solid order
could not be observed throughout. At length, when they
had gained a brookside at the very edge of the wood, the
column staggered, quailed, fell into disorder, and then fell
back. Some of the more desperate dashed singly into the
thicket, bayoneting their enemies, and falling in turn in
the fierce grapple. Others of the Confederates ran from the
wood, and engaged hand to hand with antagonists, and, in
places, a score of combatants met sturdily upon the plain,
lunging with knife and sabre bayonet, striking with clubbed
musket, or discharging revolvers. But at last the broken
lines regained the shelter of the timber, and there was a
momentary lull in the thunder.

For a time, each party kept in the edges of the timber,
firing at will, but the Confederates were moving forward in
masses by detours, until some thousands of them stood in
the places of the few who were at first isolated. Distinct

charges were now made, and a large body of Federals attempted to capture the battery before Slaughter's house, while separate brigades charged by front and flank upon the impenetrable timber. The horrible results of the previous effort were repeated ; the Confederates preserved their position, and, at nightfall, the Federals fell back a mile or more. From fifteen hundred to two thousand of the latter were slain or wounded, and, though the heat of the battle had lasted not more than two hours, nearly four thousand men upon both sides were maimed or dead. The valor of the combatants in either cause was unquestionable. But no troops in the world could have driven the Confederates out of the impregnable mazes of the wood. It was an error to expose columns of troops upon an open plain, in the face of imperceptible sharpshooters. The batteries should have shelled the thickets, and the infantry should have retained their concealment. The most disciplined troops of Europe would not have availed in a country of bog, barren, ditch, creek, forest, and mountain. Compared to the bare plain of Waterloo, Cedar Mountain was like the antediluvian world, when the surface was broken by volcanic fire into chasms and abysses. In this battle, the Confederate batteries, along the mountain side, were arranged in the form of a crescent, and, when the solid masses charged up the hill, they were butchered by enfilading fires. On the Confederate part, a thorough knowledge of the country was manifest, and the best possible disposition of forces and means ; on the side of the Federals, there was zeal without discretion, and gallantry without generalship.

During the action, "Stonewall" Jackson occupied a commanding position on the side of the mountain, where, glass in hand, he observed every change of position, and directed all the operations. General Banks was indefatigable and courageous ; but he was left to fight the whole battle, and not a regiment of the large reserve in his rear, came forward to succor or relieve him. As usual, McDow-

22*

ell was cursed by all sides, and some of Banks's soldiers threatened to shoot him. But the unpopular Commander had no defence to make, and said nothing to clear up the doubts relative to him. He exposed himself repeatedly, and so did Pope. The latter rode to the front at nightfall, — for what purpose no one could say, as he had been in Culpepper during the whole afternoon, — and he barely escaped being captured. The loss of Federal officers was very heavy. Fourteen commissioned officers were killed and captured out of one regiment. Sixteen commissioned officers only remained in four regiments. One General was taken prisoner and several were wounded. A large number of field-officers were slain.

During the progress of the fight I galloped from point to point along the rear, but could nowhere obtain a panoramic view. The common sentiment of civilians, that it is always possible to see a battle, is true of isolated contests only. Even the troops engaged, know little of the occurrences around them, and I have been assured by many soldiers that they have fought a whole day without so much as a glimpse of an enemy. The smoke and dust conceal objects, and where the greatest execution is done, the antagonists have frequently fired at a line of smoke, behind which columns may, or may not have been posted.

It was not till nightfall, when the Federals gave up the contested ground, and fell back to some cleared fields, that I heard anything of the manner of action and the resulting losses. As soon as the firing ceased, the ambulance corps went ahead and began to gather up the wounded. As many of these as could walk passed to the rear on foot, and the spectacle at eight o'clock was of a terrible character. The roads were packed with ambulances, creaking under fearful weights, and rod by rod, the teams were stopped, to accommodate other sufferers who had fallen or fainted on the walk. A crippled man would cling to the tail of a wagon, while the tongue would be burdened with two, sustaining themselves by the backs of the horses. Water was sought for everywhere, and all were hungry. I met at sundry times, friends who had passed me, hopeful and humorous the day before, now crawling wearily with a shattered leg or dumb with a stiff and dripping jaw. To realize the horror of the night, imagine a common clay road, in a quiet, rolling country, packed with bleeding people, — the fences down, horsemen riding through the fields, wagons blocking the way, reinforcements in dark columns hurrying up, the shouting of the well to the ill, and the feeble replies, — in a word, recall that elder time when the " earth was filled with violence," and add to the idea that the time was in the night.

I assumed my old rôle of writing the names of the wounded, but when, at nine o'clock, the 10th Maine regiment — a fragment of the proud column which passed me in the morning — returned, I hailed Colonel Beale, and reined with him into a clover-field, the files following wearily. Tramping through the tall garbage, with few words, and those spoken in low tones, we stopped at length in a sort of basin, with the ground rising on every side of us. The men were placed in line, and the Company Sergeants called the rolls. Some of the replies were thrilling, but all were prosaic : —

" Smith ! "

" Smithe fell at the first fire, Sergeant. Bill, here, saw him go down."

" Sturgis ! "

" Sam's in the ambulance, wi' his thigh broke. I don't believe he'll live, Sergeant ! "

" Thompson ! "

" Dead."

" Vinton ! "

" Yar ! (feebly said) four fingers shot off ! "

In this way, the long lists were read over, while the survivors chatted, laughed, and disputed, talking of the incidents of the day. Most of the men lay down in the clover, and some started off in couples to procure water. The field-officers gave me some items relative to the conflict, and as they were ordered to remain here, I resolved to pass the night with them. Obtaining a great fence-rail, I lashed my horse to it by his halter, and, removing his saddle and bridle, left him free to graze in the vicinity. Then I unfolded my camp-bed, covered myself with a rubber blanket, and continued to listen to the conversation. Of course, accusations, bitter mutterings, moodiness, and melancholy, prevailed. I heard these for some time, interspersed with sententious eulogies upon particular persons, and references to isolated events. The evening was one of the pleasantest of the year, in all that nature could contribute; a fine starlight, a transparent atmosphere, a coolness, and a fragrance of sweet-clover blossoms. I had laid my head upon my arm, and shut my eyes, and felt drowsiness come upon me, when something hurtled through the air, and another gun boomed on the stillness. A shell, describing an arc of fire, fell some distance to our left, and, in a moment, a second shell passed directly over our heads.

"——!" said an officer; "have they moved a battery so close? See! it is just at the end of this field!"

I looked back! At the top of the basin in which we lay, something flashed up, throwing a glare upon the woody background, and a shell, followed by a shock, crashed ricochetting, directly in a line with us, but leaped, fortunately, above us, and continued its course far beyond.

"They mean 'em for us," said the same voice; "they see these lights where the fools have been warming their coffee. Halloo!"

Another glare of fire revealed the grouped men and horses around the battery, and for a moment I thought the missile had struck among us. There was a splutter, as of shivering metal flying about, and, with a sort of intuition, the whole regiment rose and ran. I started to my feet and looked for my horse. His ears were erect, his eyeballs distended, and his nostrils were tremulous with fright. A fifth shell, so perfectly in range that I held my breath, and felt my heart grow cold, came toward and passed me, and, with a toss of his head, the nag flung up the rail as if it had been a feather. He seemed literally to juggle it, and it flitted here and there, so that I dared not approach him. A favorable opportunity at length ensued, and I seized the animal by his halter. He was now wild with panic, and sprang toward me as if to trample me. In vain I endeavored to pull him toward the saddle. Fresh projectiles darted beside and above us, and the last of these seemed to pass so close that I could have reached and touched it. The panic took possession of me. I grasped my camp-bed, rather by instinct than by choice, and, holding it desperately under my arm, took to my heels.

It was a long distance to the bottom of the clover-field, and the swift iron followed me remorselessly. At one moment, when a shell burst full in my face, half blinding me, I felt weak to faintness, but still I ran. I had wit enough to avoid the high road, which I knew to be packed with fugitives, and down which, I properly surmised, the enemy would send his steady messengers. Once I fell into a ditch, and the breath was knocked out of my body, but I rolled over upon my feet with marvellous sprightliness, till, at last, when I gained a corn-field, my attention was diverted to a strange, rattling noise behind me. I turned and looked. It was my horse, the rail dangling between his legs, his eyes on fire in the night. As we regarded each other, a shell burst between us. He dashed away across the inhospitable fields, and I fell into the high road among the routed. Expletives like these ensued : —

"Sa-a-ay ! Hoss ! Pardner ! Are you going to ride over this wounded feller ? "

"Friend, have you a drop of water for a man that's fainted here ? "

"Halloo ! Buster ! Keep that bayonit out o' my eye, if you please ! "

" Where's Gen. Banks ? I hearn say he's a prisoner."

" I do' know ! "

" Was we licked, do you think ? "

" No ! We warn't nothin' o' the kind. Siegel's out-flanked 'em and okkepies the field. A man jus' told me so."

" Huzza ! Hearties, cheer up ! Siegel's took the field, and Stonewall Jackson's dead."

" Three cheers for Siegel."

" Hoorooar, hoor —— "

" Oh ! Get out ! That's all blow. Don't try stuff me ! We're lathered ; that's the long and shawt of it."

" Is that so ? Boys, I guess we're beat ! "

Such was the character of exclamations that ran here and there, and after a little volley of them had been let off, a long pause succeeded, when only the sighs of the injured and the tramp of men and nags broke the silence. Over-head the starlight and the blue sky ; on either side the rolling, shadowy fields ; and wrapping the horizon in a gray, grisly girdle, the reposing woods plentiful with dew. Na-ture was putting forth all her still, sweet charms, as if to make men witness the damned contrast of their own wrath, violence, and murder. Even thus, perhaps, — I reasoned, — in the days of old, did the broken multitudes of Xerxes return by the shores of the golden Archipelago ; and the Hellespont shone as peacefully as these silvernesses of earth and firmament. The dulness of history became in-vested with new intelligence. I filled in the details of a thousand routs conned in school-days, when only the dry outlines lay before me. They were mysteries before, and lacked the warmness of life and truth ; but now I *saw* them ! The armor and the helmets fell away, with all other trappings of custom, language, and ceremony. This pale giant, who walked behind the ambulance, leaning upon the footboard, was the limping Achilles, with the arrow of Paris festering in his heel. This ancient veteran, with his back to the field, was the fugitive Æneas, leaving Troy behind. And these, around me, belonged to the columns of Barbazona, scattered at Legnano by the revengeful Milanese. Cobweb, and thick dust, and faded parchment had somewhat softened those elder events; but in their day they were tangible, practical, and prosaic, like this scene. Years will roll over this, as over those, and folks will read at firesides, half doubtfully, half wonderingly, the story of this bafflement, when no fragment of its ruin remains. It was a profound feeling that I should thus be walking down the great retreat of time, and that the occurrences around me should be remembered forever!

There were a few prisoners in the mass, walking before cavalry-men. Nobody interfered with them, and they were not in a position to feel elated. Now and then, when we reached an ambulance, the fugitives would press around it to inquire if any of their friends were within. Rough recognitions would ensue, as thus:—

"Bobby, is that you, back there?— Bobby Baker?"

"Who is it?" (feebly uttered.)

"Me, Bobby—Josh Wiggins. Are you shot bad, Bobby?"

"Shot in the thigh; think the bone's broke. You haven't got a drop of water, have you?"

"No, Bobby; wish I had. Have any more of our boys been hurt that you know of?"

"Switzer is dead; Bill Cringle and Jonesy are prisoners; 'Pud' White is in the ambulance ahead; 'Fol' Thompson's lost an arm; that's all I know."

When we had gone two miles or more, we found a provost column drawn across the road, and a mounted officer interrogating all who attempted to pass:—

"Stop there! You're not wounded."

"Yes, I am."

"Pass on! Halt boy! Go back. Men, close up there. Stop that boy."

"I am sun-struck, Major."

"You lie! Drive him back. Go back, now!"

Beyond this the way was comparatively clear; but as I knew that other guards held the road further on, I passed to the right, and with the hope of finding a rill of water, went across some grass fields, keeping toward the low places. The fields were very still, and I heard only the subdued noises wafted from the road; but suddenly I found myself surrounded by men. They were lying in groups in the tall grass, and started up suddenly, like the clansmen of Roderick Dhu. At first I thought myself a prisoner, and these some cunning Confederates, who had lain in wait. But, to my surprise, they were Federal uniforms, and were simply skulkers from various regiments, who had been hiding here during the hours of battle. Some of these miserable wretches asked me the particulars of the fight, and when told of the defeat, muttered that they were not to be hood-winked and slaughtered.

"I was sick, anyway," said one fellow, "and felt like droppin' on the road."

"I didn't trust my colonel," said another; "he ain't no soldier."

"I'm tired of the war, anyhow," said a third, "and my time's up soon; so I shan't have my head blown off."

As I progressed, dozens of these men appeared; the fields were strewn with them; a true man would rather have been lying with the dead on the field of carnage, than here, among the craven and base. I came to a spring at last, and the stragglers surrounded it in levies. One of them gave me a cup to dip some of the crystal, and a prayerful feeling came over me as the cooling draught fell over my dry palate and parched throat. Regaining the road, I encountered reinforcements coming rapidly out of Culpepper, and among them was the 9th New York. My friend, Lieutenant Draper, recognized me, and called out that he should see me on the morrow, if he was not killed meantime. Culpepper was filling with fugitives when I passed up the main street, and they were sprinkled along the sidewalks, gossiping with each other. The wounded were being carried into some of the dwellings, and when I reached the Virginia Hotel, many of them lay upon the porch. I placed my blanket on a clean place, threw myself down exhaustedly, and dropped to sleep directly.

23

CHAPTER XXV.

OUT WITH A BURYING PARTY.

When I rose, at ten o'clock on the morning of Sunday, August 10, the porch was covered with wounded people. Some fierce sunbeams were gliding under the roof, shining in the poor fellows' eyes, and they were stirring wearily, though asleep. Picking my way among the prostrate figures, I resorted to the pump in the rear of the tavern for the purpose of bathing my face. A soldier stood there on guard, and he refused to give me so much as a draught of water. The wounded needed every drop, and there were but a few wells in the town. I strolled through the main street, now crowded with unfortunates, and pausing at the Court House, found the seat of justice transmuted to a headquarters for surgeons, where amputations were being performed. Continuing by a street to the left, I came to the depot, and here the ambulances were gathered with their scores of inmates. A tavern contiguous to the railway was also a hospital, but in the basement I found the transportation agents at breakfast, and they gave me a bountiful meal.

It was here arranged between myself and an old friend — a newspaper correspondent who had recently married, and whose wife awaited him at Willard's in Washington — that he should proceed at once to New York with the outline of the fight, and that I should follow him next day (having, indeed, to report for duty and fresh orders at

(266)

Head-quarters of the army in Washington,) with particulars and the lists of killed. I commenced my part of the labors at once, employing three persons to assist me, and we districted Culpepper, so that no one should interfere with the grounds of the other. My own part of the work embraced both hotel-hospitals, the names and statements of the prisoners of the Court House loft, and interviews with some of the generals and colonels who lay at various private residences. The business was not a desirable one; for hot hospital rooms were now absolutely reeking, and many of the victims were asleep. It would be inhuman to awaken these; but in many cases those adjacent knew nothing, and with all assiduity the rolls must be imperfect. I found one man who had undergone a sort of mental paralysis and could not tell me his own name. However, I groped through the several chambers where the bleeding littered the bare floors. Some of them were eating voraciously, and buckets of ice-water were being carried to and fro that all might drink. Some male nurses were fanning the sleeping people with boughs of cedar; but the flies filled the ceiling, and, attracted by the wounds, they kept up a constant buzzing. I imagined that mortification would rapidly ensue in this broiling atmosphere. A couple of trains were being prepared below, to transport the sufferers to Washington, and from time to time individuals were carried into the air and deposited in common freight-cars upon the hard floors. Here they were compelled to wait till late in the evening, for no trains were allowed to leave the village during the day. At the Virginia Hotel, I visited, among others, the room in which I had lodged when I first came to Culpepper. Eight persons now occupied it, and three of them lay across the bed. I took the first man's name, and as the man next to him seemed to be asleep, I asked the first man to nudge him gently.

"I don't think he is alive," said the man; "he hasn't moved since midnight. I've spoken to him already."

I pulled a blanket from the head of the figure, and the tangled hair, yellow skin, and stiffened jaw told all the story. The other man looked uneasily into the face of the corpse and then lay down with his back toward it.

"I hope they'll take it out," said he, "I don't want to sleep beside it another night."

The guard at the Court House allowed me to ascend to the loft, and the prisoners — forty or fifty in number — clustered around me. They had received, a short time before, their day's allotment of crackers and bread, and some of them were sitting in the cupola, with their bare legs hanging over the rails. They were anxious to have their names printed, and I learned from the less cautious the names of the brigades to which they belonged. Before I left the room I had obtained the number of regiments in Jackson's command and the names of his brigadier-generals. Some prisoners arrived while I was noting these matters. They had been sent to pick up arms, canteens, cartridge-boxes, etc., from the battle-field, and some of our cavalry had ridden them down and captured them. They were a little discomposed, but said, for the most part, that they were weary of the war and glad to be in custody. As a rule, Northern and Southern troops have the same general manners and appearances. These were more ragged than any Federals I had ever known, and their appetites were voracious.

I found General Geary, a Pennsylvania brigade Commander, in the dwelling of a lady near the end of the town. He had received a bullet in the arm, and, I believe, submitted to amputation afterward. He was a tall, athletic man, upwards of six feet in height, and a citizen of one of the mountainous interior counties of the Quaker State. His life had been marked by much adventure, and he had been elevated to many important civil positions in various quarters of the Republic. He occupied a leading place in the Mexican war, and was afterward Mayor of San Francisco and Governor of Kansas. He acted with the Southern wing of the Democratic party, and was discreetly ambitious, promoting the agricultural interests of his commonwealth, and otherwise fulfilling useful civil functions. He was a fine exemplar of the American gentleman, preserving the better individualities of his countrymen, but discarding those grosser traits, which have given us an unenviable name abroad. Geary could not do a mean thing, and his courage came so naturally to him that he did not consider it any cause of pride. The bias of party, which in America diseases the best natures, had in some degree affected the General. He was prone to go with his party in any event, when often, I think, his fine intelligence would have prompted him to an independent course. But I wish that all our leading men possessed his manliness, for then more dignity and self-respect, and less "smartness," might be apparent in our social and political organizations.

He was lying on his back, with his shattered arm bandaged, and resting on his breast. Twitches of keen pain shot across his face now and then, but he received me with a simple courtesy that made his patience thrice heroic. He did not speak of himself or his services, though I knew both to be eminent; but McDowell had insulted him, as he rode disabled from the field, and Geary felt the sting of the word more than the bullet. He had ventured to say to McDowell that the Reserves were badly needed in front, and the proud "Regular" had answered the officious "Volunteer," to the effect that he knew his own business. Not the least among the causes of the North's inefficiency will be found this ill feeling between the professional and the civil soldiery. A Regular contemns a Volunteer; a Volunteer hates a Regular. I visited General Augur — badly wounded — in the drawing-room of the hotel, and paused a moment to watch Colonel Donnelly, mortally wounded, lying on a spread in the hall. The latter lingered a day in fearful agony; but he was a powerful man in physique, and he

23*

fought with death through a bloody sweat, never moaning nor complaining, till he fell into a blessed torpidity, and so yielded up his soul. The shady little town was a sort of Golgotha now. Feverish eyes began to burn into one's heart, as he passed along the sidewalks. Red hospital flags, hung like regalia from half the houses. A table for amputations was set up in the open air, and nakedness glared hideously upon the sun. How often have they brought out corpses in plain boxes of pine, and shut them away without sign, or ceremony, or tears, driving a long stake above the headboard. The ambulances came and went, till the line seemed stretching to the crack of doom ; while, as in contemplation of further murder, the white-covered ammunition-teams creaked southward, and mounted Provosts charged upon the skulkers, driving them to a pen, whence they were forwarded to their regiments. Old Mr. Paine, the landlord, tottered up to me, with a tear in his eye, and said—

"My good Lord, sir ! Who is responsible for this ? "

He did not mean to suggest argument. It was the language of a human heart pitying its brotherhood.

At twelve o'clock I started anew for the field, and fell in with Captain Chitty on the way. He stated that his courage during the fight surpassed his most heroic expectations, and added, in an undertone, that he was deliberating as to whether he should allow his name to be mentioned officially, since several military men were urging that honor upon him. I dissuaded Chitty from this intent, upon the ground that his reputation for modesty might be sacrificed. Chitty at once said that he would take my advice. We encountered Surgeon Ball, of Ohio, after a time, and he informed us that a day's armistice had been agreed upon, to allow for the burial of the dead. The work of interment was already commenced in front, and the surgeon had been ordered to see to the wounded, some of whom still lay on the places where they fell. He allowed us to accompany him in the capacity of cadets, but we first diverged a little from the road, that he might obtain his portmanteau of instruments. I fell into a little difficulty here, by unwittingly asking aloud of the 28th Pennsylvania regiment, if that was not the organization which hid itself during the fight? The 28th had been ordered, on the morning of Saturday, to occupy Telegraph Mountain, — an elevation in the rear of Cedar Mountain, — which was used for a Federal signal-post. Nobody having notified the 28th to return to camp, they remained on the mountain, passively witnessing the carnage, and came away in the night. But although my remark was jestingly said, the knot of soldiers who heard it were intensely excited. They spoke of taking me " off that hoss," and called me a New York "Snob," who " wanted his head punched." This irate feeling may be attributed to the rivalry which exists between the " Empire " and the " Keystone " States, the latter being very jealous of the former, and claiming to have sent more troops to the war than any other commonwealth. The 28th volunteers doubtless expected a terrific onslaught from the next issue of the Philadelphia papers.

The reserve, which had lain some miles in the rear the previous evening, were now massed close to the field, but in the woods, that the enemy might not count their numbers from his high position. Stopping at times to chat with brother officers, at last I reached the meadow whence I had been driven the previous evening. I looked for my nag in vain. One soldier told me that he had seen him at daylight limping along the high road ; but after sundry wild-goose chases, I gave up the idea of recovering him.

At last I passed the outlying batteries, with their black muzzles scanning the battle-ground, and ascending the clover field, came upon the site of the battery which had so discomfited us the previous night. A signal vengeance had overtaken it. Some splinters of wheel and an over-turned caisson, with eight horses lying in a group, — their hoofs extended like index boards, their necks elongated

along the ground, and their bodies swollen — were the results of a single shell trained upon the battery by a cool
artillerist.   Beyond, the road and fields were strown with
knapsacks, haversacks, jackets, canteens, cartridge-boxes,
shoes, bayonets, knives, buttons, belts, blankets, girths, and
sabres.   Now and then a mule or a horse lay at the roadside, with the clay saturated beneath him ; and some of the
tree-tops, in the depth of the woods, were scarred, split,
and barked, as if the lightning had blasted them.   Now
passing a disabled wagon, now marking a dropped horse-
shoe, now turning a capsized ambulance, now regarding a
perfect wilderness of old clothes, we emerged from the timber at last, and came to the place where I had slept on the
eve of the battle.   A hurricane had apparently swept the
country here, and the fences had been transported bodily.
Sometimes the ground looked, for limited areas, as if there
had been a rain of kindling-wood ; and there were furrows
in the clay, like those made by some great mole which had
ploughed into the bowels of the earth.   All the tree boles
were pierced and perforated, and boughs had been severed
so that they littered the way.   Cedar Creek ran merrily
across what had been the road, — the waters limpid and cool
as before, — and when I passed beyond, I entered the region
of dead men.   Some poisonous Upas had seemingly grown
here, so that adventurers were prostrated by its exhalations.
A tributary rivulet formed with the creek a triangular enclosure of ground, where most of the Federals had fallen.
To the left of the road stood a cornfield ; to the right a
stubble-field, dotted with stone heaps : deep woods formed
the background to these, and scrub-timber, irregularly disposed, the foreground.   On the right of the stubble lay a
great stretch of ''barren,'' spotted with dwarf cedars, and
on the left of the cornfield stood a white farm-house, with
orchards and outbuildings ; beyond, the creek had hollowed
a ravine among the hills, and the far distance was bounded
by the mountains on the Rapidan.   In the immediate front,

towered Cedar Mountain, with woods at its base ; and the roadway in which I stood, lost itself a little way on in the mazes of the thicket. Looking down one of the rows of corn, I saw the first corpse — the hands flung stiffly back, the feet set stubbornly, the chin pointing upward, the features losing their sharpness, the skin blackening, the eyes great and white —

"A heap of death — a chaos of cold clay."

Turning into the cornfield, we came upon one man with a spade, and another man lying at his feet. He was digging a grave, and when we paused to note the operation, he touched his cap : —

"Pardner o' mine," he said, indicating the body ; "him and I fit side by side, and we agreed, if it could be done, to bury each other. There ain't no sich man as that lost out o' the army, private or officer, — with all respect to you."

It was a eulogy that sounded as if more deserved, because it was homely. There are some that I have read, much finer, but not as honest. At little distances we saw parties of ten or twenty, opening trenches, the tributary brook, only, dividing the Confederate and Federal fatigue parties. Close to this brook, in the cornfield, lay a fallen trunk of a tree, and four men sat upon it. Two of them wore gray uniforms, two wore blue. The latter were Gens. Roberts and Hartsuff of the Federal army. They were waiting for Gens. Stuart and Early, of the Confederate army : and the four were to define the period of the armistice. The men in gray were Major Hintham of Mississippi, and Lieut. Elliott Johnston of Maryland. Hintham was a lean, fiery, familiar man, who wore the uniform of several field-marshals. An ostrich feather was stuck in his soft hat and clasped by a silver star upon a black velvet ground. A golden cord formed his hat-band, and two tassels, as huge as those of drawing-room curtains, fell upon his back. His collar was plentifully embroidered as well as his coat-sleeves, and a black seam ran down his trousers. He wore spurs of prodigious size, and looked, in the main, like a tragedian about to appear upon the stage. The other man was young, stout, and good humored ; and he talked sententiously, with a little vanity, but much courtesy. The Federals had nothing to say to these, they dealt only with equals in rank. It became a matter of professional ambition, now, to obtain the greatest amount of information from these Confederates, without appearing to depart from any conventionality of the armistice. I got along very well till Chitty came up, and his interrogatives were so pert and pointed that he very nearly spoiled the entire labor. Young Johnston was a Baltimorean, and wished his people to know something of him ; he gave me a card, stated that he was one of Gen. Garnett's aids, and had opened the armistice, early in the day, by riding into the Federal lines with a flag of truce. By detachments, new bodies of Confederate officers joined us, most of them being young fellows in gray suits : and at length Gen. Early rode down the hillside and nodded his head to our party.

It was the custom of our newspapers to publish, with its narrative of each battle, a plan of the field ; and in furtherance of this object, having agreed to act for my absent friend, I moved a little way from the place of parley, and laying my paper on the pommel of my saddle proceeded to sketch the relative positions of road, brook, mountain, and woodland. While thus busily engaged, and congratulating myself upon the fine opportunities afforded me, a lithe, indurated, severe-looking horseman rode down the hill, and reining beside me, said —

"Are you making a sketch of our position ? "

"Not for any military purpose."

"For what ? "

"For a newspaper engraving."

"Umph ! "

The man rode past me to the log, and when I had finished my transcript, I resumed my place at the group. The new comer was Major General J. E. B. Stuart, one of the most famous cavalry leaders in the Confederate army. He was inquiring for General Hartsuff, with whom he had been a fellow-cadet at West Point; but the Federal General had strolled off, and in the interval Stuart entered into familiar converse with the party. He described the Confederate uniform to me, and laughed over some reminiscences of his raid around McClellan's army.

"That performance gave me a Major-Generalcy, and my saddle cloth there, was sent from Baltimore as a reward, by a lady whom I never knew."

Stuart exhibited what is known in America as "airiness," and evidently loved to talk of his prowess. Directly Gen. Hartsuff returned, and the forager rose, with a grim smile about his mouth —

"Hartsuff, God bless you, how-de-do?"

"Stuart, how are you?"

They took a quiet turn together, speaking of old school-days, perhaps; and when they came back to the log, Surgeon Ball produced a bottle of whiskey, out of which all the Generals drank, wishing each other an early peace.

"Here's hoping you may fall into our hands," said Stuart; "we'll treat you well at Richmond!'

"The same to you!" said Hartsuff, and they all laughed.

It was a strange scene,— this lull in the hurricane. Early was a North Carolinian, who lost nearly his whole brigade at Williamsburg. He wore a single star upon each shoulder, and in other respects resembled a homely farmer. He kept upon his horse, and had little to say. Crawford was gray and mistrustful, calmly measuring Stuart with his eye, as if he intended to challenge him in a few minutes. Hartsuff was fair and burly, with a boyish face, and seemed a little ill at ease. Stuart sat upon a log, in careless posture, working his jaw till the sandy gray beard brushed his chin and became twisted in his teeth. Around, on foot and on

horse, lounged idle officers of both armies ; and the little
rill that trickled behind us was choked in places with
corpses. A pleasanter meeting could not have been held,
if this were a county training. The Surgeon told Gen.
Stuart that some of his relatives lived near the Confederate
Capital, and as the General knew them, he related trifling
occurrences happening in their neighborhoods, so that the
meeting took the form of a roadside gossip, and Stuart
might have been a plain farmer jaunting home from market.
The General, who was called "JEB" by his associates, so
far relented finally as to give me leave to ride within the
Confederate outer lines, and Lieut. Johnson accompanied
me. The corpses lay at frequent points, and some of the
wounded who had not been gathered up, remained at the
spots where they had fallen. One of these, whose leg had
been broken, was incapable of speaking, and could hardly
be distinguished from the lifeless shapes around him. The
number of those who had received their death wound on the
edge of the brook, while in the act of leaping across was very
great. I fancied that their faces retained the mingled ardor
and agony of the endeavor and the pang. There seemed to
be no system in the manner of interment, and many of the
Federals had thrown down their shovels, and strolled across
the boundary, to chaff and loiter with the "Butternuts."
No one, whom I saw, exhibited any emotion at the strewn
spectacles on every side, and the stories I had read of the
stony-heartedness during the plague, were more than
rivalled by these charnel realities. Already corruption was
violating the "temples of the living God." The heat of the
day and the general demoralizing influences of the climate,
were making havoc with the shapely men of yesterday, and
nature seemed hastening to reabsorb, and renew by her
marvellous processes, what was now blistering and bur-
dening her surface. Enough, however, of this. Satiated
with the scenes of war, my ambition now was to extend my
observations to the kingdoms of the Old World.

CHAPTER XXVI.

OUR OWN CORRESPONDENT IN ENGLAND.

THE boy's vague dream of foreign adventure had passed away ; my purpose was of a tamer and more practical cast ; it was resolved to this problem : "How could I travel abroad and pay my expenses ? "

Evidently no money could be made by home correspondence. The new order of journals had no charity for fine moral descriptions of church steeples, ruined castles, and picture galleries ; I knew too little of foreign politics to give the Republic its semi-weekly " sensation ; " and exchange was too high at the depreciated value of currency to yield me even a tolerable reward. But might I not reverse the policy of the peripatetics, and, instead of turning my European experiences into American gold, make my knowledge of America a bill of credit for England ?

What capital had I for this essay ? I was twenty-one years of age ; the last three years of my minority had been passed among the newspapers ; I knew indifferently well the distribution of parties, the theory of the Government, the personalities of public men, the causes of the great civil strife. And I had mounted to my saddle in the beginning of the war, and followed the armies of McClellan and Pope over their sanguinary battle-fields. The possibility thrilled me like a novel discovery, that the Old World might be willing to hear of the New, as I could depict it, fresh from the theatre of action. At great expense foreign correspond-

24 (277)

ents had been sent to our shores, whose ignorance and confidence had led them into egregious blunders; for their
travelling outlay merely, I would have guaranteed thrice
the information, and my sanguine conceit half persuaded me
that I could present it as acceptably. I did not wait to
ponder upon this suggestion. The guns of the second
action of Bull Run growled a farewell to me as I resigned
my horse and equipments to a successor. With a trifle of
money, I took passage on a steamer, and landed at Liverpool on the first of October, 1862.

Among my acquaintances upon the ship was a semi-
literary adventurer from New England. I surmised that his
funds were not more considerable than my own; and
indeed, when he comprehended my plans, he confessed as
much, and proposed to join enterprises with me.

"Did you ever make a public lecture?" he asked.

Now I had certain blushing recollections of having entertained a suburban congregation, long before, with didactic
critiques upon Byron, Keats, and the popular poets. I replied, therefore, misgivingly, in the affirmative, and Hipp,
the interrogator, exclaimed at once —

"Let us make a lecturing tour in England, and divide the
expenses and the work; you will describe the war, and I
will act as your agent."

With true Yankee persistence Hipp developed his idea,
and I consented to try the experiment, though with grave
scruples. It would require much nerve to talk to strange
people upon an excitable topic; and a camp fever, which
among other things I had gained on the Chickahominy, had
enfeebled me to the last degree.

However, I went to work at once, inditing the pages in a
snug parlor of a modest Liverpool inn, while Hipp sounded
the patrons and landlord as to the probable success of our
adventure. Opinions differed; public lectures in the Old
World had been generally gratuitous, except in rare cases,
but the genial Irish proprietor of the *Post* advised me to go
on without hesitation.

We selected for the initial night a Lancashire sea-side town, a summer resort for the people of Liverpool, and filled at that time with invalids and pleasure-seekers. Hipp, who was a sort of American Crichton, managed the business details with consummate tact. I was announced as the eye-witness and participator of a hundred actions, fresh from the bloodiest fields and still smelling of saltpetre. My horse had been shot as I carried a General's orders under the fire of a score of batteries, and I was connected with journals whose reputations were world-wide. Disease had compelled me to forsake the scenes of my heroism, and I had consented to enlighten the Lancashire public, through the solicitation of the nobility and gentry. Some of the latter had indeed honored the affair with their patronage.

We secured the three village newspapers by writing them descriptive letters. The parish rector and the dissenting preachers were waited upon and presented with family tickets ; while we placarded the town till it was scarcely recognizable to the oldest inhabitant.

On the morning of the eventful day I arrived in the place. The best room of the best inn had been engaged for me, and waiters in white aprons, standing in rows, bowed me over the portal. The servant girls and gossips had fugitive peeps at me through the cracks of my door, and I felt for the first time all the oppressiveness of greatness. As I walked on the quay where the crowds were strolling, look-ing out upon the misty sea, at the donkeys on the beach, and at the fishing-smacks huddled under the far-reaching pier, I saw my name in huge letters borne on the banner of a bill-poster, and all the people stopping to read as they wound in and out among them.

How few thought the thin, sallow young man, in wide breeches and square-toed boots, who shambled by them so shamefacedly, to be the veritable Mentor who had crossed the ocean for their benefit. Indeed, the embarrassing responsibility I had assumed now appeared to me in all its vividness.

My confidence sensibly declined; my sensitiveness amounted to nervousness; I had half a mind to run away and leave the show entirely to Hipp. But when I saw that child of the Mayflower stolidly, shrewdly going about his business, working the wires like an old operator, making the largest amount of thunder from so small a cloud, I was rebuked of my faintheartedness. In truth, not the least of my misgivings was Hipp's extraordinary zeal. He gave the townsmen to understand that I was a prodigy of oratory, whose battle-sketches would harrow up their souls and thrill them like a martial summons. It brought the blush to my face to see him talking to knots of old men after the fashion of a town crier at a puppet-booth, and I wondered whether I occupied a more reputable rank, after all, than a strolling gymnast, giant, or dwarf.

As the twilight came on my position became ludicrously unenviable. The lights in the town-hall were lit. I passed pallidly twice or thrice, and would have given half my fortune if the whole thing had been over. But the minutes went on; the interval diminished; I faced the crisis at last and entered the arena.

There sat Hipp, taking money at the head of the stairs, with piles of tickets before him; and as he rose, gravely respectful, the janitor and some loiterers took off their hats while I passed. I entered the little bare dressing-room; my throat was parched as fever, my hands were hot and tremulous; I felt my heart sag. How the rumble of expectant feet in the audience-room shook me! I called myself a poltroon, and fingered my neck-tie, and smoothed my hair before the mirror. Another burst of impatient expectation made me start; I opened the door, and stood before my destiny.

The place was about one third filled with a representative English audience, the males preponderating in number. They watched me intently as I mounted the steps of the rostrum and arranged my port-folio upon a musical tripod;

then I seated myself for a moment, and tried to still the beating of my foolish heart.

How strangely acute were my perceptions of everything before me ! I looked from face to face and analyzed the expressions, counted the lines down the corduroy pantaloons, measured the heavily-shod English feet, numbered the rows of benches and the tubes of the chandeliers, and figured up the losing receipts from this unremunerative audience.

Then I rose, coughed, held the house for the last time in severe review, and repeated —

"LADIES AND GENTLEMEN — A grand contest agitates America and the world.   The people of the two sections of the great North American Republic, having progressed in harmony for almost a century, and become a formidable power among the nations, are now divided and at enmity; they have consecrated with blood their fairest fields, and built monuments of bones in their most beautiful valleys," etc.

For perhaps five minutes everything went on smoothly. I was pleased with the clearness of my voice ; then, as I referred to the origin of the war, and denounced the traitorous conspiracy to disrupt the republic, faint mutterings arose, amounting to interruptions at last.   The sympathies of my audience were, in the main, with the secession.   There were cheers and counter cheers ; storms of " Hear, hear," and " No, no," until a certain youth, in a sort of legal monkey-jacket and with ponderously professional gold seals, so distinguished himself by exclamations that I singled him out as a mark for my bitterest periods.

But while I was thus the main actor in this curious scene, a strange, startling consciousness grew apace upon me ; the room was growing dark ; my voice replied to me like a far, hollow echo ; I knew — I knew that I was losing my consciousness — that I was about to faint ! Words cannot describe my humiliation at this discovery.   I set my lips hard and straightened my limbs ; raised my voice to a

24*

shrill, defiant pitch, and struggled in the dimming horror to select my adversary in the monkey-jacket and overwhelm him with bitter apostrophes. In vain! The novelty, the excitement, the enervation of that long, consuming fever, mastered my overtaxed physique. I knew that, if I did not cease, I should fall senseless to the floor. Only in the last bitter instant did I confess my disability with the best grace I could assume.

"My friends," I said, gaspingly, "this is my first appearance in your country, and I am but just convalescent; my head is a little weak. Will you kindly bear with me a moment while the janitor gets me a glass of water?"

A hearty burst of applause took the sting from my mortification. A bald old gentleman in the front row gravely rose and said, "Let me send for a drop of brandy for our young guest." They waited patiently and kindly till my faintness passed away, and when I rose, a genuine English cheer shook the place.

I often hear it again when, here in my own country, I would speak bitterly of Englishmen, and it softens the harshness of my condemnation.

But I now addressed myself feverishly to my task, and my disgrace made me vehement and combative. I glared upon the individual in the monkey-jacket as if he had been Mr. Jefferson Davis himself, and read him a scathing indictment. The man in the monkey-jacket was not to be scathed. He retorted more frequently than before; he was guilty of the most hardy contempt of court. He was determined not to agree with me, and said so.

"Sir," I exclaimed at last, "pray reserve your remarks till the end of the lecture, and you shall have the platform."

"I shall be quite willing, I am sure," said the man in the monkey-jacket with imperturbable effrontery.

Then, as I continued, the contest grew interesting; explosions of "No, no," were interrupted with volleys of "Ay, ay," from my adherents.   Hipp, who had squared accounts, made all the applause in his power, standing in the main threshold, and the little auditory became a ringing arena, where we fought without flinching, standing foot to foot and drawing fire for fire.   The man in the monkey-jacket broke his word : silence was not his forte ; he hurled denials and counter-charges vociferously ; he was full of gall and bitterness, and when I closed the last page and resumed my chair, he sprang from his place to claim the platform.

"Stop," cried Hipp, in his hard nasal tone, striding forward; "you have interrupted the lecturer after giving your parole ; we recall our promise, as you have not stood by yours.   Janitor, put out the lights ! "

The bald old gentleman quietly rose.   "In England," he said, "we give everybody fair play ; tokens of assent and dissent are commonly made in all our public meetings ; let us have a hearing for our townsman."

"Certainly," I replied, giving him my hand at the top of the stairs ; "nothing would afford me more pleasure."

The man in the monkey-jacket then made a sweeping speech, full of loose charges against the Americans, and expressive of sympathy with the Rebellion ; but, at the finishing, he proposed, as the sentiment of the meeting, a vote of thanks to me, which was amended by another to include himself.   Many of the people shook hands with me at the door, and the bald old gentleman led me to his wife and daughter, whose benignities were almost parental.

"Poor young man ! " said the old lady ; "a must take care of 'is 'ealth ; will a come hoom wi' Tummas and me and drink a bit o' tea ? "

I strolled about the place for twenty-four hours on good terms with many townsmen, while Hipp, full of pluck and business, was posting me against all the dead walls of a farther village.   Again and again I sketched the war-episodes I had followed, gaining fluency and confidence as by degrees my itinerant profession lost its novelty, but we as steadily lost money. The houses were invariably bad ; we had the same fiery discussions every evening, but the same meagre receipts, and in every market town of northwestern Lancashire we buried a portion of our little capital, till once, after talking myself hoarse to a respectable audience of empty benches, Hipp and I looked blankly into each other's faces and silently put our last gold pieces upon the table. We were three thousand miles from home, and the possessors of ten sovereigns apiece. I reached out my hand with a pale smile : —

"Old fellow," I said, "let us comfort ourselves by the assurance that we have deserved success. The time has come to say good by."

"As you will," said Hipp: "it is all the fault of this pig-headed nation. Now I dare say if we had brought a panorama of the war along, it would have been a stunning success ; but standing upon high literary and forensic ground, of course they can't appreciate us. Confound 'em !"

I think that Hipp has since had but two notions, — the exhibition of that panorama, or, in the event of its failure, a declaration of war against the British people. He followed me to Liverpool, and bade me adieu at Birkenhead, I going Londonward with scarcely enough money to pay my passage, and he to start next day for Belfast, to lecture upon his own hook, or, failing (as he afterward did), to recross the Atlantic in the steerage of a ship.

My feelings, as the train bore me steadily through the Welsh border, by the clustering smoke-stacks of Birmingham, by the castled tower of Warwick, and along the head waters of the Thames and Avon, were not of the most enthusiastic description. I had no money and no friends ; I had sent to America for a remittance, but in the interval of six weeks required for a reply, must eat and drink and lodge, and London was wide and pitiless, even if I dared stoop to beg assistance.

Let no young man be tempted to put the sea between his home and himself, how seductive soever be the experiences of book-makers and poetic pedestrians. One hour's contemplation of poverty in foreign lands will line the boy's face with the wrinkles of years, and burn into his soul that withering dependency which will rankle long after his privations are forgotten.

In truth, my circumstances were so awkward that my very desperation kept me calm. I had a formal letter to one English publisher, but not any friendly line whatever to anybody ; and as the possibilities of sickness, debt, enemies, came to mind, I felt that I was no longer the hero of a romance, but face to face with a hard, practical, terrible reality. It was night when I landed at the Paddington Station, and taking an omnibus for Charing Cross, watched the long lines of lamps on Oxford Street, and the glitter of the Haymarket theatres, and at last the hard plash of the fountains in Trafalgar Square, with the stony statues grouped so rigidly about the column to Nelson.

I walked down Strand with my carpet-bag in my hands, through Fleet Street and under Temple Bar, till, weary at last from sheer exercise, I dropped into a little ale-house under a great, grinning lantern, which said, in the crisp tone of patronage, the one word, "beds." They put me under the tiles, with the chimney-stacks for my neighbors, and I lay awake all night meditating expedients for the morrow : so far from regret or foreboding, I longed for the daylight to come that I might commence my task, confident that I could not fail where so many had succeeded. They were, indeed, inspirations which looked in upon me at the dawn. The dome of St. Paul's guarding Paternoster Row, with Milton's school in the background, and hard by the Player's Court, where, in lieu of Shakespeare's company, the American presses of the *Times* shook the kingdom and the continent. I thought of Johnson, as I passed Bolt Alley, of Chatterton at Shoe Lane, of Goldsmith as I put my foot upon his grave under the eaves of the Temple.

The public has nothing to do with the sacrifices by which my private embarrassment received temporary relief. Though half the race of authors had been in similar straits, I would not, for all their success, undergo again such self-humiliation. It is enough to say that I obtained lodgings in Islington, close to the home of Charles Lamb, and near Irving's Canterbury tower; and that between writing articles on the American war, and strategic efforts to pay my board, two weeks of feverish loneliness drifted away.

I made but one friend; a young Englishman of radical proclivities, who had passed some years in America among books and newspapers, and was now editing the foreign column of the *Illustrated London News.* He was a brave, needy fellow, full of heart, but burdened with a wife and children, and too honestly impolitic to gain money with his fine abilities by writing down his own unpopular sentiments. He helped me with advice and otherwise.

"If you mean to work for the journals," he said, "I fear you will be disappointed. I have tried six years to get upon some daily London paper. The editorial positions are always filled; you know too little of the geography and society of the town to be a reporter, and such miscellaneous recollections of the war as you possess will not be available for a mere newspaper. But the magazines are always ready to purchase, if you can get access to them. In that quarter you might do well."

I found that the serials to which my friend recommended me shared his own advanced sentiments, but were unfortunately without money. So I made my way to the counter of the Messrs. Chambers, and left for its junior partner an introductory note. The reply was to this effect. I violate no confidence, I think, in reproducing it : —

"SIR, — I shall be glad to see any friend of —— ——, and may be found," etc., etc. "I fear that articles upon the American war, written by an American, will not, however, be acceptable in this journal, as the public here take a widely different view of the contest from that entertained in your own country, and the feeling of horror is deepening fast."

Undeterred by this frank avowal, I waited upon the publisher at the appointed time, — a fine, athletic, white-haired Scotchman, whose name is known where that of greater authors cannot reach, and who has written with his own hand as much as Dumas *père*. He met me with warm cordiality, rare to Englishmen, and when I said —

" Sir, I do not wish the use of your paper to circulate my opinions, — only my experiences," he took me at once to his editor, and gave me a personal introduction. Fortunately I had brought with me a paper which I submitted on the spot ; it was entitled, " Literature of the American War," collated from such campaign ballads as I could remember, eked out with my own, and strung together with explanatory and critical paragraphs. The third day following, I received this announcement in shockingly bad handwriting : —

" D'r S'r,
" Y'r article will suit us.
"The ed. C. J."

For every word in this communication, I afterward obtained a guinea. The money not being due till after the appearance of the article, I anticipated it with various sketches, stories, etc., all of which were largely fanciful or descriptive, and contained no paragraph which I wish to recall. In other directions, I was less successful. Of two daily journals to which I offered my services, one declined to answer my letter, and the other demanded a quarto of credentials.

So I lived a fugitive existence, a practical illustration of Irving's " Poor Devil Author," looking as often into pastry-shop windows, testing all manner of cheap Pickwickian veal-pies, breakfasting upon a chop, and supping upon a herring in my suburban residence, but keeping up pluck and *chique* so deceptively, that nobody in the place suspected me of poverty.

I went for some American inventors, to a rifle ground, and explained to the Lords of the Admiralty the merits of a new projectile ; wrote letters to all the Continental sovereigns for an itinerant and independent embassador, and was at last so poor that my only writing papers were a druggist's waste bill-heads.   An article with no other "backing" than this was fortunate enough to stray into the *Cornhill Magazine.*   I found that its proprietor kept a banking-house in Pall Mall, and doubtful of my welcome on Cornhill, ventured one day in my unique American costume, — slouched hat, wide garments, and squared-toed boots, — to send to him directly my card.   He probably thought from its face that a relative of Mr. Mason's was about to open an extensive account with him.   As it was, once admitted to his presence, he could not escape me.   The manuscript lay in his hands before he fully comprehended my purpose.   He was a fine specimen of the English publisher, — robust, ruddy, good-naturedly acute, — and as he said with a smile that he would waive routine and take charge of my copy, I knew that the same hands had fastened upon the crude pages of Jane Eyre, and the best labors of Hazlitt, Ruskin, Leigh Hunt, and Thackeray.

Two more weary weeks elapsed ; I found it pleasant to work, but very trying to wait.   At the end my courage very nearly failed.   I reached the era of self-accusation ; to make myself forget myself I took long, ardent marches into the open country ; followed the authors I had worshipped through the localities they had made reverend ; lost myself in dreaminesses, — those precursors of death in the snow, — and wished myself back in the ranks of the North, to go down in the frenzy, rather than thus drag out a life of civil indigence, robbing at once my brains and my stomach.

One morning, as I sat in my little Islington parlor, wishing that the chop I had just eaten had gone farther, and taking a melancholy inventory of the threadbare carpet and rheumatic chairs, the door-knocker fell ; there were steps in the hall ; my name was mentioned.

A tall young gentleman approached me with a letter : I received him with a strange nervousness ; was there any crime in my record, I asked fitfully, for which I had been traced to this obscure suburb for condign arrest and decapitation ? Ha ! ha ! it was my heart, not my lips, that laughed. I could have cried out like Enoch Arden in his dying apostrophe : —

> "A sail ! a sail !
> I am saved ! "

for the note, in the publisher's own handwriting, said this, and more : —

"DEAR SIR, — I shall be glad to send you fifteen guineas immediately, in return for your article on General Pope's Campaign, if the price will suit you."

But I suppressed my enthusiasm. I spoke patronizingly to the young gentleman. Dr. Johnson, at the brewer's vendue, could not have been more learnedly sonorous.

" You may say in return, sir, that the sum named will remunerate me."

At the same time the instinct was intense to seize the youth by the throat, and tell him that if the remittance was delayed beyond the morning, I would have his heart's-blood ! I should have liked to thrust him into the coal-hole as a hostage for its prompt arrival, or send one of his ears to the publishing house with a warning, after the manner of the Neapolitan brigands.

That afternoon I walked all the way to Edmonton, over John Gilpin's route, and boldly invested two-pence in beer at the time-honored Bell Inn. I disdained to ride back upon the omnibus for the sum of threepence, but returned on foot the entire eight miles, and thought it only a league. Next day my check came duly to hand, — a very formidable check, with two pen-marks drawn across its face. I carried it to Threadneedle Street by the unfrequented routes, to avoid having my pockets picked, and presented it to the cashier, wondering if he knew me to be a foreign gentleman who had written for the *Cornhill Magazine*. The cashier looked rather contemptuous, I thought, being evidently a soulless character with no literary affinities.

" Sir," he said, curtly, " this check is crossed."

" Sir ! "

" We can't cash the check ; it is crossed."

" What do you mean by crossed ? "

" Just present it where you got it, and you will find out."

The cashier regarded me as if I had offered a ticket of leave rather than an order for the considerable amount of seventy-five dollars. I left that banking-house a broken man, and stopped with a long, long face at a broker's to ask for an explanation.

" Yesh, yesh," said the little man, whose German silver spectacles sat upon a bulbously Oriental nose ; " ze monish ish never paid on a crossed shequc. If one hash a bank-account, you know, zat is different. Ze gentleman who gif you dis shequc had no bishness to crosh it if you have no banker."

I was too vain to go back to Cornhill and confess that I had neither purse nor purser ; so I satisfied the broker that the affair was correct, and he cashed the bill for five shillings.

That was the end of my necessities ; money came from home, from this and that serial ; my published articles were favorably noticed, and opened the market to me. Whatever I penned found sale ; and some correspondence that I had leisure to fulfil for America brought me steady receipts.

Had I been prudent with my means, and prompt to advantage myself of opportunities, I might have obtained access to the best literary society, and sold my compositions for correspondingly higher prices. Social standing in English literature is of equal consequence with genius. The poor Irish governess cannot find a publisher, but Lady Morgan takes both critics and readers by storm. A duchess's name on the title-page protects the fool in the letter-press ; irreverent republicanism is not yet so great a respecter of persons. I was often invited out to dinner, and went to the expense of a dress-coat and kids, without which one passes the genteel British portal at his peril ; but found that both the expense and the stateliness of "society" were onerous. In this department I had no perseverance ; but when, one evening, I sat with the author of "Vanity Fair," in the concert rooms at Covent Garden, as Colonel Newcome and Clive had done before me, and took my beer and mutton with those kindly eyes measuring me through their spectacles, I felt that such grand companionship lifted me from the errantry of my career into the dignity of a renowned art.

I moved my lodgings, after three months, to a pleasant square of the West End, where I had for associates, among others, several American artists. Strange men were they to be so far from home ; but I have since found, that the poorer one is the farther he travels, and the majority of these were quite destitute. Two of them only had permanent employment ; a few, now and then, sold a design to a magazine ; the mass went out sketching to kill time, and trusted to Providence for dinner. But they were good fellows for the most part, kindly to one another, and meeting in their lodgings, where their tenure was uncertain, to score Millais, or praise Rosetti, or overwhelm Frith.

My own life meantime passed smoothly. I had no rivals of my own nationality ; though one expatriated person, whose name I have not heard, was writing a series of prejudiced articles for *Fraser*, which he signed " A White Republican." I thought him a very dirty white. One or two English travellers at the same time were making amusingly stupid notices of America in some of the second-rate monthlies; and Maxwell, a bustling Irishman, who owns *Temple Bar*, the *Saint James*, and *Sixpenny Magazine*, and some half dozen other serials, was employing a man to invent all varieties of rubbish upon a country which he had never beheld nor comprehended.

After a few months the passages of the war with which I was cognizant lost their interest by reason of later occurrences. I found myself, so to speak, wedged out of the market by new literary importations. The enforcement of the draft brought to Europe many naturalized countrymen of mine, whose dislike of America was not lessened by their unceremonious mode of departure from it; and it is to these, the mass of whom are familiarly known in the journals of this country, that we owe the most insidious, because the best informed, detraction of us. *Macmillan's Magazine* did us sterling service through the papers of Edward Dicey, the best literary *feuilletonist* in England; and Professor Newman, J. Stuart Mill, and others, gave us the limited influence of the *Westminster Review*. The *Cornhill* was neutral; *Chambers's* respectfully inimical; *Bentley* and *Colburn* antagonistically flat; Maxwell's tri-visaged publications grinningly abusive; *Good Words* had neither good nor bad words for us; *Once a Week* and *All the Year Round* gave us a shot now and then. *Blackwood* and *Fraser* disliked our form of Government, and all its manifestations. The rest of the reviews, as far as I could see, pitied and berated us pompously. It was more than once suggested to me to write an experimental paper upon the failure of republicanism; but I knew only one American — a New York correspondent — who lent himself to a systematic abuse of the Government which permitted him to reside in it. He obtained a newsboy's fame, and, I suspect, earned considerable. He is dead : let any who love him shorten his biography by three years.

However, I at last concluded a book, — if I may so call what never resulted in a volume, — at which, from the first, I had been pegging away. I called it "The War Correspondent," and made it the literal record of my adventures in the saddle. When some six hundred MS. pages were done I sent it to a publisher; he politely sent it back. I forwarded it to a rival house; in this respect only both houses were agreed. Having some dim recollection of the early trials of authors I perseveringly gave that copy the freedom of the city; the verdict upon it was marvellously identical, but the manner of declension was always soothing. They separately advised me not to be content with one refusal, but to try some other house, though I came at last to think, by the regularity of its transit to and fro, that one house only had been its recipient from the first.

At last, assured of its positive failure, I took what seemed to be the most philosophic course, — neither tossing it into the Thames, after the fashion of a famous novelist, nor littering my floor with its fragments, and dying amidst them like a *chiffonnier* in his den : I cut the best paragraphs out of it, strung them together, and published it by separate articles in the serials. My name failed to be added to the British Museum Catalogue; but that circumstance is, at the present time, a matter of no regret whatever.

When done with the war I took to story-writing, using many half-forgotten incidents of American police-reporting, of border warfare, of the development of civilization among the pioneers, of thraldom in the South, and the gold search on the Pacific. The majority of these travelled across the water, and were republished. And when America, in the garb of either fact or fiction, lost novelty, I entered the wide field of miscellaneous literature among a thousand competitors.

An author's ticket to the British Museum Reading-room

25*

put the whole world so close around me that I could touch it everywhere. I never entered the noble rotunda of that vast collection without an emotion of littleness and awe. Lit only from the roof, it reminded me of the Roman Pantheon ; and truly all the gods whom I had worshipped sat, not in statue, but in substance, along its radiating tables, or trod its noiseless floors. Half the literature of our language flows from thence. One may see at a glance grave naturalists knee-deep in ichthyological tomes, or buzzing over entomology ; pale zealots copying Arabic characters, with the end to rebuild Bethlehem or the ruins of Mecca ; biographers gloating over some rare original letter ; periodical writers filching from two centuries ago for their next " new " article. The Marquis of Lansdowne is dead ; you may see the *Times* reporter yonder running down the events of his career. Poland is in arms again, and the clever compiler farther on means to make twenty pounds out of it by summing up her past risings and ruins. The bruisers King and Mace fought yesterday, and the plodding person close by from *Bell's Life* is gleaning their antecedents. Half the *literati* of our age do but like these bind the present to the past. A great library diminishes the number of thinkers ; the grand fountains of philosophy and science ran before types were so facile or letters became a trade.

The novelty of this life soon wore away, and I found myself the creature of no romance, but plodding along a prosy road with very practical people.

I carried my MSS. into Paternoster Row like anybody's book-keeper, and accused the world of no particular ingratitude that it could not read my name with my articles, and that it gave itself no concern to discover me. Yet there was a private pleasure in the congeniality of my labor, and in the consciousness that I could float upon my quill even in this vast London sea. Once or twice my articles went across the Channel and returned in foreign dress. I wonder if I shall ever again feel the thrill of that first recognition of

my offspring coming to my knee with their strange French
prattle.

I was not uniformly successful, but, if rejected, my MSS.
were courteously returned, with a note from the editor. As
a sample I give the following. The original is a litho-
graphed fac-simile of the handwriting of Mr. Dickens,
printed in blue ink, the date and the title of the manuscript
being in another handwriting.

OFFICE OF "ALL THE YEAR ROUND."

A WEEKLY JOURNAL CONDUCTED BY CHARLES DICKENS.

NO. 26 WELLINGTON STREET, STRAND, LONDON, W. C.
January 27, 1863.

Mr. Charles Dickens begs to thank the writer of the paper entitled
"A Battle Sunday" for having done him the favor to offer it as a con-
tribution to these pages. He much regrets, however, that it is not
suited to the requirements of "All the Year Round."

The manuscript will be returned, under cover, if applied for as
above.

The prices of miscellaneous articles in London are remu-
nerative. Twenty-four shillings a magazine page is the
common valuation : but specially interesting papers rate
higher. Literature as a profession, in England, is more certain and more progressive than with us. It is not debased
with the heavy leaven of journalism. Among the many
serial publications of London, ability, tact, and industry
should always find a liberal market. There is less of the
vagrancy of letters, — Bohemianism, Mohicanism, or what
not, — in London than in either New York or Paris.

I think we have the cleverer fugitive writers in America,
but those of England seemed to me to have more self-respect
and conscientiousness. The soul of the scribe need never
be in pledge if there are many masters.

While a good writer in any department can find work
across the water, I would advise no one to go abroad with
this assurance solely. My success — if so that can be

called which yielded me life, not profit — was circumstantial, and cannot be repeated. I should be loth to try it again upon purely literary merits.

After nine months of experiment I bade the insular metropolis adieu, and returned no more. The Continent was close and beckoning; I heard the confusion of her tongues, and saw the shafts of her Gothic Babels probing the clouds, and for another year I roamed among her cities, as ardent and errant as when I went afield on my pony to win the spurs of a War Correspondent.

CHAPTER XXVII.

SPURS IN THE PICTURE GALLERIES.

FLORENCE, city of my delight! how do I thrill at the recollection of the asylum afforded me by thee in the Via Parione. The room was tiled, and cool, and high, and its single window looked out upon a real palace, where the family of Corsini, presided over by a porter in cocked hat and an exuberance of gold lace, gave me frequent glimpses of gauze dresses and glorious eyes, whose owners sometimes came to the casement to watch the poor little foreigner, writing so industriously.

Every young traveller has two or three subjects of unrest. Mine were girls and art. The copyists in the galleries were more beautiful studies to me than the paintings. The next time I go to Europe, I shall take enough money along to give all the pretty ones an order; this will be an introduction, and I shall know how they live, and how much money they make, and what passions have heaved their beautiful bosoms, to make their slow, quiet lives forever haunted and longing.

Love, love! There are only two grand, unsatiated passions, which keep us forever in freshness and fever, — love and art.

In Italy I breathed the purest atmosphere; all the world was a landscape picture; all the skies were spilling blueness and crimson upon the mountains; all the faces were Madonnas; all the perspectives were storied architecture.

(297)

Westward the star of Empire takes its way, but that of art shines steadily in the East. Thither look our American young men, no matter at which of its altars they make their devotions, — painting, sculpture, or architecture. And I, who had known some fondness for the pencil till lured into the wider, wilder field of letters, felt almost an artist's joy when I stood in the presence of those solemn masters whose works are inspired and imperishable, like religion.

Having passed the first thrill and disappointment, — for pure art speaks only to the pure by intuition or initiation, and I was yet a novice, — my old newspaper curiosity revived to learn of the successful living rather than of the grand dead.

Correspondents, like poets, are born, not made : the venerable associations around me — monuments, cloisters, palaces, the homes and graves of great men whom I revered, the aisles where every canvas bore a spell name — could not wean me from that old, reportorial habit of asking questions, peeping into private nooks, and making notes upon contemporary things, just as I had done for three years, in cities, on routes, on battle-fields. And as the old world seemed to me only a great art museum, I longed to look behind the tapestry at the Ghobelin weavers, pulling the beautiful threads.

"Where dwell these gay and happy students, who quit our hard, bright skies, and land of angularities, to inhale the dews of these sedative mosses, and, by attrition with masterpieces, glean something of the spirit of the masters ?"

Straightway the faery realm opened to me, and two months of Italian rambling were spent in association with the folk I esteemed only less than my own exemplars.

Art, in all ages, is the flowery way. No pursuit gives so great joy in the achieving, none achieved yields higher meed of competence, contentment, and repute. Its ambition is more genial and subdued than that of literature, its rivalry more courteous and exalting ; its daily life should be pastoral and domestic, free from those feverish mutations and adventures which cross the incipient author, and it is forever surrounded by bright and beautiful objects which linger too long upon the eye to stir the mind to more than emulation.

Is it harsh to say that artists have been too well rewarded, and thinkers and writers too ill ? Vasari dines at the ducal table, while Galileo's pension is the rack ; the mob which carries Cimabue's canvas in triumph, drives Dante into exile ; Rubens is a king's ambassador, and Grotius is sent to jail ; to Reynolds's levees, poor, bankrupt Goldsmith steals like an unwelcome guest, and Apelles's gold is paid to him in measures, while Homer, singing immortal lines, goes blind and begging.

Art students take rank in Italy among the best of travellers, but Bohemianism in art is at one's peril. There are many wasted lives among the clever fellows who go abroad ostensibly for study. I recall Jimman, who was an expert with the pencil, and who colored with excellent discrimination. He went to Dusseldorf at first, and became known to Leutze, who praised his sketches. He began to associate at once with students and tipplers, and dissipated less by drinking than by talking. I have a theory that more men are lost to themselves and the age by a love of " gabbing " than by drinking. It is not hard to eschew cognac and claret, but there is no cure for "buzzing." There is a drunkenness of talk which takes possession of one, and Jimman would have had the *delirium tremens* in a week, with nobody to listen to him. To my mind the Trappiste takes the severest of monastic vows.

Jimman used to rise in the morning betimes, full of inflexible resolution. Having stretched his canvas, and carefully prepared his pigments, he went to breakfast, pondering great achievements. Here he fell in with a lot of Germans, — the most incurable race of gossipers in the world, — and while they discussed, in a learned way, every subject under the sun, the meal extended into the afternoon, and Jimman concluded that it was then too late to undertake anything. In this way his ambition burnt away, his money was squandered, he lost facility of manipulation, and came back to Paris at the age of twenty-eight, to pursue the same listless, garrulous existence; debts and grisettes, buzzing and brandy, the utterance of resolves which expired in the utterance, and Jimman finally became, perforce, a common apprentice to a moulder, that he might not entirely starve.

I saw him, for the last time, in the Louvre, looking at Zurbaran's "Kneeling Monk."

"Ah, Townsend," he said, "I might have done something like that. All my zeal is gone."

And he began to chat in the same loose, familiar way. Dumbness and deafness would have been endowments rather than deprivations for him.

I had rooms in Florence with Gypsum and Stagg. The former was a young, industrious fellow, of German descent, who worked hard, but not wisely. He spent half a year in copying a face by Paul Veronese, and the other half in sketching an old convent yard. But he did not visit, and an artist, to get orders and take rank, must be seen as well as be earnest. He need not be hail-fellow, but should keep well in the circle of respectable travellers; for these are to be his patrons, if he pleases them. Gypsum was over-modest and too conscientious; he had only a trifle of money, and was careless of his attire. So he disregarded society, and society forgot him. Therefore, at dawn, he betook himself to the old convent-yard, and stood at his easel bravely, never so unhappy as when one of the church's innumerable holy days arrived, for then he was forbidden to work upon the convent premises. With all his conscientiousness he received no orders; while Stagg, who was not more clever, proportioned to his longer experience, was befriended on every hand, because he went to the American chapel regularly and wore a dress-coat at the sociables.

Stagg used the old studio of Buchanan Read, just off the Via Seragli.

I stumbled upon him one morning, and saw more than I anticipated.

A young, plump girl, without so much as a fig-leaf upon her, was posing before his easel, so motionless that she scarcely winked, one hand extended and clasping her loosened tresses, and bending upon one white and dimpled knee.

She had the large dark eyes of the professional *modello*, and a bosom as ripe as Titian's Venus. Her feet were small, and her hands very white and beautiful. But of me she took no more notice than if I had been a bird alighting upon the window, or a mouse peeping at her from the edge of his knot-hole.

Old Stagg, who was commonly grave as a clergyman, now and then left his easel to alter her position, and when he was done, she gathered up her clothes, which had lain in a heap on the floor, and took her few silver pieces with a "*Mille grazie, Signore!*" and went home to take dinner with her little brothers.

A studio in Florence costs only fifteen or twenty francs a month, — seldom so much. There are a series of excellent ones in the same Via Seragli, in a very large dismantled convent. There is a well in the centre of its great court-yard, and innumerable ropes lead from it to the various high windows of the building, on which buckets of water are for-ever ascending. All this of which I speak refers to a year ago, when Florence was not a capital; doubtless, studios command more at present.

The models at Florence were to me strange personages. There was a drawing-school which I sometimes attended, where one old woman kept three daughters, aged respec-tively twenty, seventeen, and thirteen years. They lived pretty much as they were born, and while they posed upon a high platform, the old woman took her seat near the door

26

and looked on with grim satisfaction. She was very careful of their moral habits, but the second one she lost by an excess of greed. She resolved to make them useful by day, as well as by night, and put them to work at the studios of individual artists. But as no one artist wanted three models, the girls had to separate, and, out of the mother's vigilance, the second one, Orsolo, went to the atelier of a wicked and handsome fellow, and met with the usual romance of her class.

The oldest girl, Luigia, married a man-model, and their nuptials must have been of a most prosaic character.

Among the many men who thus stood for the artists, was one old fellow, tall, and bearded, and massively characterized, who used to remain motionless for hours, until he seemed to be dead. He had been a model in every stage of life, from childhood to the grave, and represented every subject from Garibaldi to Moses.

The walks in and around Florence occupied all my Sabbaths. Stagg and I used to stroll up to Fiesole, by the villa where Boccaccio's party of story-tellers met, and look up old pictures in the village church; we measured the proportions of the chapel on the hill of Saint Miniato, and he endeavored in vain to imitate the hue of the light as it fell through the veined marble of Serravezza; we spent contemplative afternoons in the house of Michael Angelo, and went up to Vallambrosa, at the risk of our necks, to look at a Giotto no bigger than a tea-plate. In Florence there is enough out-of-door statuary to make one of the finest galleries in the world. The majesty of Donatello's "Saint George" arises before me when I would conceive of any noble humanity, and the sweep of Orgagna's great arches give me an idea of vastness like the sea; in the Pitti palace only giants should abide; the Campanile goes up to heaven as beautiful as Jacob's ladder, and in the perpetual twilight of the Duomo I was not of half the stature I believed when roaming under the loftier sky.

I saw a jail in Florence, and it troubled me ; who in that beautiful city could do a crime ? How should old age, or bad passions, or sickness, or shame, exist in that limpid atmosphere, in the shadow of such architecture, in the presence of those pictures ?

CHAPTER XXVIII.

A CORRESPONDENT ONCE MORE.

AGAIN on the way to Washington! I have made the trip more than sixty times. I saw the Gunpowder Bridge in flames when Baltimore was in arms and the Capital cut off from the North. I saw from Perryville the State flag of Maryland waving at Havre de Grace across the Susquehanna. I saw at the Washington Navy Yard the blackened body of Ellsworth, manipulated by the surgeons. I moved through the city with McClellan's onward army toward the transports which were to carry it to the Peninsula. The awful tidings of the seven days' retreat came first through the Capital in my haversack, and before Stonewall Jackson fell upon the flank of Pope, I crossed the Long Bridge with the story of the disaster of Cedar Mountain. In like manner the crowning glory of Five Forks made me its earliest emissary, and the murder of the President brought me hot from Richmond to participate in the pursuit of Booth and chronicle his midnight expiation.

Again am I on the way to the city of centralization, to paint by electricity the closing scenes of the conspirators, and, as I pass the Pennsylvania line, the recollection of those frequent pilgrimages — pray God this be the last! — comes upon me like the sequences of delirium.

As I look abroad upon the thrifty fields and the rich glebe of the ploughman, I wonder if the revolutions of peace are not as sweeping and sudden as those of war. He who

(304)

wrote the certain downfall of this Nation, did not keep his eye upon the steadily ascending dome of the capitol, nor remark, during the thunders of Gettysburg, the as energetic stroke of the pile-drivers upon the piers of the great Susquehanna bridge. We built while we desolated. No fatalist convert to Mohammed had so sure faith in the eternity of his institutions. More masonry has been laid along the border during the war than in any five previous years. We have finished the Treasury, raised the bronze gates on the Capitol, double-railed all the roads between New York and the Potomac, and gone on as if architecture were imperishable, while thrice the Rebels swept down toward the Relay.

And we have done one strategic thing, which, I think, will compare with the passing of Vicksburg or the raid of Sherman; we have turned Philadelphia.

This modern Pompeii used to be the stumbling-block on the great highway. It was to the direct Washington route what Hell-gate was to the Sound Channel. We were forbidden the right of way through it, on the ground that by retarding travel Philadelphia would gain trade, and had to cross the Delaware on a scow, or lay up in some inn over night. New Jerseymen, I hear, pray every morning for their daily stranger; Philadelphia has much sinned to entrap its daily customer. But Maillefert — by which name I designate the inevitable sledge which spares the grand and pulverizes the little — has built a road around the Quaker City. It is a very curious road, going by two hypothenuses of about fifteen miles to make a base of three or four, so that we lose an hour on the way to the Capital, all because of Philadelphia's overnight toil.

The bridge at Perryville will be one of the staunchest upon our continent: the forts around Baltimore make the outlying landscapes scarcely recognizable to the returning Maryland Rebels. At last, — woe be the necessity! we have garrisoned our cities. The Relay House is the most picturesque spot between the two foci of the country. Wandering through the woods, I see the dirty blouses of the remnant of "the boys" and the old abatis on the height looks sunburnt and rusty; away through the gorge thunders the Baltimore and Ohio train, over what ruins and resurrections, torn up a hundred times, and as obstinately relaid, until all its engineers are veteran officers, and can stand fire both of the furnace and the musket. Everybody in the country is a veteran; the contractor, who ran his schooner of fodder past the Rebel batteries; the correspondent, whose lean horse slipped through the crevices of dropping shells; the teamster, who whipped his mule out of the mud-hole, while his ammunition wagon behind grew hot with the heaviness of battle; the old farmer, who took to his cellar while the fight raged in his chimneys, but ventured out between the bayonet charges to secure his fatted calf.

Annapolis Junction has still the sterile guise of the campaign, where the hills are bare around the hospitals, and the railway taverns are whittled to skeletons. I have really seen whole houses, little more than shells, reduced to meagreness by the pocket-knife. The name of almost everybody on the continent is cut somewhere in the South; Virginia has more than enough names carved over her fireside altars to inscribe upon all her multitudinous graves.

There are close to the city fine bits of landscape, where the fields dip gracefully into fertile basins, and rise in swells of tilled fields and orchard to some knoll, enthroning a porticoed home. Two years ago all these fields were quagmires, where stranded wheels and the carcasses of hybrids, looked as if a mud-geyser had opened near by. The grass has spread its covering, as the birds spread their leaves over the poor babes in the wood, and we walk we know not where, nor over what struggles, and shadows, and sorrows.

I pity the army mule, though he never asked me for sympathy. Who ever loved a mule? You can love a lion, and make him lick your hand : some people love parrots, and owls ; and I once knew a person who could catch black snakes and carry them lovingly in his bosom ; but I never knew a beloved mule. Yet this war has been fought and won by hybrids. They have pulled us out of ruts and fed us, and starved for us. The mule is the great quartermaster. See him and his brethren yonder in corral, — miserable veterans of no particular race, slab-sided, and capable of holding ink between their ribs. They mounch, and mounch, and wear the same stolid eye which you have seen under the driver's lash, and in the vaulting moment of victory. No stunning receptions greet them, no cheers and banquets when Muley comes marching home ; over at *Giesboro* they come in crippled, die by the musket without a murmur, and are immediately boiled down and forgotten.

I was once beaten by a rival correspondent upon a prominent battle, by riding a mule with my despatches. He walked into a mud-puddle just half way between the field and the post-office, and stopped there till morning.

Here we are, at Washington. I have been in most of the cities of Europe : some of them have dirty suburbs, but the first impression of the Capitol City is dreary in the extreme ; a number of the lost tribes have established booths contiguous to the terminus, wherein the filthiest people in the world eat the filthiest dishes ; a man's sense of cleanliness vanishes when he enters the District of Columbia. I have been astonished to remark how greatness loses its stature here. Mr. Charles Sumner is a handsome man on Broadway or Beacon Street, but eating dinner at Thompson's, his shoulders seem to narrow and his fine face to grow commonplace.

Above the squalid wideness of ungraded streets and the waste of shanties propped upon poles above abysses of vacant lots, where two drunken soldiers are pummelling

each other, towers the marvellous dome with its airy genius
firmly planted above, like the ruins of Palmyra above contemporary meanness.   Moving up the streets, in dust and
mud-puddle, you see shabbily ambitious churches, with
wooden towers ; hotels, the curbs whereof are speckled with
human blemishes, sustaining like hip-shotten caryatides the
sandstone-wooden columns.   Within there is a pandemo-
nium of legs in the air, and an agglomeration of saliva,
ending with an impertinent clerk and two crescents of lazy
waiters, who shy whisks, and are ambitious to run superflu-
ous errands, for the warrant to rob you.   Of people, you see
squads ; of residents, none.   The public edifices have not
picked their company, neither have the public functionaries.
There is a quantity of vulgar statuary lying around, horses
standing on their tails, and impossible Washingtons imbed-
ded in arm-chairs ; but the noble façade of the treasury
always suggests to me Couture's great picture of the Deca-
dence, where, under a pure colonnade, some tipplers are
carousing.   If we are to have statues at the Capital, let us
make them with uplifted hands, and shame upon their
grave, contemplative faces.

Shall we ever make Washington the representative Capital of the country ?

Certainly all efforts to improve the site worthy of the
seat of gigantic legislation have hitherto failed.   The sword
and the malaria have attacked it.   Every year sees the
President driven from his Mansion by pestilential vapors,
and the sanitary condition of the city is extraordinarily bad.
The carcasses of slain horses at Giesboro send their effluvia
straight into Washington on the wind, and the " Island,"
or that part of the city between the river and the canal, is
dangerous almost all the year.

Moreover, the entire river front of the city seems to be
untenable, except for negroes ; the Washington monument
stands on the yielding plain in the rear of the Chief Magistrate's, a stunted ruin, finding no foundation ; and much of

the great Capital reserve near by, would be a dead weight, if any effort were made to dispose of it, as building lots. The small portion of Washington lying upon Capitol Hill, is the most salubrious and covetable; but it is a lonesome journey by night around the Capitol grounds to the city. The finest residences lie north of the President's house, but the number of these grows apace, and the quantity of capital invested in private real estate, remains almost stationary.

We recall but two or three citizens of Washington who have spent their money on the spot where they have made it. Corcoran was the most generous; he erected a museum of art, and Government has made it a Commissary depot! But how few of the illustrious Senators, Chief Justices, Generals, etc., who draw their sustenance from the Capital, care a penny to decorate it? Compare the home of Governor Sprague on 6th Street, to his splendid mansion at Providence, or the Club House of the Secretary of State, to his place at Auburn. Washington has power, but it cannot attract. It is the solitary monarch, at whose feet all kneel, but by none beloved. Strangers repair to it, grow rich, and quit it with their earnings. Government works nobly to imitate the Palaces of the Cæsars, and the public edifices leave our municipal structures far beneath, but these marble and granite piles seem to mock the littleness of individual ambition. Two hotels have been built during the war, both of the caravansary class, but the city, for four years, has been miserably incompetent to entertain its guests, or to command their respect.

Washington, to be a city, lacks three elements, — commerce, representation, health; the environs are picturesque, and the new forts on the hill-tops little injure the landscape.

But the question is not premature, whether Washington city will ever answer the purposes of a stable seat of government, and reflect the enterprise, patriotism, and taste of the American people.

I have sometimes thought that these huge public build-ings, — now inadequate to accommodate the machinery of the Government, — would, at some future day, be the nucleus of a great *lycee*, and that Washington would become the Padua of the Republic, its University and Louvre, while legislation and administration, despairing of giving dignity to the place, would depart for a more congenial locality.

At any rate, the old Federal theory of a sylvan seat of government has failed.

For a sequestered and virtuous retreat of legislation, we have corruption augmented by dirt, and business stagnation aggravated by disease. There are virtues in the town ; but these must be searched for, and the vices are obvious.

CHAPTER XXIX.

FIVE FORKS.

I COMMENCE my account on the battle-field, but must soon make the long and lonely ride to Humphrey's Station, where I shall continue it.

I am sitting by Sheridan's camp-fire, on the spot he has just signalized by the most individual and complete victory of the war. All his veterans are around him, stooping by knots over the bright fagots, to talk together, or stretched upon the leaves of the forest, asleep, with the stains of powder yet upon their faces. There are dark masses of horses blackened into the gray background, and ambulances are creaking to and fro. I hear the sobs and howls of the weary, and note, afar off, among the pines, moving lights of burying parties, which are tumbling the slain into the trenches. A cowed and shivering silence has succeeded the late burst of drums, trumpets, and cannon ; the dead are at rest ; the captives are quiet ; the good cause has won again, and I shall try to tell you how.

Many months ago the Army of the Potomac stopped before Petersburg, driven out of its direct course to Richmond. It tried the Dutch Gap and the powder-ship, and shelled and shovelled till Sherman had cut five States in half, and only timid financiers, sutlers, and congressional excursionists paid the least attention to the armies on the James. We had fights without much purpose at our breast-works, and at Hatcher's Run, but the dashing achievements

(311)

of Sheridan in the Shenandoah Valley overtoppped all our dull infantry endeavors, and he shared with Sherman the entire applause of the country. No one knows but that behind these actors stood the invisible prompter, Grant; yet prompters, however assiduous, never divide applauses with the *dramatis personæ*; and, therefore, when Sheridan, the other day, by one of those slashing adventures which hold us breathless, appeared on the Pamunkey and crossed the peninsula to City Point, even the armies of the Potomac and James were agitated. The *personnel* of the man, not less than his renown, affected people. A very Punch of soldiers, a sort of Rip Van Winkle in regimentals, it astonished folks, that with so jolly and grotesque a guise, he held within him energies like lightning, the bolts of which had splintered the fairest parts of the border. But nobody credited General Sheridan with higher genius than activity; we expected to hear of him scouring the Carolina boundary, with the usual destruction of railways and mills, and therefore said at once that Sheridan would cut the great Southside road. But in this last chapter Sheridan must take rank as one of the finest military men of our century. The battle of "Five Forks" was, perhaps, the most ingeniously conceived and skilfully executed that we have ever had on this continent. It matches in secretiveness and shrewdness the cleverest efforts of Napoleon, and shows also much of that soldier's broadness of intellect and capacity for great occasions.

Sheridan had scarcely-time to change his horses' shoes before he was off, and after him much of our infantry also moved to the left. We passed our ancient breastworks at Hatcher's Run, and extended our lines southwestward till they touched Dinwiddie Court House, thirty miles from City Point. The Rebels fell back with but little skirmishing, until we faced northward and reached out toward their idolized Southside Railway; then they grew uneasy, and, as a hint of their opposition, fought us the sharp battle of

Quaker Road on Thursday. Still, we reached farther and farther, marvelling to find that, with his depleted army, Lee always overmatched us at every point of attack; but on Friday we quitted our intrenchments on the Boydtown plank-road, and made a bold push for the White Oak road. This is one of the series of parallel public ways running east and west, south of the Southside, the Vaughan road being the first, the Boydtown plank-road the second, and the old Court-House road the third. It became evident to the Rebels that we had two direct objects in view: the severing of their railway, and the occupation of the "Five Forks." The latter is a magnificent strategic point. Five good roads meet in the edge of a dry, high, well-watered forest, three of them radiating to the railway, and their tributaries unlocking all the country. Farther south, their defences had been paltry, but they fortified this empty solitude as if it had been their capital. Upon its principal road, the "White Oak," aforenamed, they had a ditched breastwork with embrasures of logs and earth, reaching east and west three miles, and this was covered eastward and southeastward by rifle-pits, masked works, and felled timber; the bridges approaching it were broken; all the roads picketed, and a desperate resolve to hold to it averred. This point of "Five Forks" may be as much as eight miles from Dinwiddie Court House, four from the Southside road, and eighteen from Humphrey's, the nearest of our military railway stations. A crooked stream called Gravelly Run, which, with Hatcher's, forms Rowanty Creek, and goes off to feed the Chowan in North Carolina, rises near "Five Forks," and gives the name of Gravelly Run Church to a little Methodist meeting-house, built in the forest a mile distant. That meeting-house is a hospital to-night, running blood, and at "Five Forks" a victor's battle-flags are flying.

The Fifth Army Corps of General Warren, has had all of the flank fighting of the week to do. It lost five or six

27

hundred men in its victory of Thursday, and on Friday rested along the Boydtown plank-road, at the house of one Butler, chiefly, which is about seven miles from Five Forks. On Friday morning, General Ayres took the advance with one of its three divisions, and marched three-quarters of a mile beyond the plank-road, through a woody country, following the road, but crossing the ubiquitous Gravelly Run, till he struck the enemy in strong force a mile and a half below White Oak road. They lay in the edge of a wood, with a thick curtain of timber in their front, a battery of field-pieces to the right, mounted in a bastioned earth-work, and on the left the woods drew near, encircling a little farm-land and negro-buildings. General Ayres's skirmish-line being fired upon, did not stand, but fell back upon his main column, which advanced at the order. Straightway the enemy charged headlong, while their battery opened a cross fire, and their skirmishers on our left, creeping down through the woods, picked us off in flank. They charged with a whole division, making their memorable yell, and soon doubled up Ayres's line of battle, so that it was forced in tolerable disorder back upon General Crawford, who commanded the next division. Crawford's men do not seem to have retrieved the character of their predecessors, but made a feint to go in, and, falling by dozens beneath the murderous fire, gave up the ground. Griffin's division, past which the fugitives ran, halted awhile before taking the doubtful way ; the whole corps was now back to the Boydtown plank-road, and nothing had been done to anybody's credit particularly.

General Griffin rode up to General Chamberlain in this extremity. Chamberlain is a young and anxious officer, who resigned the professorship of modern languages in Bowdoin College to embrace a soldier's career. He had been wounded the day before, but was zealous to try death again.

" Chamberlain," said Griffin, " can't you save the honor of the Fifth corps ? "

The young General formed his men at once, — they had tasted powder before, — the One Hundred and eighty-fifth New York and the One Hundred and ninety-eighth Pennsylvania. Down they went into the creek waist deep, up the slope and into the clearing, muskets to the left of them, muskets in front of them, cannon to the right of them ; but their pace was swift, like their resolve ; many of them were cut down, yet they kept ahead, and the Rebels, who seemed astonished at their own previous success, drew off and gave up the field. Almost two hours had elapsed between the loss and the recovery of the ground. The battle might be called Dabney's Farm, or more generally the fight of Gravelly Run. The brigades of Generals Bartlett and Gregory rendered material assistance in the pleasanter finale of the day. An order was soon after issued to hasten the burial of the dead and quit the spot, but Chamberlain petitioned for leave to charge the Rebel earthwork in the rear, and the enthusiasm of his brigade bore down General Warren's more prudent doubt. In brief, Griffin's division charged the fort, drove the Rebels out of it, and took position on the White Oak road, far east of Five Forks. While Griffin's division must be credited with this result, it may be said that their luck was due as much to the time as the manner of their appearance ; the Rebel divisions of Pickett and Bushrod Johnston were, in the main, by the time Griffin came up, on their way westward to attack Sheridan's cavalry. Ayres and Crawford had charged as one to four, but the forces were quite equalized when Chamberlain pushed on. The corps probably lost twelve hundred men. In this action, the Rebels, for the first time for many weeks exhibited all their traditional irresistibility and confidence. The merit of the affair, I am inclined to think, should be awarded to them ; but a terrible retribution remained for them in the succeeding day's decrees.

The ill success of the earlier efforts of Sheridan, show conclusively the insufficiency of ever so good cavalry to resist well organized and resolute infantry. Concentrating at Dinwiddie Court House, he proceeded to scour so much of the country that he almost baffled conjecture as to where his quarters really were. As many thousand cavalry as constitute his powerful force seem magnified, thus mounted and ever moving here and there, to an incredible number. The Court House, where he remained fittingly for a couple of days, is a cross-road's patch, numbering about twelve scattered buildings, with a delightful prospect on every side of sterile and monotonous pines. This is, I believe, the largest village in the district, though Dinwiddie stands fourth in population among Virginia counties. At present there is almost as great a population underground as the ancient county carried on its census. Indeed, one is perplexed at every point to know whence the South draws its prodigious armies. Some English officers have been visiting Dinwiddie during the week, and one of them said, curtly : "Blast the country ! it isn't worth such a row, you know. A very good' place to be exiled, to be sure, but what can you ever make of it ! "

This soulless Briton had never read any of the poems about the " boundless continent," and had no distinct conception of " size."

From Dinwiddie fields, Sheridan's men went galloping, by the aid of maps and cross-examination, into every by-road ; but it was soon apparent that the Rebel infantry meant to give them a push. This came about on Friday, with a foretaste on Thursday.

Little Five Forks, is a cross-road not far from Dinwiddie Court House in the direction of Petersburg. Big Five Forks, which, it must be borne in mind, gives name to the great battle of Saturday, is farther out by many miles, and does not lie within our lines. But, if the left of the army be at Dinwiddie, and the right at Petersburg, Little Five Forks will be first on the front line, though when Sheridan fought there, it was neutral ground, picketed but not possessed.

Very early in the week, when the Rebels became aware of
the extension of our lines, they added to the regular force
which encamped upon our flank line at least a division of
troops. These were directed to avoid an infantry fight, but
to seek out the cavalry, and, by getting it at disadvantage,
rid the region both of the harmfulness of Sheridan, and that
prestige of his name, so terrifying to the Virginia house-
wife. So long as Sheridan remained upon the far left, the
Southside road was unsafe, and the rapidity with which his
command could be transferred from point to point rendered
it a formidable balance of power. The Rebels knew the
country well, and the peculiar course of the highways gave
them every advantage. The cavalry of Sheridan's army
proper, is divided into two corps, commanded by Generals
Devin and Custer; the cavalry of the Potomac is commanded by General Crook; Mackenzie has control of the
cavalry of the James. On Friday, these were under separate orders, and the result was confusion. The infantry
was beaten at Gravelly Run, and the cavalry met in flank
and front by overwhelming numbers, executed some movements not laid down in the manual. The centre of the
battle was Little Five Forks, though the Rebels struck us
closer to Dinwiddie Court House, and drove us pell mell up
the road into the woods, and out the old Court House road
to Gravelly Run. We rallied several times, and charged
them into the woods, but they lay concealed in copses, and
could go where sabres were useless. The plan of this battle-
field will show a series of irregular advances to puzzle anybody but a cavalry-man. The full division of Bushrod
Johnston and General Pickett, were developed against us,
with spare brigades from other corps. Our cavalry loss
during the day was eight hundred in killed and wounded;
but we pushed the Rebels so hard that they gave us the
field, falling back toward Big Five Forks, and we intrenched
immediately. Two thousand men comprise our losses of

27*

Friday in Warren's corps and Sheridan's command, including many valuable officers. We shall see how, under a single guidance, splendid results were next day obtained with half the sacrifice.

On Friday night General Grant, dissatisfied, like most observers, with the day's business, placed General Sheridan in the supreme command of the whole of Warren's corps and all the cavalry. General Warren reported to him at nightfall, and the little army was thus composed : —

General Sheridan's Forces, Saturday April 1, 1865.

Three divisions of infantry, under Generals Griffin, Ayres, and Crawford.

Two divisions of cavalry, formerly constituting the Army of the Shenandoah, now commanded by General Merritt, under Generals Devin and Custer.

One division cavalry of the Army of the Potomac, under General Crook.

Brigade or more cavalry Army of the James, under General Mackenzie.

In this composition the infantry was to the cavalry in the proportion of about two to one, and the entire force a considerable army, far up in the teens. Sheridan was absolute, and his oddly-shaped body began to bob up and down straightway ; he visited every part of his line, though it stretched from Dinwiddie Court House to the Quaker road, along the Boydtown Plank and its adjuncts. At daybreak on Saturday he fired four signal-guns, to admonish Warren he was off ; and his cavalry, by diverging roads, struck their camps. Just south of Culpepper is a certain Stony creek, the tributaries to which wind northward and control the roads. Over Stony creek went Crook, making the longest detour. Custer took a bottom called Chamberlain's bed ; and Devin advanced from Little Five Forks, the whole driving the Rebels toward the left of their works on White Oak road.

We must start with the supposition that our own men far

outnumbered the Rebels. The latter were widely separated from their comrades before Petersburg, and the adjustment of our infantry as well as the great movable force at Sheridan's disposal, renders it doubtful that they could have returned. At any rate they did not do so, whether from choice or necessity, and it was a part of our scheme to push them back into their entrenchments. This work was delegated to the cavalry entirely, but, as I have said before, mounted carbineers, are no match for stubborn, bayoneted infantry. So when the horsemen were close up to the Rebels, they were dismounted, and acted as infantry to all intents. A portion of them, under Gregg and Mackenzie, still adhered to the saddle, that they might be put in rapid motion for flanking and charging purposes; but fully five thousand indurated men, who had seen service in the Shenandoah and elsewhere, were formed in line of battle on foot, and by charge and deploy essayed the difficult work of pressing back the entire Rebel column. This they were to do so evenly and ingeniously, that the Rebels should go no farther than their works, either to escape eastward or to discover the whereabouts of Warren's forces, which were already forming. Had they espied the latter they might have become so discouraged as to break and take to the woods; and Sheridan's object was to capture them as well as to rout them. So, all the afternoon, the cavalry pushed them hard, and the strife went on uninterruptedly and terrifically. I have no space in this hurried despatch to advert either to individual losses or to the many thrilling episodes of the fight. It was fought at so close quarters that our carbines were never out of range; for had this been otherwise, the long rifles of the enemy would have given them every advantage. With their horses within call, the cavalry-men, in line of battle, stood together like walls of stone, swelling onward like those gradually elevating ridges of which Lyell speaks. Now and then a detachment of Rebels would charge down upon us, swaying the lines and threatening to annihilate us ; for at no part of the action, till its crisis, did the Southern men exhibit either doubt or dismay, but fought up to the standard of the most valiant treason the world has ever had, and here and there showing some of those wonderful feats of individual courage which are the miracles of the time.

A colonel with a shattered regiment came down upon us in a charge. The bayonets were fixed ; the men came on with a yell ; their gray uniforms seemed black amidst the smoke ; their preserved colors, torn by grape and ball, waved yet defiantly ; twice they halted, and poured in volleys, but came on again like the surge from the fog, depleted, but determined ; yet, in the hot faces of the carbineers, they read a purpose as resolute, but more calm, and, while they pressed along, swept all the while by scathing volleys, a group of horsemen took them in flank. It was an awful instant ; the horses recoiled ; the charging column trembled like a single thing, but at once the Rebels, with rare organization, fell into a hollow square, and with solid sheets of steel defied our centaurs. The horsemen rode around them in vain ; no charge could break the shining squares, until our dismounted carbineers poured in their volleys afresh, making gaps in the spent ranks, and then in their wavering time the cavalry thundered down. The Rebels could stand no more ; they reeled and swayed, and fell back broken and beaten. And on the ground their colonel lay, sealing his devotion with his life.

Through wood and brake and swamp, across field and trench, we pushed the fighting defenders steadily. For a part of the time, Sheridan himself was there, short and broad, and active, waving his hat, giving orders, seldom out of fire, but never stationary, and close by fell the long yellow locks of Custer, sabre extended, fighting like a Viking, though he was worn and haggard with much work. At four o'clock the Rebels were behind their wooden walls at Five Forks, and still the cavalry pressed them hard, in feint rather than solemn effort, while a battalion dismounted, charged squarely upon the face of their breastworks which lay in the main on the north side of the White Oak road. Then, while the cavalry worked round toward the rear, the infantry of Warren, though commanded by Sheridan, prepared to take part in the battle.

The genius of Sheridan's movement lay in his disposition of the infantry. The skill with which he arranged it, and the difficult manœuvres he projected and so well executed, should place him as high in infantry tactics as he has heretofore shown himself superior in cavalry. The infantry which had marched at 2½ P. M. from the house of Boisseau, on the Boydtown plank-road, was drawn up in four battle lines, a mile or more in length, and in the beginning facing the White Oak road obliquely ; the left or pivot was the division of General Ayres, Crawford had the center and Griffin the right. These advanced from the Boydtown plank-road, at ten o'clock, while Sheridan was thundering away with the cavalry, mounted and dismounted, and deluding the Rebels with the idea that he was the sole attacking party ; they lay concealed in the woods behind the Gravelly Run meeting-house, but their left was not a half-mile distant from the Rebel works, though their right reached so far off that a novice would have criticized the position sharply. Little by little, Sheridan, extending his lines, drove the whole Rebel force into their breastworks ; then he dismounted the mass of his cavalry and charged the works straight in the front, still thundering on their flank. At last, every Rebel was safe behind his intrenchments. Then the signal was given, and the concealed infantry, many thousand strong, sprang up and advanced by echelon to the right. Imagine a great barndoor shutting to, and you have the movement, if you can also imagine the door itself, hinge and all, moving forward also. This was the door : —

AYRES —— CRAWFORD —— GRIFFIN.

Stick a pin through Ayres and turn Griffin and Crawford

forward as you would a spoke in a wheel, but move your
pin up also a very little.   In this way Ayres will advance,
say half a mile, and Griffin, to describe a quarter revolution,
will move through a radius of four miles.   But to compli-
cate this movement by echelon, we must imagine the right
when half way advanced cutting across the centre and re-
forming, while Crawford became the right and Griffin the
middle of the line of battle.   Warren was with Crawford on
this march.   Gregory commanded the skirmishers.   Ayres
was so close to the Rebel left that he might be said to hinge
upon it; and at 6 o'clock the whole corps column came
crash upon the full flank of the astonished Rebels.   Now
came the pitch of the battle.

We were already on the Rebel right in force, and thinly
in their rear.   Our carbineers were making feint to charge in
direct front, and our infantry, four deep, hemmed in their
entire left.   All this they did not for an instant note, so
thorough was their confusion; but seeing it directly, they, so
far from giving up, concentrated all their energy and fought
like fiends.   They had a battery in position, which belched
incessantly, and over the breastworks their musketry made
one unbroken roll, while against Sheridan's prowlers on
their left, by skirmish and sortie, they stuck to their sinking
fortunes, so as to win unwilling applause from mouths of
wisest censure.

It was just at the coming up of the infantry that Sheridan's little band was pushed the hardest.   At one time,
indeed, they seemed about to undergo extermination; not
that they wavered, but that they were so vastly overpowered.   It will remain to the latest time a matter of
marvel that so paltry a cavalry force could press back sixteen thousand infantry; but when the infantry blew like a
great barndoor — the simile best applicable — upon the
enemy's left, the victory that was to come had passed the
region of strategy and resolved to an affair of personal
courage.   We had met the enemy; were they to be ours?

To expedite this consummation every officer fought as if he were the forlorn hope. Mounted on his black pony, the same which he rode at Winchester, Sheridan galloped everywhere, his flushed face all the redder, and his plethoric, but nervous figure all the more ubiquitous. He galloped once straight down the Rebel front, with but a handful of his staff. A dozen bullets whistled for him together ; one grazed his arm, at which a faithful orderly rode ; the black pony leaped high, in fright, and Sheridan was untouched, but the orderly lay dead in the field, and the saddle dashed afar empty. General Warren rode with Crawford most of the afternoon, mounted likewise, and making two or three narrow escapes. He was dark, dashing, and individual as ever, but for some reason or other was relieved of his command after the battle, and Griffin was instated in his place. General Sheridan ordered Warren to report to General Grant's head-quarters, sending the order by an aid. Warren, on his own hook, did not meet on Friday with his general success, and on Saturday Sheridan was the master-spirit ; but Warren is a General as well as a gentleman, and is only overshadowed by a greater genius, — not obliterated. Ayres, accounted the best soldier in the Fifth corps, but too quietly modest for his own favor, fought like a lion in this pitch of battle, making all the faint-hearted around him ashamed to do ill with such an example contiguous. General Bartlett, keen-faced and active like a fiery scimitar, was leading his division as if he were an immortal ! He was closest at hand in the most gallant episodes, and held at nightfall a bundle of captured battle-flags. But Griffin, tall and slight, was the master-genius of the Fifth corps, to which by right he has temporarily succeeded. He led the charge on the flank, and was the first to mount the parapet with his horse, riding over the gunners as May did at Cerro Gordo, and cutting them down. Bartlett's brigade, behind him, finished the business, and the last cannon was fired for the day against the conquering Federals. General Crawford fulfilled his full share of duties throughout the day, amply sustained by such splendid brigade commanders as Baxter, Coulter, and Kellogg, while Gwin and Boweryman were at hand in the division of General Ayres; not to omit the fallen Winthrop, who died to save a friend and win a new laurel. What shall I say for Chamberlain, who, beyond all question, is the first of our brigade commanders, having been the hero of both Quaker Road and Gravelly Run, and in this action of Five Forks making the air ring with the applauding huzzas of his soldiers, who love him? His is one of the names that will survive the common wreck of shoulder-straps after the war.

But I am individualizing; the fight, as we closed upon the Rebels, was singularly free from great losses on our side, though desperate as any contest ever fought on the continent. One prolonged roar of rifle shook the afternoon; we carried no artillery, and the Rebel battery, until its capture, raked us like an irrepressible demon, and at every foot of the intrenchments a true man fought both in front and behind. The birds of the forest fled afar; the smoke ascended to heaven; locked in so mad frenzy, none saw the sequel of the closing day. Now Richmond rocked in her high towers to watch the impending issue, but soon the day began to look gray, and a pale moon came tremulously out to watch the meeting squadrons. Imagine along a line of a full mile, thirty thousand men struggling for life and prestige; the woods gathering about them — but yesterday the home of hermit hawks and chipmonks — now ablaze with bursting shells, and showing in the dusk the curl of flames in the tangled grass, and, rising up the boles of the pine trees, the scaling, scorching tongues. Seven hours this terrible spectacle had been enacted, but the finale of it had almost come.

It was by all accounts in this hour of victory when the modest and brave General Winthrop of the first brigade, Ayres division, was mortally wounded. He was riding along the breastworks, and in the act as I am assured, of saving a friend's life, was shot through to the left lung. He fell at once, and his men, who loved him, gathered around and took him tenderly to the rear, where he died before the stretcher on which he lay could be deposited beside the meeting-house door.   On the way from the field to the hospital he wandered in mind at times, crying out, "Captain Weaver how is that line?   Has the attack succeeded?" etc.   When he had been resuscitated for a pause he said: "Doctor, I am done for." His last words were : "Straighten the line !"   And he died peacefully.   He was a cousin of Major Winthrop, the author of "Cecil Dreeme."   He was twenty-seven years of age.   I had talked with him before going into action, as he sat at the side of General Ayres, and was permitted by the guard of honor to uncover his face and look upon it.   He was pale and beautiful, marble rather than corpse, and the uniform cut away from his bosom showed how white and fresh was the body, so pulseless now.

General Griffin said to me : "This victory is not worth Winthrop's life."

Winthrop went into the service as a simple color-bearer. He died a brevet brigadier.

At seven o'clock the Rebels came to the conclusion that they were outflanked and whipped,   They had been so busily engaged that they were a long time finding out how desperate were their circumstances; but now, wearied with persistent assaults in front, they fell back to the left, only to see four close lines of battle waiting to drive them across the field, decimated.   At the right the horsemen charged them in their vain attempt to fight "out," and in the rear straggling foot and cavalry began also to assemble ; slant fire cross fire, and direct fire, by file and volley rolled in perpetually, cutting down their bravest officers and strewing the fields with bleeding men ; groans resounded in the intervals

28

of exploding powder, and to add to their terror and despair, their own artillery, captured from them, threw into their own ranks, from its old position, ungrateful grape and canister, enfilading their breastworks, whizzing and plunging by air line and ricochet, and at last bodies of cavalry fairly mounted their intrenchments, and charged down the parapet, slashing and trampling them, and producing inexplicable confusion. They had no commanders, at least no orders, and looked in vain for some guiding hand to lead them out of a toil into which they had fallen so bravely and so blindly. A few more volleys, a new and irresistible charge, a shrill and warning command to die or surrender, and, with a sullen and tearful impulse, five thousand muskets are flung upon the ground, and five thousand hot, exhausted, and impotent men are Sheridan's prisoners of war.

Acting with his usual decision, Sheridan placed his captives in care of a provost-guard, and sent them at once to the rear. Those which escaped, he ordered the fiery Custer to pursue with brand and vengeance ; and they were pressed far into the desolate forest, spent and hungry, many falling by the way of wounds or exhaustion, many pressed down by hoof or sabre-stroke, and many picked up in mercy and sent back to rejoin their brethren in bonds. We captured in all fully six thousand prisoners. General Sheridan estimated them modestly at five thousand, but the provost-marshal assured me that he had a line four abreast a full mile long. I entirely bear him out, having ridden for forty minutes in a direction opposite to that they were taking, and growing weary at last of counting or of seeing them. They were fine, hearty fellows, almost all Virginians, and seemed to take their capture not unkindly. They wore the gray and not very attractive uniform of the Confederacy, but looked to be warm and fat, and passing along in the night, under the fir-trees, conveyed at most a romantic idea of grief and tribulation. They were put in a huge pen, midway between Big and Little Five Forks, for the night, the officers sharing the same fare with the soldiers, from whom, indeed, they were undistinguishable.

Thus ended the splendid victory of Five Forks, the least bloody to us, but the most successful, proportionate to numbers engaged, that has been fought during the war. One man out of every three engaged took a prisoner. We captured four cannon, an ambulance train and baggage-teams, eight thousand muskets, and twenty-eight battle-flags. General Longstreet, it is thought, commanded. Neither he nor Pickett nor Bushrod Johnston, division commanders, were taken; they were wise enough to see that the day was lost, and imitated Bonaparte after Waterloo.

I attribute this victory almost entirely to Sheridan; it was won by strategy and persistence, and in great part by men who would not stand fire the day before. The happy distribution of duties between cavalry and infantry excited a fine rivalry, and the consciousness of Sheridan's guidance inspired confidence. Has any battle so successful ever been fought in Virginia? or, indeed, in the East? I think not. It has opened to us the enemy's flank, so that we can sweep down upon the Appomattox and inside of his breastworks, enabling us to shorten our lines of intrenchments one half, if no more, and putting out of Lee's service fifteen thousand of his choicest troops. And all this, General Sheridan tells me, has cost him personally no more than eight hundred men, and the service no more than fifteen hundred. Compare this with Chancellorsville, Williamsburg, the Wilderness, Bull Run, and what shall we say? The enemy must have lost in this fight three thousand in killed and wounded.

The scene at Gravelly Run meeting-house at 8 and at 10 o'clock on Saturday night, is one of the solemn contrasts of the war, and, I hope, the last of them. A little frame church, planted among the pines, and painted white, with cool, green window-shutters, holds at its foot a gallery for the negroes, and at the head a varnished pulpit. I found its pews moved to the green plain over the threshold, and on its bare floors the screaming wounded. Blood ran in little rills across the planks, and, human feet treading in them, had made indelible prints in every direction; the pulpit-lamps were doing duty, not to shed holy light upon holy pages, but to show the pale and dusty faces of the beseeching; and as they moved in and out, the groans and curses of the suffering replace the gush of peaceful hymns and the deep responses to the preacher's prayers. Federal and Confederate lay together, the bitterness of noon assuaged in the common tribulation of the night, and all the while came in the dripping stretchers, to place in this golgotha new recruits for death and sorrow. I asked the name of the church, but no one knew any more than if it had been the site of some obsolete heathen worship. At last, a grinning sergeant smacked his thumbs as if the first idea of his life had occurred to him, and led me to the pulpit. Beneath some torn blankets and rent officers' garments, rested the hymn book and Bible, which he produced. Last Sunday these doled out the praises of God, and the frightened congregation worshipped at their dictation. Now they only served by their fly leaves to give me my whereabouts, and said : —

Presented to Gravelly Run Meeting House by the Ladies.

Over the portal, the scenes within were reiterated, except that the greatness of a starry night replaced the close and terrible arena of the church. Beneath the trees, where the Methodist circuit-rider had tied his horse, and the urchins, during class-meeting, had wandered away to cast stones at the squirrels, and measure strength at vaulting and running, the gashed and fevered lay irregularly, some soul going out at each whiff of the breeze in the fir-tops; and the teams and surgeons, and straggling soldiers, and galloping orderlies passed all the night beneath the old and gibbous moon and the hushed stars, and by the trickle of Gravelly Run stealing off, afeared. But the wounded had no thought that night; the victory absorbed all hearts; we had no losses to notice where so much was won.

A mile past the church, going away from head-quarters all the time, lies Five Forks, the object and name of the battle. A large open field of perhaps thirty acres, interposes between the church and the commencement of the Rebel works. Their left is only some rails and logs to mask marksmen, but the work proper is a very long stretch of all obstructions of a man's height in relief.

The White Oak road runs directly in front of these intrenchments, and was, at the time I passed, the general highway for infantry returning from the field and cavalrymen concentrating at General Sheridan's bivouac. Riding a mile I came upon the Five Forks proper, and just to the left, at the foot of some pines, the victor and his assistants were congregated. Sheridan sat by some fagots, examining a topographical map of the country he had so well traversed; possibly with a view to design further aggressive movements in the morning. He is opposite me now as I pen these paragraphs by the imperfect blaze of his bivouac fire. He is good humored and talkative, like all men conscious of having achieved a great work, and has been good enough to sketch for me the plan of the day's operations, from which I have compiled much of the statement above. Close by lies Custer, trying to sleep, his long yellow hair covering his face; and General Griffin, now commanding the Fifth corps, goes here and there issuing orders, while aides and orderlies rode in and out, bearing further fresh messages of deeds consummated or proposed. We shall have a hot night no doubt, for away off to the right, continue volleys of musketry and discharges of artillery, intermixed with what seem to be thunderbolts of our men-of-war at anchor in the Appomatox and James, — if such can be heard at this great distance, — which tell us that the lines are in motion.

28*

CHAPTER XXX.

RICHMOND DESOLATE.

THE scenes of entering the doomed stronghold, when Grant had burst its gates, ought to be made vivid as the spectacle of death. With my good and talented associate, Mr. Jerome B. Stillson, I hold the Spotswood Hotel, and from this caravansary of the late capital as thoroughly identified with Rebellion as the inn at Bethlehem with the gospel, we date our joint paragraphs upon the condition of the city. A week cannot have exhausted the curiosity of the North to learn the exact appearance of a city which has stood longer, more frequent, and more persistent sieges, than any in Christendom. This town is the Rebellion; it is all that we have directly striven for; quitting it, the Confederate leaders have quitted their sheet-anchor, their roof-tree, their abiding hope. Its history is the epitome of the whole contest, and to us, shivering our thunderbolts against it for more that four years, Richmond is still a mystery.

Know then, that, whether coming from Washington or Baltimore, the two points of embarkation, all bound hitherward must rendezvous at Fortress Monroe; thence, in such excellent steamers as the *Dictator*, start up the broad James River. To own a country-house upon the "Jeems" river is the Virginia gentleman's ultimate aspiration. There, with a tobacco-farm, and wide wheatlands, his feet on his front-porch rails, a Havana cigar between his teeth, and a colored person to bring him frequent juleps, the Virginia gentleman, confident in the divinity of slavery, hopes in his natural, refined idleness, to watch the little family grave-yard close up to his threshold, till it shall kindly open and give him sepulture.

Elsewhere men aim to be successful, or enterprising, or eloquent, or scholarly, but that nobleness of hospitality, high spirit, dignity, and affability which constitute our idea of chivalry is everywhere save here an exotic. We say that chivalry is "played out," and that the prestige of "first families" is gone with the hurried retreat before Grant's salamanders. Not so. Secession as a cause is past the range of possibilities. But no people in their subjugation wear a better front than these brave old spirits, whose lives are not their own. Fire has ravaged their beautiful city, soldiers of the color of their servants, guard the crossings and pace the pavement with bayoneted muskets. But gentlemen they are still, in every pace, and inch, and sylla-ble, — such men as we were wont to call brothers and countrymen. However, the James River, at which we commenced, has not a town upon it between the sea and the head of navigation. It is a strong commentary upon this patriarchal civilization, judged by our gregarious tastes, that one of the noblest streams in the world should show to the traveller only here and there a pleasant mansion, flanked by negro cabins, but nowhere a church-spire nor a steam-mill. All that we see from Fortress Monroe to City Point are ridges of breastworks, rifle-pits, and forts, lying bare, yellow, and deserted, to defend its passage, excepting at James Island, where the solitary and broken tower of the ancient colony holds guard over some bramble and ruin. Here Smith founded the celebrated settlement, which wooed to its threshold the gentle Pocahontas, and fell to fragments at the behest of the fiery Bacon. The ramparts on the James will remain forever ; great as they are, they would hardly hold the bones of the slain in the capture and defence.

Four hours from Fortress Monroe we pass Harrison's Landing, where two grand armies, *beaten* aside from Richmond, sought the shelter of the river, and at City Point quit our large craft, to be transferred to a light draught vessel, which is to carry the first mail going to Richmond under the national flag since the beginning of the war.

City Point is still a populous place, and the millions of mules upon it bray hoarsely; but we leave all these behind, as well as the national standard, which flaunts over General Grant's late head-quarters, and steam past the mouth of the Appomattox to go through the enemy's lines.

Henceforward every foot of the way is freshly interesting. The Rebel ram *Atlanta* in tow of a couple of tugs, goes past us with a torpedo boat at the rear. She is raking, slant, and formidable; but "old glory" is waving on her. Directly our own leviathan, the *Roanoke* drifts up, and all her storm-throated tars cheer like the belch of her guns. We see to the right, the tip of Malvern Hill, ever sorrowful and sacred, and soon a great unfinished ram careens by, which never grew to battle-size; the true colors shine above her bulwarks like a flower growing in a carcass. Then at little intervals there are frequent prizes from the docks of Richmond, tugs, transports, barges, some of which show under our beautiful banner the Rebel cross, pale and contemptible. These malcontents committed as great crime against good taste in substituting for our starry emblem this artistic abomination, as against law and policy in changing the configuration of the Union. There is another flag, however, which we see, half exultantly, half vindictively, — the cross of St. George, — flying from a British cutter.

By and by we come to our intrenchments upon the upper James and at Bermuda Hundred. Now they are very listless and half empty. The boys have gone off to tread on Lee's shanks. Only a few vessels stand at the landings, and the few remnants have laid down the rifle, and taken up the fishing-pole. One should come up this river to get a conception of our splendid navy. Sharp-pointed gun-boats, with bullet-proof crows' nests and swivels that are the gentlest murderers ever polished ; monitors through whose eyeholes a ball a big as a cook-stove squints from a columbiad socket ; ferry-boats which are speckled with brass cannon, and all sorts of craft that can float and manœuvre, provided they look at us through deadly muzzles are there to the number of fifty or sixty, as many as make the entire navies of all other American nations. After the war we must have a great naval review, and invite all the crowned heads to attend it. Soon we reach Dutch Gap, where lies Butler's canal, or " Butler's gut," as the sailors call it. The river at this point is so crooked that Butler must have laid it out by the aid of his wrong eye. The canal is meant to cut on a long elbow ; but being almost at right angles to the course of the river, only the most obliging tide would run through it. As a consequence, it is a sort of a sluice merely, of insufficient width, and as a " sight " very disappointing to great expectations. Between the points of debouch of this canal crosses a drawbridge of pontoons, for the use of our troops, and just beyond it Aiken's Landing, where the flag of truce boat stopped. A fine brick mansion stands in shore, with a wharf abreast it. The banks around it are trodden here with many feet. These are the traces of the poor prisoners who reached here, fevered, and starving and naked, to catch for the first time the sight of cool waters and friends, and the bright flag which they had followed to the edge of the grave. How they threw up their hats, and cheered to the feeblest, and wept, and danced, and laughed. Long be the place remembered, as holy, neutral ground, where death never trod, and multitudes passed from suffering, to freedom and home. Beyond this point, the most formidable Rebel works we have seen, line the high bluffs and ridges. They are monuments of patient labor, and make of themselves hills as great as nature's. But the siege pieces, which often bellowed upon them like thunderbolts along the mountain-tops, are gone now, and only straggling, meddling fellows pass them at all. The highest of these works commands both ends of the Dutch Gap-canal, and while our lads were digging they often hid themselves in caves which they dug in the cliff-sides.

We reach the first torpedo at length; a little red flag marks it, by which the boat slips tremulously, though another and another are before, at the sight of which our nervous folks are agitated. Here is a monitor with a drag behind it, which has just fished up one; and the sequel is told by a bloody and motionless figure upon the deck. These torpedoes are the true dragon teeth of Cadmus, which spring up armed men.

Happily for us, the Rebels have sown but few of them, and the position of these was pointed out by one of their captains who deserted to our side. In the midst of these lie the obstructions. Great hulks of vessels and chained spars, and tree-tops which reach quite across the river, except where our pioneers have hewn a little gap to let the steamer through. Upon these obstructions a hundred cannon bear from the cliffs before us, and as we go further we see the whole river-bed sprinkled with strange contrivances to keep back our thunder-bearers. We think it absolutely impossible, under any circumstances, that our fleet could have got to Richmond so long as the Rebels contested the passage; each step forward finds new and greater obstacles. The channel is as narrow as Harlem River and as crooked as a walk in the ramble of Central Park. Each elbow of the stream is muscular with snag and snare wherever the swift stream swoops around abruptly. Jagged abatis, driven piles, and artificial lumber, bar the way before us. To the right of us, to the left of us, behind us, stand up the bare parapets, crowned with airy lookout towers, where, at the coming of a nautilus, the whole horizon and foreground would rain crossfires of shell and iron bolts, to sweep into annihilation the tiniest or the staunchest opposition from the earth's surface, and under the earth and above the earth death waited to leap up and draw the daring to its bosom.   Not one, nor two, nor three lines of defences frowned down as we cautiously steamed along, but every precipice was bristling with defiance, as if the deep subterranean fires underlying our race had burst here fitfully and frequently, heaving up the swells of the hills till they lay hard and barren for human ingenuity to garnish them with anxious artillery.   All along were the deep funnel-shaped cases of the torpedoes just disentombed.   But at nightfall Drury's Bluff flitted by like the battlemented wall of a city, and then we saw no more.

The band that greeted us from a distance stops playing as the boat nears the wharf.

There is a stillness, in the midst of which Richmond, with her ruins, her spectral roof, afar, and her unchanging spires, rests beneath a ghastly, fitful glare,— the night stain which a great conflagration leaves behind it for weeks,— struggling silently with colossal shadows along the foreground, two hideous walls alone arise in front, shutting these gleams. They are the Libby Prison and Castle Thunder.   Right and left, and far in the moonlighted perspective beyond, there is a soft glitter upon cornices and domes.   A haggard glow of candles, faintly defines the thoroughfares that have not suffered ruin ; while massive, and upon a height overlooking all, stands the Capitol, flying its black shadow from the sinking moon across a hundred crumbling walls, until its edges touch the windows of the Libby.

But over its massive roof, dimly seen through the mists of the river, and, as before, " through the mists of the deep," the banner of the Union, banished for four years, is shaken out again, broad and beautiful, by the breath of an April night.   Upon the face of every leaning figure on the steamer's deck, in sight of that radiant signal, is the same half-melancholy, half-triumphant smile.

The thought of the battle which has passed, of the army,

which, after struggling through years for this majestic procession, has swept by and beyond without the view for which its straining eyes have yearned, is sad and strange. There comes back dimly suggestive, a story of Iran and his host, thundering at the gates of Tupelo, for the possession of a wondrous jewel, and awakening once upon a dawn to learn that Tupelo was an empty casket,— to turn back longing, "wondering eyes upon the city, and to hunt the fleeing prize afar." Yet unto those legions of the republic which have emptied Richmond of a prize which yet they may have easily clutched, there go out reverence and blessing even larger than might be bestowed upon them resting in camp, upon these overlooking hills. That true allegiance, that calm and stern self-sacrifice which impels an army forward past the sweet applauses and rewarding calms to which great victories might entitle it, are the purest sources of its glory and its fame. God bless the army that has permitted us to consummate this journey and to gaze upon this spectacle, while it does not impress us too proudly, too triumphantly. Both pride and triumph have, of course, a place in the tumultuous feeling that surges through the hearts of all ; yet as in every true man is born an instinct of compassion for a fallen foe, we prefer that the shout should go up in honor of our victory alone, and not because these have suffered.

The boat touches the shore at Rockett's, the foot of Richmond. A few minutes' walk and we tread the pavements of the capital. There are no noisy and no beseeching runners ; there is no sound of life, but the stillness of a catacomb, only as our footsteps fall dull on the deserted sidewalk, and a funeral troop of echoes bump their elfin heads against the dead walls and closed shutters in reply, and this is Richmond. Says a melancholy voice : " And this is Richmond."

We are under the shadow of ruins. From the pavements where we walk far off into the gradual curtain of the night, stretches a vista of desolation.   The hundreds of fabrics, the millions of wealth, that crumbled less than a week ago beneath one fiery kiss, here topple and moulder into rest. A white smoke-wreath rising occasionally, enwraps a shattered wall as in a shroud.   A gleam of flame shoots a grotesque picture of broken arches and ragged chimneys into the brain.   Huge piles of debris begin to encumber the sidewalks, and even the pavements, as we go on.   The streets in some places are quite choked up from walking. We are among the ruins of half a city.   The wreck, the loneliness, seem interminable.   The memory of lights in houses above, beheld while upon the steamer, alone keeps despondency from a victory over hope ; and although the continued existence of the Spottswood Hotel is vouched for by authority, my lodge in such a wilderness seems next to impossible.   Away to the right, above the waste of blackened walls, around the phantom-looking flag upon the capitol, — the only sign betwixt heaven and earth, or upon the earth, that Richmond is not wholly deserted, — beyond and out of the ruins, we walk past one of two open doorways where the moon serves as candle to a group of talking negroes.   The gas works, injured by fire, are not working, and "ile" has not been struck in the Confederacy. Not a white man appears until we reach the Spottswood, — there before the entrance is a conclave of officers, — then, at last, entering, we stand in that most famous of Southern hotels, the interior of which is filled with the very aroma of the Rebellion.   A thankful yielding up of carpet-bags and valises to the indignant negro waiters, and then a brief moonlight stroll toward the capitol.

Within the gates of the Square, that swing on their hinges silent as the hour we pass alone, before us stands the magnificent monument crowned with Crawford's equestrian statue of Washington.   The right hand of the rider, lifted against the sky, points a prophetic finger toward the southwest.   Dark, and motionless, and grand, it is the one

29

symbol belonging solely to the Union, which they have not dared to desecrate; which they have strangely chosen to consider neither as an insult nor a rebuke.

Gazing beyond at the capitol itself, and back again at the figure which overlooks the building, it is not hard to imagine that, while the noisy debates of a congress of traitors to the Union that he founded were in progress, those bronze lips sometimes smiled in scorn.

Leaving Richmond proper, and descending into the low, squalid portion of the town known as Rocketts, one sees among the many large warehouses, used without exception for the storage of tobacco, a certain one more irregular than the rest. An archway leads into it, and upon the outside of the second story windows runs a long ledge or footway, whereupon sentries used to stride, guarding the miserable people within. This is the jail of Castle Thunder, and it was the civil or State prison of the capital. Ill as were the accommodations of prisoners of war, the treatment of their own unoffending citizens by the Rebel government was ten times more infamous. We could not repress indignation, nor by any philosophic or charitable effort excuse the atrocious tyranny which here lashed, chained, handcuffed, tortured, shot, and hung, hundreds of people whom it could not stultify or impress. We may grant that the Confederacy had become a government; that, in its perilous incipiency, it had apology for severity and rigor with all malcontents; that, in its own struggle for death or life, it might, in self-defence, absorb all private liberty; but even thus the terrible testimony of this Castle Thunder is an everlasting stigma upon the Southern cause. We entered its strong portal, and there in the new commandant's room lay the record left behind by the Confederates. Its pages made one shudder.

These are some of the entries : —

" George Barton, — giving food to Federal prisoners of

war ; forty lashes upon the bare back. Approved. Sentence carried into effect July 2.

"Peter B. Innis, — passing forged government notes ; chain and ball for twelve months ; forty lashes a day. Approved.

"Arthur Wright, — attempting to desert to the enemy ; sentenced to be shot. Approved. Carried into effect, March 26.

"John Morton, — communicating with the enemy ; to be hung. Approved. Carried into effect, March 26."

In an inner room are some fifty pairs of balls and chains, with anklets and handcuffs upon them, which have bent the spirit and body of many a resisting heart. Within are two condemned cells, perfectly dark, — a faded flap over the window peep-hole, — the smell from which would knock a strong man down.

For in their centre lies the sink, ever open, and the floors are sappy with uncleanliness. To the right of these, a door leads to a walled yard not forty feet long, nor fifteen wide, overlooked by the barred windows of the main prison rooms, and by sentry boxes upon the wall-top. Here the wretched were shot and hung in sight of their trembling comrades. The brick wall at the foot of the yard is scarred and crushed by balls and bullets which first passed through some human heart and wrote here their damning testimony. The gallows had been suspended from a wing in the ledge, and in mid-air the impotent captive swung, none daring or willing to say a good word for him ; and not for any offence against God's law, not for wronging his neighbor, or shedding blood, or making his kind miserable, but for standing in the way of an upstart organization, which his impulse and his judgment alike impelled him to oppose. This little yard, bullet-marked, close, and shut from all sympathy, is to us the ghastliest spot in the world. Can Mr. Davis visit it, and pray as he does so devoutly afterward? When men plead the justice of the South, and arguments are prompt to favor them, let this prison yard rise up and say that no such crimes in liberty's name have ever been committed, on this continent, at least. Up stairs, in Castle Thunder, there are two or three large rooms, barred and dimly lit, and two or three series of condemned cells, pent-up and pitchy, where, by a refinement of cruelty, the ceiling has been built low so that no man can stand upright. Here fifteen or twenty were crowded together, and, in the burning atmosphere, they stripped themselves stark naked, so that when in the morning the cell-doors were opened, they came forth as from the grave, begging for death. There are women's cells too ; for this great and valiant government recognized women as belligerents, and locked them up close to a sentry's cartridge, so that, in the bitterness of solitude, they were unsexed, and railed, and blasphemed, like wanton things. On the pavements before the jail, were hidden numberless guards, who shot at every rag fluttering from the cages, and all this little circle of death and terror was enacted close to the bright river, and airy pediment of that high capitol, where bold men hoped by war to wring from a reluctant Union, acknowledgment of arrogant independence to rein civilization as it pleased, and warp the destinies of our race.

CHAPTER XXXI.

THE RUINS OF THE REBELLION.

WHEN Richmond was a plain city, a county seat, and the residence of a governor and commonwealth legislature, its enterprise was as gradual as its hospitality and private probity were steadfast. It was always a fierce political arena, and its two great journals, the *Whig* and *Enquirer*, were not more violently partisan than its hustings. In the latter its debaters were wide-famed. No such "stump" has ever existed in America, commencing with Patrick Henry, whose eloquence was as intense and telling as his statesmanship was errant and inconsistent, and passing through the shrill and bitter apostrophes of John Randolph down to the latest era of Henry A. Wise, the most sufferable and interminable campaign orator extant, and John Minor Botts, scarcely his inferior. With us, out of door rhetoric is dry, studied, and argumentative; here an inspiration, based upon feeling rather than reason, and so earnest that it knew no personal friendship where its political affinities stopped. Whig and Democrat were not men of the same race or family in Richmond; they passed each other on the sidewalk with a sneer or a scowl, and knew no coalition even in the house of God. Even when the Whig party as an organization deceased, the Whigs, as individuals, retained their traditional antipathy, and the advent of secession was decried by these, not because they loved the Union more, but the triumphant Democracy the less. Sep-

29*   (341)

aration was a feature of the hated faith, and no good could come out of Nazareth. The Union men of Richmond who have hungered in Castle Thunder, and been driven, needy and naked, from the South, were all old line Whigs, distrusting the North, but disliking Democracy. However, the war burst at last, heralded by that mysterious lunatic who appeared like a warning giant in the twilight day of the Union, — old John Brown; and as the Gulf States wheeled into line and pulled down the old colors, the Old Dominion, Southern and slaveholding, was too impulsive not to follow the whirlwind. She did not go for policy's sake, nor for principle's sake, but for emotion's sake. How wild and jubilant, and confident, were those Richmond mass meetings, at which separation was counselled! How awful seems their levity at this distance, with the city conquered and in ruins! On the Capitol Hill the mad orators inveighed; within the Capitol met the disunion assembly in secret and prolonged session; before the American, the Exchange, and the Spottswood hotels, visiting commissioners harangued the crowd; the people went to ballot on the day of State suicide, with laughing and wagging, and at the decree that Virginia and her people had resolved to quit the fabric of their fathers, bonfires and illuminations lit up the river and the sky.

Done, these were the men to stand fast. Done in dream, the first acts were mirages rather than comprehensible events. They marched upon Harper's Ferry; they suppressed the Unionists in their midst; they erased the sacred mottoes of amity and unity from their monuments, and won to the new cause they so blindly embraced every inch of their soil except Old Point, where Fortress Monroe still stood defiant, to be in the end the source of their downfall. Gayly went the populace of Richmond, and splendid parties made the nights lustrous. When they heard that their town was mentioned, among many others, as the probable Confederate capital, they threw their hearts into the suggestion and offered lands and edifices as free gifts for the honor of being the centre of the South. A few, more interested, beheld in the coming of the seat of government higher rents and increased patronage, crowded hotels, and railway stock at a premium; but the mass, with the enthusiasm of women or children, thought only of their beloved city growing in rank and power; the home of legislators, orators, and savans; the seat of all rank and the depository of archives. At last the good news came; Richmond was the capital of a great nation; that courtesy bound all grateful Virginian hearts to the common cause forever; the heyday and gratulation were renewed; the new President, and the reverend senators appeared on Richmond streets; the citizens were proud and happy.

There was no spectre of the mighty North, slowly rising from lethargy like those Medicean figures of Michael Angelo, which leap from stone to avengers. There was no mutter of coming storm, no clank of coming sabres and bayonets, no creak of great wheels rolling southward, and war in its extremest and most deadly phase. Richmond and Virginia laughed at these, flushed in the present, and invincible in the past. They only held high heads, — and trade, with vanity, grew strong, till every citizen wondered why all this glory had been so long delayed, and despised the ten years preceding the rupture, if not, indeed, the whole past of the Union.

The President of the United States proclaimed war; an army marched upon the city. Not until the battle of Bull Run, when the dead and mangled came by hundreds into the town, did any one discover the consequences of Richmond's new distinction; but by this time the Rebel government had absorbed Virginia, and was master of the city. Thenceforward Richmond was the scene of all terrors, the prey of all fears and passions. Campaign after campaign was directed against her; she lived in the perpetual thunder of cannon; raiders pressed to her gates; she was a great garrison and hospital only, besieged and cut off from her own provinces; armies passed through her to the sound of drums, and returned to the creak of ambulances. She lost her social prestige, and became a barrack-city, filled with sutlers, adventurers, and refugees, till, bearing bravely up amid domestic riot and horrible demoralization, — a jail, a navy-yard, a base of operations, — she grew pinched, and base, and haggard, and, at last, deserted. Given over to sack and fire, the wretches who used her retreated in the night, and the enemies she had provoked marched over her defences, and laid her — spent, degenerate, and disgraced — under martial law.

The outline of the scenes immediately associated with the evacuation of Richmond has been told by telegraph. Now that the stupefied citizens have recovered reason and memory so well as to tell us the story, it seems the most dramatic and fearful of the war. On Saturday the city was calm and trusting; Lee, its idol, held Grant, at Petersburg, fast; the daily journals came out as usual, filled with soothing accounts; that night came vague rumors of reverses; in the morning vaguer rumors of evacuation; by Sunday night the public records were burned in the streets, and the only remaining railway carried off the specie of the banks; before daylight on Monday, the explosions of bridges and half-built ships of war shook the houses; in the imperfect day, women, and old men, and children began to sway and surge before the guarded depot, which refused to admit them; then the town fell afire; no remonstrance could pacify the incendiaries; the spring wind carried the flame from the burning boats on the canal to the great Galligo Mills, to files of massive warehouses groaning with tobacco, into the heart of the town, where stores, and vaults, and banks, and factories lined the wide, undulating streets; it filled the gray concave with flame till the stars of the dawn shrank to pale invisibility in the advancing glare, and the crackle of hot roofs and beams, and the crash of walls and timbers, drowned the cries of the frightened and bankrupt, who beheld their fortunes wither in an hour, and the inheritance of their children fall to ashes. By the red, consuming light, poured past the straggling Confederate soldiers, dead to the acknowledgment of private rights, and sacking shop and home with curses and ribaldry; the suburban citizens and the menial negroes adopted their examples; carrying off whatever came next their hands, and with arms full of "swag," dropping it in the highway, lured by some dearer plunder. Negroes, with baskets of stolen champagne and rare jars of tamarinds, sought their dusky quarters to swill and carouse; and whites of the middle, and even of the higher class, lent themselves to theft, who, before this debased era, would have died before so surrendering their honor. All was peril, terror, and license; all who had nothing to lose were thieves; all who had anything left to lose were cowards. The conflagration swept through the densest, proudest blocks, driving off, not only the resident worthy, but the resident corrupt. Where were the lewd contractors, who had hoarded Confederate scrip by the basest exactions? With the fall of the capital their dollars dwindled to dust; four years of crime had resulted in beggary; still, with grasping palms, they adhered to their valueless paper, bearing it away. But of all the wretched, the Cyprians were the foremost. These inhabited the dense and business part of the town, where their houses were serried and compact; and, driven forth by the fire, they sought the street in their plumes and calicoes, to spend a cold and shivering bivouac in the square of the Capitol. From afar, the rich men of Sunday watched the flames of Monday sweeping on in terrible impetuosity, knowing that every tongue of light which leaped on high carried with it the competence they had sinned to acquire. And behind all, plunderer, incendiary, and straggler, came the one vague, overlapping, dreadful fear of — the enemy. Would they finish what friends had commenced, — the sack,

the desolation, the slaughter of the place ?   Richmond had
cost them half a million of lives, a mountain of blood and
wealth, four years of deadly struggle; would they not
complete its ruin ?

The morning came; the Confederates were gone; cavalry
in blue galloped up the streets; a brigade of white infantry
filed after them; then came the detested negroes.   Behold !
the victors, the subjugators, assist to quench the flames, —
and Richmond is captured, but secure !

Many of the churches were open on the Sunday of April
9, 1865, and were thinly attended by the more adventurous
of the citizens, with a sprinkling of soldiers and Northern
civilians.   Mr. Woodbridge, at the Monument Church,
built on the site of a famous burnt theatre, prayed for " all
in authority," and held his tongue upon dangerous topics.
The First Baptist Negro Church has been occupied all the
week by Massachusetts chaplains, and Northern negro
preachers, who have talked the gospel of John Brown to
gaping audiences of wool, white-eyeball, and ivory, telling
them that the day of deliverance has come, and that they
have only to possess the land which the Lord by the bayonet
has given them.   To-day, Mr. Allen, the regular white
preacher, occupied the pulpit, and told the negroes that
slavery was a divine institution, which would continue forever, and that the duty of every good servant was to stay
at home and mind his master.   Half of the enlightened
Africans got up midway of the discourse and left; the rest
were in doubt, and two or three black class-leaders, whom
the parson had wheeled over, prayed lustily that the Lord
would keep Old Virginny from new ideas and all Yankee
salvations; so that in the end the population were quite
tangled up, as much so as if they had read the book of
Revelation.   I attended Saint Paul's, the fashionable Episco-
palian church, where Lee, Davis, Memminger, and the rest
had been communicants, and heard Doctor Minnegerode
discourse.   He was one of the Prussian refugees of 1848,

and, though a hot Jacobin there, became a more bitter secessionist here. He is learned, fluent, and thoughtful, but speaks with a slight Teutonic accent. Jeff Davis's pew was occupied by nobody, the door thereof being shut. Jeff was a very devout man, but not so much so as Lee, who made all the responses fervently, and knelt at every requirement. This church is capable of "seating" fifteen hundred persons, has galleries running entirely around it, and is sustained at the roof within by composite pilasters of plaster, and at the pulpit by columns of mongrel Corinthian; the *tout ensemble* is very excellent; a darkey sexton gave us a pew, and there were some handsome ladies present, dark Richmond beauties, haughty and thinly clothed, with only here and there a jockey-feathered hat, or a velvet mantilla, to tell of long siege and privation. We saw that those who dressed the shabbiest had yet preserved some little article of jewelry — a finger-ring, a brooch, a bracelet, showing how the last thing in woman to die is her vanity. Poor, proud souls! Last Sunday many of them were heiresses; now many of them could not pay the expenses of their own funerals. There were some Confederate officers in the house. They reminded me of the captive Jews holding worship in their gutted Temple. Some ruffians broke into this church after the occupation, and wrote ribaldry in the Bible and hymn-book. Dr. Minnegerode dared not pray for the Confederate States, and his sermon was trite, based upon the text of the eleventh chapter of the Acts — "The disciples were first called Christians in Antioch." In the opening lesson, however, he aimed poison at the North, selecting the forty-fourth and following Psalms, commencing, "We have heard with our ears, O God! our fathers have told us, what work Thou didst in their days, in the times of old." Then it spoke of the heathen being driven out and the chosen people planted; afflicted by God's disfavor, the forefathers held the territory, and the generation extant would yet rout its enemies. But now the old stock were put to shame, a reproach to their neighbors and those that dwelt round about them.   "Thou hast broken us in the place of dragons, and covered us with the shadow of death," going not forth with our armies, bowing our souls to the dust till our bellies cleave unto the earth ; we are killed all the day long, and counted as sheep for the slaughter.

Let all who would drink the essence of sorrow and anguish, read this wonderful Psalm, to learn how after this recapitulation, the parson said aloud the thrilling invocation.

"Arise ! for our help, and redeem us for thy mercies' sake."

Then came the next Psalm, light and tripping, full of praise for the king and his bride, coming to the nuptials with her virgin train : "instead of thy fathers, shall be thy children, whom thou mayst make princes in all the earth." A poetic parallel might be drawn between all this and the early hopes of Richmond ; but the third Psalm came in like a beautiful peroration.

"God is our refuge and strength, a very present help in trouble, — the Lord of Hosts is with us, the God of Jacob is our refuge.   Selah !   He maketh wars to cease unto the end of the earth ; he breaketh the bow and cutteth the spear in sunder ; he burneth the chariot in the fire."

Clear, direct, and in meaning monotone, the captive high-priest read all this, so fearfully applicable to the subjugated and ruined town, and then the organ threw its tender music into the half-empty concave, sobbing like a far voice of multitudes, until the sweet singing of Madame Ruhl, the chorister, swept into the moan of pipes, and rose to a grand peal, quivering and trilling, like a nightingale wounded, making more tears than the sublimest operatic effort and the house reeled and trembled, as if Miriam and her chanting virgins were lifting praises to God in the midst of the desert.

That part of the New Testament read, by some strange

fatuity, touches also the despair of the city. It told of Christ betrayed by Iscariot, deserted by his disciples, saying to his few trusty ones : "I will smite the shepherd, and the sheep of the flock shall be scattered abroad." "Can ye not watch with me one hour ?" he says to the timid and sleeping ; and turning to his conquerors, avers that the Son of Man shall return to Jerusalem, " sitting on the right hand of power, and coming in the clouds of heaven." All this, of course, was the prescribed lesson for the Sunday before Easter, which to-day happened to be ; but had the pastor searched it out to meet the exigencies of the place and time, it could not have been more *apropos*. He read also from Daniel, where the king's dream was interpreted ; his realm, like a tree worn down to the root, and the king himself making his dwelling with the wild asses, but in the end " thy kingdom shall be sure unto thee, after that thou shalt have known that the heavens do rule."

Again the organ rang, and the wonderful voice of the choristers alternated with deep religious prayers, whose refrain was, " Have mercy upon us."

Only one Sunday gone by, the church was densely packed with Rebel officers and people ; Mrs. Lee was there, and the president, in his high and whitened hairs. Midway of the discourse a telegram came up the aisle, borne by a rapid orderly. The president read it, and strode away ; the preacher read it, and faltered, and turned pale ; it said :

My lines are broken ; Richmond must be evacuated by midnight.
ROBERT E. LEE.

Ill news travels without words ; the whole house felt that the great calamity had come ; they broke for the doors, and left the rector, alone and frightened, to finish the solemn services.

Now the enemy is here ; the music and the prayer are not interrupted. God is over all, whether Davis or Lincoln be uppermost.

30

This campaign, so gloriously and promptly finished, has consumed just eleven days. It took three to flank the Rebel army, one to capture Petersburg, one to occupy Richmond, and six to pursue, overtake, and capture the Army of Northern Virginia. No such memorable fighting has ever been known on our continent, and it parallels the Italian, the Austerlitz, and the Jena campaigns; in breadth of conception, it outrivals them all; it took less men to do it than the last two; it shows equal sagacity with any of them, but none of their brilliant episodes; and, unlike them, we cannot trace its full credit to any single personality. It has made the army immortal, but the lustre of it is diffused, not concentrating upon any single head. Grant must be credited with most of the combinations; yet without the genius and activity of Sheridan, the bewildering rapidity of Sherman, and the steadfastness of such reliable men as Wright, Parke, and Griffin, these combinations would have fallen apart. It is said that Stoneman and Sheridan were to have joined their separate cavalry commands at Lynchburg, and effect a simultaneous junction with the Army of the Potomac. This failed, through a miscalculation of distance or time; but had they succeeded, we should have been less than three days in turning Lee's right, and so made the campaign even more concise. But Grant's talent has been marked and signal. He is the long-expected "coming man." None can be lukewarm in surveying the nice adjustment of so many separate and converging routes to a grand series of victories. Sherman leaves the Rebellion no Gulf city to inhabit, and cuts off Lee's retreat while he absorbs Johnston; the navy closes the last seaport; Sheridan severs all communication with Richmond, and swells the central forces; then the Rebels are lured from their lines and scattered on their right; the same night the intrenchments of Petersburg are stormed, Richmond falls as this prop is removed, being already hungry-hearted, and the flushed army falls upon Lee and finishes the war. Is not this work for gratulation?   Glory to the army, perfect at last, and to Grant, to Sheridan, to each of its commanders!

Let us not do injustice to Lee.   His tactics at the close of his career were as brilliant as necessity would permit. He could not feed Richmond, even though its impregnable works were behind him to retire to.   So he gave his government time to evacuate, and, with his thinned and famishing ranks, made a bold push to join Johnston, some of whose battalions had already reinforced him; overtaken on the way, and punished anew, he did as any great and humane commander would do, — stopped the effusion of blood uselessly, and gave up his sword.

Unless Davis has been captured, we would think it improbable that he had given up the Rebel cause.   He was born to revolutionize, containing within himself all the elements of a Rebel leader, and too proud to yield, even when, like Macbeth, pursued to his castle-keep.   I am assured by those who know him best that he has been, throughout, the absolute master of the Confederacy, overawing Lee, who, from the first, was a reluctant Rebel; and his design was, until abandoned by his army, to hold Richmond, even through starvation, making, behind its tremendous fortifications, a defence like that of Leyden or Genoa.

There is no more faith in the Rebellion; it will be a long time before the United States is greatly beloved, but it will be always obeyed.   Our soldiers look well, most of them being newly uniformed, and behave like gentlemen.   Courtesy will conquer all that bayonets have not won.   The burnt district is still hideously yawning in the heart of the town, a monument to the sternness of those bold revolutionists who are being hunted to their last quarry.   Despotism, under the plea of necessity, has met with its end here as it must everywhere.   We shall have no more experiments for liberty out of the Union, if the new Union will grant all that it gave before.   Yesterday, when our splendid levies were paraded in the street, with foot, cavalry, and cannon, in admirable order, and kindly-eyed men in command, I looked across their cleanly lines, tipped with bayonets, to the Capitol they had won, bearing at last the tri-color we all love and honor, as the symbol of our homes and the hope of the world, and thought how more grandly, even in her ruin, Richmond stood in the light of its crowding stars, rather than the den of a desperate cabal, whose banner was known in no city nor sea, but as the ensign of corsairs, and hailed only by fustian peers, now rent in the grip of our eagle, and without a fane or an abiding-place. Let us go on, not conquerors, but Republicans, battering down only to rebuild more gloriously, — not narrowing the path of any man, but opening to high and low a broader destiny and a purer patriotism.

CHAPTER XXXII.

WAR EXECUTIONS.

To have looked upon seventeen beings of human organism, ambition, sense of pain and of disgrace, brought forward with all the solemnities of a living funeral, and launched from absolute cognition to direct death, should put one in the category of Calcraft, Ketch, and Isaacs.

Yet, I do not think it would be right to so classify me. I know an excellent clergyman, who has seen and assisted in fifty odd executions. He says, as I say, that each new one is an augmented terror. But he is upon the spot to smooth the felon's troubled spirit, and I am with him to teach the felon's boon companions the direness of the penalty. Without either the Chaplain or myself, capital punishment would lose half its effectiveness.

And this is why I write the present article, — to relieve myself from the pertinacious inquiries with which I have been assailed since my return from the melancholy episodes of the executions at Washington. I am button-holed at every corner, and put through a cross-examination, to which Holt's or Bingham's had no searchingness: "How did Mrs. Suratt die?" "Was the rope attached to her left ear?" "What sort of rope was it, for example?" "Do her pictures look like her?" "Pray describe how Payne twisted, and whether you think Atzeroth's neck was dislocated?"

And, after answering these questions, replete as they are

with horrible curiosity, the questioner turns away, saying, "Dear me! I wouldn't see a man hung for a thousand dollars."

I am weary of such hypocrisy, and I shall, in this paper, speak of some executions I have witnessed.

I was quite a small boy, at school, when my chum and model, Bill Everett, dragged me off to Wayland's Mill, to see old Mrs. Kitty White suspended. She was a very infamous old woman, who had been in the habit of kidnapping black children, and running them by night from the Eastern shore across the bay to Virginia, where they were sold. If they became noisy and obstreperous before they left her house, and suspicion fell upon her, she clove their skulls with a hatchet, and buried them in her garden. When finally discovered, the remains of nearly a score marked how wholesale had been her wickedness.

This old woman was very drunk when she came to be hanged, and so was the sheriff who assisted her. She called him impolite names, and carried a pipe in her mouth, and went off smoking and cursing. I remember that I cried very loudly, so that Bill Everett had to choke me, and saw ghosts for so many nights succeeding, that Crouch, our maid of all work, had to sit at my bedside till I fell asleep.

The atrocity of a crime makes great difference in one's desire to see its after tragedy; and the next hanging I attended was almost world-famed. Four men were suspended for shooting down an entire family in cold blood. They had embarked on a raid of robbery, and emerging from the barren scrub of Delaware Forest, fell upon a snug and secluded Maryland farm-house, where the farmer's family were taking their supper. They fired through the ruddy windows, and brought the man down at his wife's feet; she, in turn, fell upon her threshold, rushing forth into the darkness, and the remnant of the family perished except two little boys, who slipped away and gave the alarm.

The jailer's boys of Chestertown went to school with me, and I was invited by the least of them to visit the jail, — a tumble-down old structure with goggly windows, and so unsafe that the felons had to be ironed to almost their own weight. And into the cell where the four fiends were lying, the jailer's big boy, for a big joke, pushed me, and locked the door upon me.

I was alone with the same bloody-handed men who had so recently, and for a trifle of gold, made the fireside a shamble, and the night a howling terror.

They appreciated the joke, and drew me to them, while their chains clanked, and pressed to my face their wild and prickly beards. There was one of them, named Drummond, who swore he would cut my heart out, and they executed a sort of death-tune on the floor with their balls and links. I lost all knowledge and perception in my fright, and cannot, at this interval, remember anything succeeding, but the execution. They were put to death upon a single long scaffold, the counterpart of that erected for the Booth conspirators, and the rope attached to the neck of the least guilty, broke when the drop fell, and cast him upon the ground, lacerated, but conscious, to be picked up and again suspended, while he begged for life, like a child.

The sixth miscreant murdered from revenge, which is just a trifle better than avarice : his girl preferred another, and the disappointed man, Bowen, went to sea. Returning, he found the united lovers in the exultation of happiness ; a child had just been born to them, and, touched by their content, Bowen gave the old rival his hand, and asked him out to accept a bumper. They drank again and again, — the spirits burning their blood to fire, and reviving again the bitter story of Bowen's love and shame. Within the hour, the husband lay at the jilted man's feet ! He was condemned to death, and I undertook to describe his exit for a weekly newspaper.

Still I see him, broad and muscular, climbing the gallows

stair with his peaked cap, deathly white, and looking up at the sun as if he dreaded its eye. There was the muttering of prayers, the spasm of one spectator taken sick at the crisis, and the dull thump of the scaffold falling in.

The preacher Harden, who fondled his wife on his knee, and fed her the while with poison, passed away so recently, that I need not revive the scene into which all his bad life should have been prolonged.

The death of Armstrong, expiating a hypocrite's life at Philadelphia, is not so well remembered: he killed an old man in the heart of the city, riding in a wagon, and dumped him out when he reached the suburbs. His life, to the end, was marked by all insolence and infamy, and on the day of the execution, he made a pretended confession, inculpating two innocent persons. One hour after this, he made the following speech: —

MY FRIENDS: I have a few words to say to you; I am going to die; and let me say, in passing, I die in peace with my Maker; and if, at this moment, a pardon was offered me on condition of giving up my Maker, I would not take it; and I die in peace with all the world, and forgive all my enemies. I desire you to take warning by my fate. Sabbath-breaking was the first cause. I bid you farewell, gentlemen, (here he mentioned various officers), and I bid you all farewell. I die in peace with everybody.

The Sheriff, very nervous, gave a signal to the drop-man too soon, and a serious accident very nearly occurred. The props were readjusted, all but the main support removed, and that unhinged; the Sheriff waved his handkerchief, and with the dead thump of the trap-lids against their cushions, and the heavy jerking of the noose knot against the victim's throat, the young murderer hung dangling in the air, not a limb quivering, and only a convulsive movement of the shoulders, to indicate the struggle which life maintained when giving up its place in the body.

There was a rush forward. The doctors grasped his wrist. Some spectators passed their hands across his knees to feel the tremulous sinews; one or two felt a faintness, and a dozen made coarse jokes; and one or more speculated as to the issue of his immortal part, or the degree of his pain, or the probability of his cognizance. In seven minutes he was beyond the reach of execution or executioner, and a hurdle being wheeled from the stable, they cut down his body, while a few scrambled for the rope, and it was wheeled on a run into the convict's corridor for his old father to claim. The neck was not broken, nor the flesh discolored. Some said that he died "game;" and all went away, leaving the old man and a brother to sit by the remains and weep, that so great calamity had darkened their home and blighted their lives. Few lamented him, for he had youth, but none of its elements of sympathy; and those who would make, even of his dying speech, a text and a lesson, are instancing a lie more grievous than the murder which he did.

In England, I saw two men and a woman suffer death on the common sidewalk; just as if we were to hang people in New York on the pavement before the Tombs.

No man, anxious to see an execution in London, need be disappointed. Once or twice a month the wolves are brought to the slaughter, and all the people are invited to enjoy the spectacle. A woman, one Catharine Wilson, was to be hanged for poisoning. She was middle aged, and had been reputable. Her manner of making way with folks was to act as sick-nurse, and mingling poison with their medicine, possess herself of the trifles upon their persons. She had sent six souls to their account in this way; but, discovered in the seventh attempt, all the other cases leaked out. She was condemned, of course, and on the Sunday evening previous to the execution, as I was returning from Spurgeon's Tabernacle, the omnibus upon which I sat passed through the Old Bailey. There were the carpenters joining the timbers of the scaffold, and building black barricades across the street. A murmuring crowd stood around in the solemn night, and the funereal walls of old Newgate glowered like a horrible vault upon the dimly-lit street. The public houses across the way were filled up with guests. All the front parlors and front bedrooms had been let at fat prices, and suppers were spread in them for the edification of their tenants. Do you remember the thrilling chapter of "The Jew's last night alive," in "Oliver Twist?" Well, this was the scene! These were the same beams and uprights. There, huge, massive, and blackened with smoky years, rose the cold, impervious stones; and yonder, casting its sharp pinnacles into the sky, is the tower of St. Sepulchre's Church, where the bell hangs muffled for the morrow's tolling away of a sinner's life. Old Fagin heard it, though it was no new sound to him; for Field Lane, where he kept his "fence," lies a very little way off, — little more than a stone's throw, and when, in the morning, I dressed at an early hour and hurried to the place of execution, I saw Charley Bates, and the Dodger, and Nancy, and Toby Crackit, and the rest, shying men's hats in the air, and looking out for the "wipes" and the "tickers." All the streets leading to Newgate were like great conduits, where human currents babbled along, emptying themselves into the Old Bailey. Mothers by the dozen were out with their infants, holding them aloft tenderly, to show them the noose and the cross-beam. Fathers came with their sons, and explained very carefully to them the method of strangulation. Little girls, on their way to workshops, had turned aside to see the playful affair, and traders in fancy soap and shoe-blacking, pea-nuts and shrimps, Banbury cakes, and Chelsea buns, and Yarmouth bloaters, were making the morning hilarious with their odd cries and speeches. Along the chimney-pots of Green Arbour Court, where Goldsmith penned the "Vicar of Wakefield," lads and maidens were climbing, that they might have commanding places. There was one young woman who had some difficulty in climbing over a battlement, and the mob hailed her failure with roars of mirth. But she persevered, though there was a high wind blowing, and then called loudly for her male attendant to follow her. He obeyed dutifully, and they both seated themselves upon a chimney-top, — a picture of love rewarded, — and waited for the show. The moments, as marked upon St. Sepulchre's clock, went grudgingly, as if the index-hands were unwilling to shoulder the responsibility of what was to come. Meantime, the police had their hands full; for some merry urchins were darting between their legs, and it was dangerous to keep one's hat on his head, for it hazarded plucking off and shying here and there. At the chamber-windows aforesaid, crowded the tipsy occupants, men and women, red-eyed with drinking, and leering stupidly upon the surging heads below. Some asked if Calcraft did the "job," and others volunteered sketches of Calcraft's life. One man boasted that he had taken a pot of beer with him, and another added that the hangman's children and his own went to school together. "He pockets," said the man, "two-pun ten for every one he drops, besides his travelling expenses, and he has put away three hundred and twenty folks. He is a clever fellow, is Calcraft, and he is going to retire soon."

So the hours passed ; the great clock-hands journeyed onward ; all eyes watched them attentively ; suddenly the deep bells struck a terrible one — two — three — four — five — six — seven — eight, and the bells of the neighborhood answered, some hoarsely, others musically, others faintly, as if ashamed.

Before the tones had died away, three persons appeared upon the scaffold, — a woman, pinioned and wearing a long, sharp, snowy, shrowdy, death-cap ; a man in loose black robes with a white neckhandkerchief, and a burly, surly fellow, in black cloth, bareheaded, and having a curling jetty beard around his heavy jaws. It is but a moment, that, standing on tiptoe, you catch this scene. The priest stretches his hand toward the people, and says some unintelligible words; those of the mob curse each other, and some scream out that they are dying in the press. Then the scaffold is clear; the woman stands alone, — God forgive her! — and when you look again, a bundle of old clothes, tipped with a sugar-loaf, is all that is visible, and the gallows-cord is very straight and tight. For the last chapter, consult the graveyard within the jail walls!

The guillotining which I witnessed in Paris, in the month of June, 1864, may be deemed worthy of an extended description: —

Couty de la Pommerais was a young physician of Paris, descended from a fine family, and educated beyond the requirements of a French Faculty. He was handsome and manly, and gave evidences of ambition at an early age. He was popularly called the Comte de la Pommerais, and at the time of his apprehension, was expecting a decoration from the Papal Government, with the rank he desired. Like all French students, he was incontinent, and had several mistresses. The last of these was a widow named Pauw, who appears to have loved him sincerely. She had some little fortune, which they consumed together; and then la Pommerais married a rich young lady, with whom he lived one year. Her mother died suddenly at the end of that time, and as la Pommerais was interested in getting certain moneys which the elder lady controlled, the manner of her death led to suspicions of poisoning. However, the woman was interred, but the son-in-law was not so fortunate as he supposed, and he ceased to live with his wife, but returned to Madame Pauw, who still adored him. Upon this fond, foolish woman he seems to have premeditated a deep and intricate crime; and it was for this that he suffered death. She must have been dishonest like himself, for she consented to a scheme of swindling the insurance companies; but, unlike himself, she lacked the wit to be silent, and was heard to hint mysteriously that she should soon be grand and happy. La Pommerais persuaded her to have her life insured, which was done for 515,000 francs, or upward of $100,000. When the matter had transpired some time, he persuaded her to feign sickness. The simple woman asked why she should do so.

"The insurance people," he replied, "will, when they consider that you are dangerously ill, prefer to give you 100,000f., rather than pay the 515,000f. in the certainty of your death. You can give them up your policy, accept the compromise, get well again, and be rich."

Yet this counterfeited sickness was meant by the villian to prepare the neighbors of Mme. Pauw for the death which he intended to ensue. He was to make it known to all, that she was dangerously ill; she was to uphold his testimony; and he was to kill her in due time, and take the whole of the insurance. At length, the farce was finished. La Pommerais gave to Mme. Pauw, a poison difficult to detect, called *digitalline*, the essential principle of our common foxglove; she died unconscious of his deception, loving him to the last, and he claimed the 515,000 francs at the insurance office. He was suspected, accused, and tried. The old suspicions relative to his mother-in-law were revived; the bodies were exhumed and examined; upon evidence entirely circumstantial and technical, he was convicted, and sentenced to be guillotined. His learning and standing made the trial a famous one; his bearing during the long proceedings was calm and collected; he was handsome, and had much sympathy: but the jury found him guilty, and the Emperor refused to extend his clemency to the case. He was put in a strait jacket and locked up in La Roquette, the prison for the condemned.

The prison of *La Roquette* (or the Rocket Prison) is situated in the eastern suburbs of Paris, a mile beyond the Bastile. It does not look unlike our American jails; a high exterior wall of rough stone, over the top of which one

31

gets a glimpse of the prison gables, with a huge gate in the arched portal, guarded forever by sentinels. Before this gate is a small open plot of ground, planted with trees. *Rue de la Roquette* passes between it and a second prison, immediately facing the first, called the *Prison des Jeunes Detenus,*or, as we would say in America, the "House of Refuge."   Standing between the two jails, and looking away from Paris, one will see the great metropolitan cemetery of *Père la Chaise*, scarcely a stone's throw distant, and behind him will be the great *abbatoir* or public slaughter-house of Menilmontant, with the vast area of roofs and spires of Paris stretching beyond it to the horizon.   It was to this region of vacant lots and lonesome, glowering houses, that thousands of Parisians bent their steps the night before the execution. The news had gone abroad that la Pommerais would not be pardoned. It was also generally credited that this would be the last execution ever held in Paris, since there is a general desire for the abolition of capital punishment in France, and a conviction that the Legislature, at its next session, will substitute life-imprisonment. This, with the rarity of the event, and that terrible allurement of blood which distinguishes all populaces, brought out all the excitable folk of the town ; and at dusk, on the night before the expiation, the whole neighborhood of La Roquette was crowded with men and women. All classes of Parisians were there, — the *blouses*, or workingmen, standing first in number ; the students from the Latin Quartier being well represented, and idlers, and well-dressed nondescripts without enumeration, — distributing themselves among women, dogs, and babies.

Venders of *gateaux*, muscles, and fruit were out in force. The "Savage of Paris," clothed in his war plumes, paint, greaves, armlets, and moccasins, was selling razors by gaslight ; here and there ballad-mongers were singing the latest songs, and boys, with chairs to let, elbowed into the intricacies of the crowd, which amused itself all the night long by smoking, drinking, and hallooing. At last, the mass became formidable in numbers, covering every inch of ground within sight of the prison, and many soldiers and *sergeants de ville*, mounted and on foot, pushed through the dense mass to restore order.

At midnight, a body of cavalry forced back the people from the square of La Roquette. A number of workmen, issuing from the prison-gates, proceeded to set up the instrument of death by the light of blazing torches. The flame lit up the dark jail walls, and shone on the helmets and cuirasses of the sabre-men, and flared upon spots of the up-turned faces, now bringing them into strong, ruddy relief, now plunging them into shadow. When the several pieces had been framed together, we had a real guillotine in view,— the same spectre at which thousands of good and bad men had shuddered; and the folks around it, peering up so eagerly, were descendants of those who stood on the *Place de la Concorde* to witness the head of a king roll into the common basket. Imagine two tall, straight timbers, a foot apart, rising fifteen feet from the ground. They are grooved, and spring from a wide platform, approached by a flight of steps. At the base, rests a spring-plank or *bascule*, to which leather thongs are attached to buckle down the victim, and a basket or *pannier* filled with sawdust to receive the severed head. Between these, at their summit, hangs the shining knife in its appointed grooves, and a cord, which may be disconnected by a jerk, holds it to its position. Two men will be required to work the instrument promptly, — the one to bind the condemned, the other to drop the axe. The *bascule* is so arranged that the whole weight and length of the trunk will rest upon it, leaving the head and neck free, and when prone it will reach to the grooves, leaving space for the knife to pass below it. The knife itself is short and wide, with a bright concave edge, and a rim of heavy steel ridges it at the top; it moves easily in the greased grooves, and may weigh forty pounds.

It has a terrible fascination, hanging so high and so lightly in the blaze of the torches, which play and glitter upon it, and cast stains of red light along its keen blade, as if by their brilliance all its past blood-marks had become visible again. A child may send it shimmering and crashing to the scaffold, but only God can fasten together the warm and throbbing parts which it shall soon dissever. And now that the terrible creature has been recreated, the workmen slink away, as if afraid of it, and a body of soldiers stand guard upon it, as if they fear that it might grow thirsty and insatiate as in the days of its youth. The multitude press up again, reinforced every hour, and at last the pale day climbs over the jail-walls, and waiting people see each other by its glimmer. The bells of Notre Dame peal out; a hundred towers fall into the march of the music; the early journals are shrieked by French newsboys, and folks begin to count the minutes on their watches. There are men on the ground who saw the first guillotine at work. They describe the click of the cleaver, the steady march of victims upon the scaffold-stairs, the rattle of the death-cart turning out of the *Rue Saint Honore*, the painted executioners, with their dripping hands, wiping away the jets of blood from the hard, rough faces; nay! the step of the young queen, white-haired with care, but very beautiful, who bent her body as she had never bent her knee, and paid the penalty of her pride with the neck which a king had fondled.

At four minutes to six o'clock on Thursday morning, the wicket in the prison-gate swung open; the condemned appeared, with his hands tied behind his back, and his knees bound together. He walked with difficulty, so fettered; but other than the artificial restraints, there was no hesitation nor terror in his movements. His hair, which had been long, dark, and wavy, was severed close to his scalp; his beard had likewise been clipped, and the fine moustache and goatee, which had set off his most interesting face, no longer appeared to enhance his romantic, expressive physi-

ognomy. Yet his black eyes and cleanly cut mouth, nostrils, and eyebrows, demonstrated that Couty de la Pommerais was not a beauty dependent upon small accessories.
There was a dignity even in his painful gait; the coarse
prison-shirt, scissored low in the neck, exhibited the
straight columnar throat and swelling chest; for the rest,
he wore only a pair of black pantaloons and his own
shapely boots. As he emerged from the wicket, the chill
morning air, laden with the dew of the truck gardens near
at hand,. blew across the open spaces of the suburbs, and
smote him with a cold chill. He was plainly seen to tremble; but in an instant, as if by the mere force of his will,
he stood motionless, and cast a first and only glance at the
guillotine straight before him. It was the glance of a man
who meets an enemy's eye, not shrinkingly, but half-defiant,
as if even the bitter retribution could not abash his strong
courage. The dramatic manner which is characteristic of
the most real and earnest incidents of French life had its
fascination for la Pommerais, even at his death-hour. Not
Mr. Booth nor Mr. Forrest could have expressed the rally-
ing, startling, almost thrilling recognition of an instrument
of death, better than this actual criminal, whose last winkful
of daylight was blackened by the guillotine. It reminded
one of Damon, in the pitch of the tragedy : —

" I stand upon the scaffold — I am standing on my throne."

His dark eye was scintillant; his nostril grew full; his
shoulders fell back as if to exhibit his broad, compact figure
in manlier outline; he seemed to feel that forty thousand
men and women, and young children were looking upon him
to see how he dared to die, and that for a generation his
bearing should go into fireside descriptions. Then he
moved on between the files of soldiers at his shuffling pace,
and before him went the *aumonier* or chaplain, swaying the

crucifix, behind him the executioner of Versailles — a rough and bearded man — to assist in the final horror.

It was at this intense moment a most wonderful spectacle. As the prisoner had first appeared, a single great shout had shaken the multitude. It was the French word " *Voila!* " which means " Behold ! " " See ! " Then every spectator stood on tiptoe ; the silence of death succeeded ; all the close street was undulant with human motion ; a few house roofs near by were dizzy with folks who gazed down from the tiles ; all the way up the heights of Père la Chaise, among the pale chapels and monuments of the dead, the thousands of stirred beings swung and shook like so many drowned corpses floating on the sea. Every eye and mind turned to the little structure raised among the trees, on the space before *La Roquette,* and there they saw a dark, shaven, dis robed young man, going quietly toward his grave.

He mounted the steps deliberately, looking toward his feet ; the priest held up the crucifix, and he felt it was there, but did not see it ; his lips one moment touched the image of Christ, but he did not look up nor speak ; then, as he gained the last step, the *bascule* or swingboard sprang up before him ; the executioner gave him a single push, and he fell prone upon the plank, with his face downward ; it gave way before him, bearing him into the space between the upright beams, and he .lay horizontally beneath the knife, presenting the back of his neck to it. Thus resting, he could look into the *pannier* or basket, into whose saw- dust lining his head was to drop in a moment. And in that awful space, while all the people gazed with their fingers tingling, the legitimate Parisian executioner gave a jerk at the cord which held the fatal knife. With a quick, keen sound, the steel became detached ; it fell hurtling through the grooves ; it struck something with a dead, dumb thump ; a jet of bright blood spurted into the light, and dyed the face of an attendant horribly red ; and Couty de la Pomme- rais's head lay in the sawdust of the pannier, while every vein in the lopped trunk trickled upon the scaffold-floor! They threw a cloth upon the carcass and carried away the pannier; the guillotine disappeared beneath the surrounding heads; loud exclamations and acclaims burst from the multitude; the venders of trash and edibles resumed their cheerful cries, and a hearse dashed through the mass, carrying the warm body of the guillotined to the cemetery of Mt. Parnasse. In thirty minutes, newsboys were hawking the scene of the execution upon all the quays and bridges. In every café of Paris some witness was telling the incidents of the show to breathless listeners, and the crowds which stopped to see the funeral procession of the great Marshal Pelissier divided their attention between the warrior and the poisoner, — the latter obtaining the preponderance of fame.

I wonder sometimes, if the ultimate penalty, however enforced, greatly assists example, or dignifies justice. But this would involve a very long controversy, over which many sage heads have sadly ached.

In the open daylight, when my face is shining, and my life secure, I take the humanitarian side, and denounce the barbarities of the gibbet.

But when I come down the dark stairs of the daily paper office, after midnight, and see three or four stealthy fellows hiding in the shadows, and go up the black city unarmed with my pocket full of greenbacks, I think the gallows quite essential as a warning, and indorse it, even after seventeen executions.

So end my desultory-chapters of desultory life. It has been, in the arranging of them, difficult to reject material, — not to select it. I am amazed to find what a world of dead leaves lies around my feet, as if I were a tree that blossomed and shed its covering every day. There are baskets-full of copy still remaining, from which the temptation is great to gather. It is sad to have written so much at twenty-five, and yet to have only drifting convictions. I may have succeeded in depicting the lives of certain young gentlemen who reported the war. All of us, who were young, loved the business, and were glad to quit it. For myself, I am weary of travel; rather than publish again from these fragments of my fugitive life, let me weave their material into a more poetic story, softened by some years cf stay at home.

CPSIA information can be obtained
at www.ICGtesting.com
Printed in the USA
BVHW070147120819
555624BV00025B/4166/P

9 781318 667161